LOVE IN HARD PLACES

Crossway books by D. A. Carson

The Difficult Doctrine of the Love of God
For the Love of God, Volume 1
For the Love of God, Volume 2

With John D. Woodbridge
Letters Along the Way

LOVE IN HARD PLACES

D. A. CARSON

CROSSWAY BOOKS

A DIVISION OF
GOOD NEWS PUBLISHERS
WHEATON, ILLINOIS

Love in Hard Places

Copyright © 2002 by D. A. Carson

Published by Crossway Books
    a division of Good News Publishers
    1300 Crescent Street
    Wheaton, Illinois 60187

Cover design: Cindy Kiple

First printing 2002

Printed in the United States of America

Library of Congress Cataloging-in-Publication Data
Carson, D. A.
   Love in hard places / D.A. Carson.
     p. cm.
   Includes bibliographical references and index.
   ISBN 1-58134-425-2 (alk. paper)
    1. Love—Religious aspects—Christianity. 2. Forgiveness—Religious aspects—Christianity. 3. Love—Biblical teaching. 4. Forgiveness—Biblical teaching. 5. Love—Biblical teaching. I. Title.
BV4639 .C315   2002
241'.4—dc21
                                2002002087
                                      CIP

15	14	13	12	11	10	09	08	07	06	05	04	03	02
15	14	13	12	11	10	9	8	7	6	5	4	3	2	1

This one is for Bob and Bernie,
with gratitude.

TABLE OF CONTENTS

PREFACE

This book began its modest life as two or three sermons prepared for the annual meeting of the Overseas Missionary Fellowship in the United Kingdom. Eventually those sermons expanded into four rather lengthy lectures and became the Oak Hill Theological College lectures of 2001. I am thankful to Dr. David Peterson, the principal, for inviting me, as the invitation stimulated me to put into more polished form things I had been thinking about for some time.

The kindnesses shown me by David Peterson and his wife, Lesley, and by other members of the Oak Hill College staff and students, are too numerous to mention, but were all deeply appreciated. The questions stirred up by the lectures, combined with further material that I had left out for want of time, lengthened the manuscript again. Then came September 11, and it occurred to me that if I were going to write on Christian love for enemies and the relation between love and forgiveness (among other things), the discussion should not remain at a merely conceptual level. It needed to deal with hard cases. What does it mean to love one's enemy if his name is Osama bin Laden? Inevitably, that question led to further expansion.

I mention this somewhat tortuous history of the manuscript for three reasons. First, I would not want anyone to think that my discussion of Osama bin Laden was prepared for the lectures at Oak Hill, delivered in the spring of 2001 several months before the destruction of the Pentagon and the World Trade Center. Prescient I am not. Second, one of the underlying themes of these lectures is that careful reflection on Christian love soon leaves behind the vapid sentimentalism with which Western culture is so heavily afflicted. Exegesis, biblical theology, historical debates, and present experience conspire to show us that thinking seriously about Christian love soon embroils us in reflection on justice, revenge, war, the authority of the state, forgiveness, hate, and much more. What begins as some introductory thoughts on some of the different ways the Bible speaks of Christian love soon grows into the embryo of a book on Christian ethics. And, third, this growth in the manuscript explains why its publication is a few months later than I (and David Peterson!) would have wished.

The opening paragraphs of the first lecture explain the relationship between this book and a slightly earlier one, *The Difficult Doctrine of the Love of God*. In both cases, I decided to keep the tone and style of the lectures.

I am grateful to Trinity Evangelical Divinity School for its very sub-stantial role in encouraging this particular faculty member to keep study-ing and writing across the years and for proving unusually flexible in allowing me to accept invitations like the ones that called this book into being. Thanks, too, to Sigurd Grindheim for compiling the indexes.

With a generous spirit my wife, Joy, has put up with my long hours in the study so that in some ways this work is as much hers as mine. *Soli Deo gloria.*

D. A. Carson
Trinity Evangelical Divinity School

1

LOVE AND THE
COMMANDMENT OF GOD

A. A PROTRACTED INTRODUCTION

Three years ago I gave some lectures that were eventually published under the title *The Difficult Doctrine of the Love of God*.[1] Almost all the focus of those lectures was on the ways in which the Bible speaks of the love of God. I said relatively little about Christian love, i.e., about the love Christians are called to display. In this book I want to redress the balance a little; indeed, by the end of the work I shall show some of the ways in which the love of Christians is a reflection of the love of God.

Before plunging into the topic, the way will be eased if I review and slightly adapt three points made in the first set of lectures.

First, popular culture saunters between a sentimental view and an erotic view of love. The erotic view is fed by television, movies, and certain popular books and articles; the sentimental view is nurtured by many streams, some of which we shall think about as we press on, but the result is a form of reductionism whose hold on the culture is outstripped only by its absurdity.

Applied to God, the sentimental view generates a deity with all the awesome holiness of a cuddly toy, all the moral integrity of a marshmallow. In the previous lectures, I briefly documented this point with

[1] Wheaton, Ill.: Crossway Books, 2000.

examples from films and books. Applied to Christians, the sentimental view breeds expectations of transcendental niceness. Whatever else Christians should be, they should be *nice*, where "niceness" means smiling a lot and never ever hinting that anyone may be wrong about anything (because that isn't *nice*). In the local church, it means abandoning church discipline (it isn't *nice*), and in many contexts it means restoring adulterers (for instance) to pastoral office at the mere hint of broken repentance. After all, isn't the church about forgiveness? Aren't we supposed to love one another? And doesn't that mean that above all we must be, well, *nice?* Similarly with respect to doctrine: the letter kills, while the Spirit gives life, and everyone knows the Spirit is nice. So let us love one another and refrain from becoming upright and uptight about this divisive thing called "doctrine."

None of this is to say that "un-niceness" has any allure for thoughtful Christians. It is merely to say that the surrounding culture's sophomoric reduction of "love," even Christian love, into niceness does not give us the scope to think through the diversities of ways in which the Bible speaks of Christian love, the diversities of contexts that demand something a great deal more profound than sentimental niceness.

Sorting these things out is not easy. Quite apart from the usual exegetical challenges, one quickly discovers that the issues, though never less than exegetical, are usually more: it is not easy to think clearly with exegetical evenhandedness when you are being told that because you say that certain behavior is wrong, you are not nice, you are not displaying Christian love. If Christians are not *nice*, they are not really loving, and that means they are hypocrites. And all of us know with shame that the church has generated its share of hypocrites, don't we? So hearing the scorn, not knowing quite how to answer, we are tempted to hunker down in our holes and resolve to be a little *nicer*. If the truth be told, the pressures along this line will as often come from inside the church as outside. The temptation to retreat into "nice" silence is immediately augmented.

Second, the different kinds of love proposed by various writers cannot safely be aligned with specific words. Probably the most famous analysis is that of Nygren, who specified three loves: sexual and erotic love, which he tied to the noun ἔρως; emotional love, or the love of friendship and feeling, which he tied to the φιλέω word-group; and willed love, the self-sacrificial commitment to the other's good, which he thought of as Christian love and tied to the ἀγαπάω word-group.[2]

Whatever the heuristic merits of this analysis of kinds of love, I have shown elsewhere that there is plenty of evidence that these different loves cannot safely be tied to these respective words. The Bible has plenty to say about sexual love, for instance, and yet never uses the word ἔρως. In the Septuagint, when Amnon rapes his half-sister Tamar, the Greek text can say that he "loved" her, using the verb ἀγαπάω (LXX 2 Sam. 13:1, 4, 15). When John tells us that the Father *loves* the Son, once he does so with φιλέω, and once with ἀγαπάω, with no discernible distinction in meaning (John 3:35; 5:20). When Demas forsakes Paul because he *loves* this present evil world, the verb is ἀγαπάω. In fact, the evidence goes way beyond a smattering of verses, but I need not repeat it here since it has been set forth often enough.[3]

Not for a moment am I suggesting that there are not different kinds of love. All I am denying is that specific kinds of love can be reliably tied to particular Greek words. Context and other factors will decide, not mere vocabulary. So although there are still plenty of studies that speak of "agapic love" or the like,[4] the transliterated adjective manages to be simultaneously unhelpful (because it is not intrinsically transparent in English) and misleading (because it gives the erroneous impression that the weight of the stipulated meaning rests on a Greek word when it doesn't).

The threefold analysis of Nygren is not the only one. Rather famously C. S. Lewis preferred to speak of *The Four Loves*.[5] Basing himself on the vocabulary available to ancient Greek writers, he added the

[2]Anders Nygren, *Agape and Eros* (New York: Harper and Row, 1969).

[3]I summarized some of the evidence in *Exegetical Fallacies*, 2nd ed. (Grand Rapids: Baker, 1996), 31-32, 51-53.

[4]E.g., Stanley J. Grenz, *The Moral Quest: Foundations of Christian Ethics* (Downers Grove, Ill.: InterVarsity Press, 1997), esp. chap. 8; Lewis B. Smedes, *Love Within Limits: Realizing Selfless Love in a Selfish World* (Grand Rapids: Eerdmans, 1978), *passim*. Both books, I hasten to add, include many good things; the latter stands within a tradition of thoughtful Christian expositions of 1 Corinthians 13. Compare, for instance, Jonathan Edwards, *Charity and Its Fruits* (London: Banner of Truth, 1969 [1852]); William Scroggie, *The Love Life: A Study of I Corinthians xiii* (London: Pickering and Inglis, n.d.). One of the reasons why some ethicists (e.g., Grenz, 280) are still claiming a distinction in the Greek words is because they rely on older works (e.g., Gustav Stählin, "φιλέω κτλ," *TDNT* 9.128,134) that *presupposed* an isomorphic relationship between form and meaning. Linguistics has long since demonstrated how impossible that view is.

[5]New York & London: Harcourt Brace Jovanovich, 1960.

term στοργή (for "affection," especially among family members) and restricted the φιλία/φιλέω word-group to friendship. Once again the analytic distinction may be helpful, but it must not be tied to particular Greek words.[6] More recently it has become common to speak of the five loves.[7] The two "loves" to be added to the three proposed by Nygren are affection for the less than fully personal, linked by many writers to στοργή (a rather different analysis from that of C. S. Lewis!), and self-love (amor sui: mercifully, no Greek word-group is associated with this category). But my immediate point is that even if one accepts that there are three or four or five distinguishable loves, they cannot be tied to distinctive words or word-groups.

Many writers whose categories are primarily those of analytic philosophy or systematic theology have debated the relationships that exist among these five kinds of love. One of the most interesting and creative of these is Timothy Jackson, whose book *Love Disconsoled: Meditations on Christian Charity*[8] argues that what he calls agapic love or *agape* "has a singular priority to all other forms of love; it both precedes them causally and governs them epistemically."[9] In other words, he sees the other four loves—erotic love, friendship love, love for the less-than-personal object, and even self-love—as "growing out of *agape* as its proper fruits, rather than being entirely discontinuous with (or even contradictory to) *agape* as its implacable rivals. The loves are distinct, but they are not antithetical."[10] I have learned much from Jackson and others,[11] and I continue to ponder what they have written. But their categories, though heuristically illuminating, are not demonstrably the controlling concerns of Scripture. So in these lectures, I have adopted the far more modest aim of understanding how the love mandated of the followers of Jesus operates in several different passages and in conjunction with other New Testament themes.

Third, it will help my developing argument if I take the time now

---

[6]The book to read is Robert Joly, *Le vocabulaire chrétien de l'amour est-il original?* Φιλεῖν et Άγαπᾶν *dans le grec antique* (Bruxelles: Presses Universitaires, 1968).
[7]See the elegant summary of this discussion in Timothy P. Jackson, *Love Disconsoled: Meditations on Christian Charity* (Cambridge: Cambridge University Press, 1999), ch. 3.
[8]Op. cit.
[9]Ibid., 56.
[10]Ibid. C. S. Lewis gave a similar priority to ἀγάπη.
[11]See especially the excellent bibliography in Jackson, *Love Disconsoled*, 231-244.

to review and summarize very briefly one of the central themes of my earlier little book, *The Difficult Doctrine of the Love of God.* There I argued that the Bible speaks of the love of God in at least five distinguishable ways.

(1) The love of the Father for the Son (e.g., John 3:35; 5:20) and of the Son for the Father (John 14:31). This intra-Trinitarian love, if I may use terms that were not developed until later, is not the love of redemption: neither the Father nor the Son needs redeeming. Nor is it love that is poured out despite the imperfections of the loved one: not only do the Father and the Son love each other, but each is to the other inestimably lovable.

(2) God's providential love over the entire universe. Not only did God make the universe and call it "very good" (Gen. 1:31), but even now in its disordered and rebellious state, Jesus teaches us that God "causes his sun to rise on the evil and the good, and sends rain on the righteous and the unrighteous" (Matt. 4:45). That this is an act of love on God's part is shown by what Jesus says next: "If you love those who love you, what reward will you get?" (Matt. 5:46). In other words, our responsibility to love our enemies is grounded in the fact that God providentially loves the just and the unjust.

(3) God's yearning, inviting, seeking, saving love. He is the God who loves the world (John 3:16) to this end—that people will believe in him and have eternal life. He is the God who cries, "As surely as I live . . . I take no pleasure in the death of the wicked, but rather that they turn from their ways and live. Turn! Turn from your evil ways! Why will you die, O house of Israel?"(Ezek. 33:11). Of course, this is rather different from the love of the Father for the Son; it is, to say the least, distinguishable from God's providential love.

(4) God's choosing love, his selective love. He is the God who chose Israel—not because Israel was greater or stronger or more impressive than other nations, but because he loved her (Deut. 7:7-8; 10:15). This is not to be confused with passages that speak of God's providential love, for everyone without exception is the recipient of that love, whereas here the entire point is that God's love is making distinctions. That is why God can summarize this love by referring to distinguishing categories: "I have loved Jacob, but Esau I have hated," God says (Mal. 1:2-3)—a

distinction, Paul points out, that was grounded in the mind of God before either Jacob or Esau "were born or had done anything good or bad" (Rom. 9:10-12). Similarly in the New Testament: "Christ loved the church and gave himself up for her" (Eph. 5:25). These ways of speaking are to be differentiated from passages that talk about God's yearning, inviting love, still more from those that talk of his providential love over all without distinction.

(5) God's conditional love. In both Testaments, numerous passages make God's love conditional on faithful obedience. In the Decalogue, for instance, God promises to show love "to a thousand generations of those who love me *and keep my commandments*" (Exod. 20:6, emphasis mine). Jesus tells his followers, "If you obey my commands, you will remain in my love, just as I have obeyed my Father's commands and remain in his love" (John 15:10). Jude warns his readers, "Keep yourselves in God's love" (21), giving the unavoidable impression that it is all too possible *not* to remain in God's love.

Three further things need to be said about the different ways the Bible speaks of the love of God.

First, it is better to speak of the entries on this list as five different ways the Bible has of speaking of the love of God than as five different "loves" of God. To speak of different "loves" of God gives the impression that God is in possession of several compartmentalized "loves" that he turns on and off for different targets or on different occasions. There is no good evidence that that is what the biblical texts mean.

Moreover, on the analogy of human beings (who, after all, have been created in the image of God), we speak of human love in highly diverse ways that reflect the complexity of our relationships as persons. For instance, in one context I may speak of my unconditional love for my children: I am committed to loving them no matter what they do or become. But in another sense, as when I tell my teenaged son to be home with the car by midnight, he knows me well enough to know that if he returns home late and without valid excuse, he will face the wrath of Dad; he knows it pays to keep himself in Dad's love, so to speak. To love a hobby is not quite the same thing as to love an enemy. So also with respect to talk about God's love: God is love, as John says (1 John 4:8), but that love works out in a diverse array of patterns that reflect the diversity of the relationships in which he as a person engages.

Second, to avoid distortion we should reflect on the love of God only in conjunction with reflection on all of God's other perfections. Otherwise there will be a tendency to pit one attribute of God against other attributes of God, to domesticate one or more of God's characteristics by appealing to the supremacy of another. If we rejoice in God's love, we shall rejoice no less in God's holiness, in God's sovereignty, in God's omniscience, and so forth, and we shall be certain that all of God's perfections work together.

Third, this analysis of the different ways the Bible speaks of God's love enables us to evaluate a number of clichés common among Christians. For example: "God's love is unconditional." Is this true? Transparently, it is true of some of the ways the Bible speaks of the love of God. For instance, God's providential love is unconditional, for it is poured out on the just and the unjust alike. God's elective love is unconditional, for absolutely nothing can separate us from it (Rom. 8:31-39). But the love of God spoken of in the Decalogue and in John 15 and Jude 21 (i.e., the fifth in the list above) is explicitly conditional. Again, Christians often say, "God loves everyone exactly the same way and to the same extent." Is this true? In passages that speak of God's love for the just and the unjust, it certainly appears to be true. In passages that speak of God's elective love, it certainly appears to be false. And in passages that speak of God's love being conditioned by obedience, then his love for different individuals will vary with their obedience.

So much for review. The primary reason why I have taken this liberty is that at several points in these lectures I shall compare what the Bible says about the love Christians ought to display with the various ways the Bible speaks of the love of God. So it is important to bear the latter in mind.

So now I turn to Christian love. Where to begin?

I should say something about the title: *Love in Hard Places*. It is a warning that I am not attempting a full-orbed and comprehensive survey of Christian love. For if I were, I would have to be more expansive about the delights of love, the pleasure of loving, about love in the (relatively) easy places. In fact, I shall say a few things about these themes, but I have chosen the title for two reasons. (1) I shall focus especially on those aspects of Christian love that are not easy and may be painful as well as difficult. (2) Because all of the expressions of our love take place in a fallen and broken world of which we are a part, we are unwise to retreat too quickly to merely sentimental notions of love. To love wisely and well, to love appropriately, to love faithfully, to love in line with biblical expectations of what it means to love, is commonly a very difficult thing to do. And that is one of the controlling themes of these lectures.

An obvious and excellent place for any Christian to begin is with:

B. THE DOUBLE COMMANDMENT TO LOVE (MARK 12:28-34)

28*One of the teachers of the law came and heard them debating. Noticing that Jesus had given them a good answer, he asked him, "Of all the commandments, which is the most important?"*

29*"The most important one," answered Jesus, "is this: 'Hear, O Israel, the LORD our God, the LORD is one. 30Love the LORD your God with all your heart and with all your soul and with all your mind and with all your strength.' 31The second is this: 'Love your neighbor as yourself.' There is no commandment greater than these."*

32*"Well said, teacher," the man replied. "You are right in saying that God is one and there is no other but him. 33To love him with all your heart, with all your understanding and with all your strength, and to love your neighbor as yourself is more important than all burnt offerings and sacrifices."*

34*When Jesus saw that he had answered wisely, he said to him, "You are not far from the kingdom of God." And from then on no one dared ask him any more questions. (Mark 12:28-34; cf. Matt. 22:34-40; Luke 10:25-28)*

For my present purposes, there is little need to work through the relatively minor differences between, say, Mark and Matthew; the most central issues will command our attention. It appears that the rising debates between Jesus and his opponents, and especially the quality of Jesus' responses, prompts one particular interlocutor to ask what he regarded as a tough question. The question hummed in the background of first-century conservative Judaism, but there was no consensus in the responses commonly offered. Of all the commandments, which is the most important?

In any complex legal system, some laws eventually take precedence over others. First-century rabbis distinguished between "light" and "heavy" laws; Jesus himself elsewhere makes a similar distinction in the relative importance of laws when he says, in effect, that matters having to do with justice and mercy take precedence over the code on tithing (Matt. 23:23), or when he says that the law mandating the circumcision of a male child on the eighth day takes precedence over the Sabbath (John 7:22-23). But if distinctions must be made as to which laws are "lighter" or "heavier," it will not be long before someone asks which law is the "heaviest" of all, the most important.

Here the rabbis differed. Some said it was the command to love God; others said it was the command to obey one's parents; the great Rabbi Akiba said that the command to love one's neighbor was "the greatest principle in the law."[12] Yet Jesus' linking of the commandment to love God and the commandment to love one's neighbor exercised a unique power in the formation of the ethical structures of his followers. In part, this was because only Jesus wielded the kind of moral authority in both his teaching and his example that compelled followers to build their ethics around a single theme;[13] in part, it was because, as we shall see, Jesus was doing something more than merely classifying what was most important. One of the great themes of his ministry was that love, rightly understood and practiced, actually *fulfilled* Old Testament law. In other words, his teaching on this subject was deeply enmeshed in his insistence that a new age was dawning, and the *eschaton*, the long-awaited final state, was already quite astonishingly being inaugurated.

Jesus' answer to the question put to him unites two traditional Jewish summaries. The first is the command to love God. The words of Scripture that Jesus cites come from Deuteronomy 6:4-5, the *Shema*, the closest thing Judaism has to a creed. It is recited by pious Jews every morning and evening.[14] The moral imperative is squarely set in the con-

---

[12]*Sipre*, on Lev. 19:18.
[13]See John P. Meier, *Matthew*, New Testament Readings 3 (Wilmington: Michael Glazier, 1980), 257.
[14]Cf. also 2 Kings 23:25.

text of the bold declaration, "Hear, O Israel, the LORD our God, the LORD is one" (12:29). Many pagans could say that there is one god because much first-century paganism espoused some form of pantheism: there is an impersonal God coextensive with the universe, the one godness from which all the finite pagan gods spring. But although they could say there is one god, they could not say, as could Jews and Christians, that God is one, for that would deny their polytheism.

This point is not a minor one. Many pagans thought that the various finite deities exercised primary dominion over specified domains. If you wanted to take a sea voyage, you would pray to Neptune, the god of the sea; if you had to give a speech, you would want Hermes (or Mercury in the Latin pantheon; cf. Acts 14:12) on your side. But if there is only one God, if God is one and not many, then he must be God of all. If there are many gods, each exercising authority in restricted and sometimes competing domains, the obligation of the pious pagan is to give each god (or as many gods as he or she can remember) its due; if God is one, he commands the allegiance and devotion of our whole being. In other words, one of the entailments of monotheism is this first and greatest command. That is the nature of the link between verse 29 and verse 30.

Because God is one, then, you are commanded to love him "with all your heart and with all your soul and with all your mind and with all your strength" (12:30).[15] We should first focus on the prepositional phrases. If we restrict ourselves to the meaning of the English words, we might think that the first phrase, "with all your heart," focuses on a love that is affective, emotional, passionate. "I love you with all my heart," Bob tells Sue, as they gaze into each other's eyes—and for us the "heart" is a symbol for the seat of the emotions. The second and fourth phrases, "with all your soul" and "with all your strength," have to do with intensity, with putting your whole being into loving God. That leaves only the third: What does it mean to love God "with all your mind"? Well,

---

[15]We need not here go into the variations of terminology from Gospel to Gospel, on which see W. D. Davies and Dale C. Allison, Jr., *A Critical and Exegetical Commentary on the Gospel According to St. Matthew* (Edinburgh: T & T Clark, 1988-97), 3.240-241. They affect little of the substance of the argument.

we might say, whatever the meaning, it emerges from only one of the four prepositional phrases, so let's not worry about it too much.

As soon as we recognize that biblical symbolism, both Hebrew and Greek, is a little different from ours, the flavor of these four prepositional phrases, taken together, changes a little. In the biblical world, of course, the heart is not the seat of the emotions; the lower organs are. Bob might well tell Sue, "I love you with all my kidneys," or "I love you with all my intestines."[16] The heart is the seat of the entire personality and is very close to what we mean today by "mind," except for the fact that for us "mind" can be a bit narrowly cerebral. Of these four prepositional phrases, then, two of them, the first and the third, focus on our thinking. The second and fourth, "with all your soul" and "with all your strength," focus on intensity, but even "soul" carries overtones of your "inner being" or the like, and therefore of who you are and how or what you think.[17]

So the question must be put in a focused way: What does it mean to love God with the way we think and with all the intensity of our being? For that is what this first commandment mandates.

There are two things it does *not* mean.

First, it is inadequate to think that the verb "to love" means something narrowly volitional, such as "seek the other's good regardless of your affection or non-affection," as if Christian love can be reduced to committed altruism. The commandment to love must not be stripped of affective content. The impetus for this reductionism springs in part from the defective word studies to which I have already alluded. Transparently, however, such reductionism will not work in the most famous love chapter of all, 1 Corinthians 13. For there, love is contrasted with the most amazing altruism, viz. giving all one's goods to feed the poor, giving one's body to be burned. But Paul is convinced that it is

---

[16]This is not too fanciful. See, for instance, in the King James Version or some earlier versions the preservation of expressions that tended to keep to the literal at the expense of comprehension: "though my reins be consumed" (Job 19:27); "God trieth the heart and reins" (Ps. 7:9); "examine me, O LORD . . . try my reins" (Ps. 26:2); "yea, my reins shall rejoice" (Prov. 23:16); "for his bowels did yearn" (Gen. 43:30); "my bowels boiled, and rested not" (Job 30:27); "my bowels, my bowels, I am pained" (Jer. 4:19); "if there be any bowels of compassion" (Phil. 2:1).

[17]I cannot here discuss the understanding of these phrases put forth by Birger Gerhardsson. They are ably evaluated in Davies and Allison, *Matthew*, 3.241-2.

possible to display such profound altruism *without* love—and in that case, he says, "I gain nothing" (1 Cor. 13:1-3).

Second, there is a danger of thinking that we are obeying this first commandment if we live and work in the domain of Christian intellectual endeavor. It is easy to understand how this comes about. Anti-intellectualism still inhabits a wide swath of evangelicalism, and sometimes serious thought is mocked and dismissed by those who prefer sentiment and emotion. Both tendencies have called forth biting denunciations,[18] and these certainly have their place. They have also called forth prophetic appeals to young Christians to devote themselves, for God's sake and for God's glory, to the life of the mind.[19]

But we should not ignore a converse danger, the danger of intellectual arrogance. Biblical scholars, theologians, and other Christian academics are easily tempted to think that they are obeying this first command simply because they work in the intellectual arena and happen to be Christians. After all, studying distinctively Christian themes can be all-absorbing, in precisely the way that studying almost anything can be all-absorbing, provided you have the right sort of temperament and education. I know first-rate scholars who are absorbed in the study of the metal alloys in the blades of jet propulsion engines and others who devote themselves to the properties of recently discovered quarks with unbelievably short half-lives or to the finer points of Sahidic Coptic. The only difference between these scholars and theologians is that the latter may delude themselves into thinking that the effort they put into *their* disciplines demonstrates that they are fulfilling these words of Jesus, while those who study the sex life of sea turtles are unlikely to be similarly deluded. We cannot ignore the brute fact that this first command of Jesus is not a command to think but a command to love, even if that command to love includes the modifiers, "with all your heart . . . with all your mind."

Moreover, it is a command to love *God*, not simply a command to love in some amorphous or sentimental or unfocused or even dissolute

---

[18]E.g., Mark Noll, *The Scandal of the Evangelical Mind* (Grand Rapids: Eerdmans, 1994); David F. Wells, *God in the Wasteland: The Reality of Truth in a World of Fading Dreams* (Grand Rapids: Eerdmans, 1994).

[19]J. P. Moreland, *Love Your God with All Your Mind: The Role of Reason in the Life of the Soul* (Colorado Springs: NavPress, 1997).

way. And in the mind of the biblical figures—whether the writer of Deuteronomy, the Gospel writers, or Jesus himself—this *God* is not the ill-defined figure of much postmodern emphasis, the god whom you define or the god who allegedly stands rather mistily behind all notions of religion, authorizing all of them equally.[20] This is the true God, the Maker of heaven and earth, the God who predicts and controls the future, the God who stands opposed to sin, the God to whom we must one day give an account, the God and Father of our Lord Jesus Christ. And that fact helps us to understand what this first commandment means.

In the context of the old covenant revelation, the command to love God with heart and soul and strength (Deut. 6:4-5) is located in the context of knowing God's Word, obeying it, and passing it on:

> *¹These are the commands, decrees and laws the LORD your God directed me to teach you to observe in the land that you are crossing the Jordan to possess, ²so that you, your children and their children after them may fear the LORD your God as long as you live by keeping all his decrees and commands that I give you, and so that you may enjoy long life. ³Hear, O Israel, and be careful to obey so that it may go well with you and that you may increase greatly in a land flowing with milk and honey, just as the LORD, the God of your fathers, promised you.*
>
> *⁴Hear, O Israel: The LORD our God, the LORD is one. ⁵Love the LORD your God with all your heart and with all your soul and with all your strength. ⁶These commandments that I give you today are to be upon your hearts. ⁷Impress them on your children. Talk about them when you sit at home and when you walk along the road, when you lie down and when you get up. ⁸Tie them as symbols on your hands and bind them on your foreheads. ⁹Write them on the doorframes of your houses and on your gates. (Deut. 6:1-9)*

What this means is that loving God cannot be divorced from fearing God and obeying him. On the one hand, obeying this God means obeying his commandments, and the particular commandment emphasized here is the commandment to love him with heart and soul and

---

[20]Indeed, in John Hick's vision even the word *god* must be abandoned in favor of *Reality*, since some religions have little or no place for a personal deity. Hick moved from *Christo*-centrism to *Theo*-centrism to *Reality*-centrism. See especially his *An Interpretation of Religion: Human Responses to the Transcendent* (London: Macmillan, 1989).

strength. On the other hand, if one truly loves this God, that love will be the motive power for obeying him wholly—and in this context, obeying him wholly brings with it the obligation and the privilege of dwelling long and hard upon his words and being committed to pass them on to the next generation. For how could a person truly love God with heart, soul, and strength, and *not* want to make him known, especially to one's own children? Neglect in this domain is therefore not only disobedience but lack of love for God.

Thus to love God with all our being, not least our "hearts" (in the biblical sense), our minds, means knowing God's words and obeying them. Why should this be surprising? There are so many texts that say similar things. For instance, a few chapters later, Deuteronomy envisages a time when there will be a king in Israel and prescribes what his *first* responsibility must be: "When he takes the throne of his kingdom, he is to write for himself on a scroll a copy of this law, taken from that of the priests, who are Levites. It is to be with him, and he is to read it all the days of his life so that he may learn to revere the LORD his God and follow carefully all the words of this law and these decrees and not consider himself better than his brothers and turn from the law to the right or to the left. Then he and his descendants will reign a long time over his kingdom in Israel" (Deut. 17:18-20).

The king's first task, in other words, is not to appoint Joint Chiefs of Staff or install a new Secretary of State. His first task is to copy over huge chunks of Scripture by hand. He is not simply to download it from a CD to his hard drive without it passing through his brain; he is to copy it out by hand so clearly that his hand-written copy becomes the copy that he reads daily for the rest of his life. The purpose of this exercise is that he may "revere" the Lord his God and "follow carefully all the words of this law and these decrees." Thus regard for the Lord leads him to read and reread Scripture; Scripture teaches him to revere the Lord and trains his mind to follow all of the Lord's words. And this in turn means he will learn not to "consider himself better than his brothers"— which is, of course, part and parcel of loving your brothers and sisters as yourself.

Or consider Deuteronomy 8. There Moses tells the people to remember how the Lord led his people for forty years in the wilderness. This journey included various tests, some suffering, even miraculous provisions. All of these things had the purpose of humbling them and of teaching them that "man does not live on bread alone but on every word that comes from the mouth of the LORD" (Deut. 8:3). Here every word from God's mouth is judged more crucial for human existence than the necessary food that sustains physical life. By this standard, Israel's failures, and ours, are shocking, deeply misguided, disturbingly perverse. By contrast, when the Lord Jesus quotes these very words, he does so in a context that shows how perfectly he keeps his priorities God-centered and thereby withstands temptation (Matt. 4:4).

One does not need to restrict oneself to the book of Deuteronomy. Psalm 1, for instance, describes the "blessed" person as the one whose "delight is in the law of the LORD, and on his law he meditates day and night" (Ps. 1:2). In other words, he is not merely committed to God's Word in some sort of theoretical way, but he positively delights in it—so much so that he thinks about it, turns it over in his mind, meditates on it day and night. In short, he loves God with heart and soul and mind and strength. The longest psalm in holy Scripture is given over to this world-shaping, people-transforming theme (Ps. 119). Small wonder, then, that when he comes to power, Joshua is told, "Do not let his Book of the Law depart from your mouth; meditate on it day and night, so that you may be careful to do everything written in it" (Josh. 1:8).

So it appears, then, that if Jesus has any respect for the context of the text in Deuteronomy he is quoting in Mark 12, he is saying that loving God with heart and soul and mind and strength is bound up with reading, cherishing, meditating on, and obeying God's words.

Intriguingly, although he is asked only for the most important commandment, Jesus stipulates not only the first but the second: "Love your neighbor as yourself" (Mark 12:31). The Old Testament passage he cites is Leviticus 19:18. The content of that chapter is primarily devoted to an array of commands that bear on social relationships: honoring parents, leaving enough gleanings in one's fields at harvest so that the poor may benefit from them, not stealing or lying or perverting justice, not taking advantage of the handicapped, and much more of the same. All of these are subsumed under the command to be holy as God is holy, to avoid idolatry (Lev. 19:1-2, 4). The crucial verse itself, 19:18, reads, "Do not seek revenge or bear a grudge against one of your people, but love your neighbor as yourself. I am the LORD."

It may clarify some issues to offer five comments.

First, the concluding clause, "I am the LORD," reminds us that in Scripture the horizontal commitment to love one's neighbor is grounded in the vertical reality: God exists, we owe him allegiance, he tells us what conduct he expects, and it is impossible to be faithful to him and confess him as Lord while nurturing lovelessness toward neighbors. "Love your neighbor," God says; "I am the LORD."

Second, the love envisaged is *not* a matter of mere performance or of willed altruism, for it is set over against attitudes. We are not to seek revenge or bear a grudge against any of the covenant community; instead, we are to love our neighbor.[21]

Third, I should mention one small detail that I will develop only in the last lecture. Contemporary culture so greatly emphasizes the importance of self-esteem, of self-love, that the little phrase "as yourself" ("love your neighbor *as yourself*") is often understood to be a *command* to love yourself, or at very least an implicit sanction of self-love. Although the idea is very popular today, it goes back at least as far as Augustine.[22] The issue of self-love and its place in the Christian scheme of things is rather complicated, but for the moment it will suffice to point out that in this passage self-love is neither commanded nor commended but presupposed.

Fourth, in this utterance Jesus does not specify how the two love commandments, the commandment to love God and the commandment to love one's neighbor, relate to each other. There have been many suggestions. Some hold that we imitate what we love. So to love God is to act like him, and since he loves our neighbors, we will love them, too. Others hold that the love of neighbor is the only tangible evidence

---

[21]The statement of Davies and Allison, *Matthew*, 3.241, is doubly mistaken: "Love of God, like love of neighbour, is not firstly an attitude or affection but—as the example of Jesus shows—a way of life, the sweat of labour for Another." Certainly love of God, like love of neighbour, is "a way of life," but the negation ("not firstly an attitude or affection") makes little sense and merely preserves an erroneous tradition; worse, the "example of Jesus" shows us nothing of the kind.

[22]*City of God*, 19.14. He goes so far as to put love of self alongside love of God and love of neighbor.

that love of God is genuine, since God cannot be seen and the neighbor can be. Still others think that because human beings are made in the image of God, to love God is necessarily to love those made in his image. All of these ideas, and others, find some warrant in other biblical passages. In the text before us, however, Jesus does not draw a specific connection.

Fifth, many passages repeat this second command or something very much like it. "Do everything in love," Paul writes (1 Cor. 16:14); or again, "The entire law is summed up in a single command: 'Love your neighbor as yourself'" (Gal. 5:14). "[A]nd live a life of love, just as Christ loved us and gave himself up for us" (Eph. 5:2). "If you really keep the royal law found in Scripture, 'Love your neighbor as yourself,' you are doing right" (James 2:8). Moreover, one must consider a somewhat narrower focus that is very common in the New Testament—the many passages where *Christians* are told to love one another. But I will return to those in the next lecture.

There is one more feature in our text that invites comment before I wrap this up with a number of theological and practical observations. That feature is the response of Jesus' interlocutor and then Jesus' further rejoinder. The man replies wisely and approvingly (Mark 12:32-33), prompting Jesus to tell him, "You are not far from the kingdom of God" (12:34). Whatever else this means, Jesus is certainly saying that he cannot imagine admittance to the kingdom without taking on board this double command to love. The text does not tell us that we *earn* admittance by our love, but it does establish an unbreakable connection between our love and entrance into the kingdom. That is precisely why Jesus can make love the characteristic mark of those who are in the kingdom, those who are his disciples: "Love one another," he says. "As I have loved you, so you must love one another. By this all men will know that you are my disciples, if you love one another" (John 13:34-35). Small wonder, then, that in his first letter, John can make love a necessary criterion of authentic Christianity (e.g., 1 John 2:3-6; 3:10b-18; 4:7-21).

But we may probe further. In his abbreviated account of Jesus' teaching on the double commandment to love, Matthew does not tell us of the interlocutor's wise response or of Jesus' comment. Instead, after articulating the two commandments, Jesus simply says, "All the Law and the Prophets hang on these two commandments" (Matt. 22:40). And there may be a theological connection between this utterance and what Jesus tells his interlocutor in Mark's account.

I shall begin from Matthew's side. What does "All the Law and the Prophets hang on these two commandments" mean? The expression "the Law and the Prophets" means "Scripture," what we today would call the Hebrew canon or the Old Testament. But what does it mean to say that all of Scripture "hangs on these two commandments"? If this were the only statement of this sort in Matthew's Gospel, our judgments about what this means would be very subjective, for any active imagination can conjure up several mutually exclusive interpretations.

In fact, however, Matthew is very interested in the relations between "the Law and the Prophets," on the one hand, and the teaching of Jesus, on the other. Already in Matthew 5:17-20, Jesus has said that he did not come to abolish the law and the prophets, but to "fulfill" them. I have argued at length elsewhere[23] that this does *not* mean that Jesus came to *preserve* the Old Testament or to *intensify* the Old Testament or to *obey* the Old Testament, but quite literally to *fulfill* it. In Matthew's use of the verb "to fulfill," he always has in mind that redemptive history is moving onward, and the revelation of the Old Testament points toward, anticipates, predicts (if you like) what is to come—and what is to come is nothing other than Jesus and what he teaches and does. Thus Jesus and the good news (the "Gospel") he preaches *fulfills* the older revelation.

A similar point recurs toward the end of the Sermon on the Mount: To "do to others what you would have them do to you" sums up the law and the prophets (Matt. 7:12). A few chapters later we are again reminded of this salvation-historical development when we are told that the "Law and the Prophets" *prophesied* until John the Baptist; from that point on, that to which they pointed—the dawning of the kingdom—is what is preached.

Similarly, Paul insists that what is *fulfilled* in one word, viz. Leviticus

---

[23]D. A. Carson, *Matthew*, EBC 8 (Grand Rapids: Zondervan, 1984), 140-147.

19:18, the command to love one's neighbor as oneself, is the entire second table of the Decalogue: love is the *fulfillment* of the law (Rom. 13:8-10). Despite arguments to the contrary, the double command to love is not some sort of deep principle from which all the other commandments of Scripture can be deduced; nor is it a hermeneutical grid to weed out the laws of the old covenant that no longer have to be obeyed while blessing those that are still operative; nor is it offered as a kind of reductionistic substitute for all the Old Testament laws. In some ways, the twin laws of love, love for God and love for neighbor, integrate all the other laws. They establish the proper motives for all the other imperatives, viz. loving God and loving one's neighbor.

But the "fulfillment" language suggests something more. All the laws of the old revelation, indeed all the old covenant Scriptures, conspire to anticipate something more, to point to something beyond themselves. They point to the coming of the kingdom, the gospel of the kingdom; they point to a time when life properly lived in God's universe can be summed up by obedience to the commandment to love God with heart and soul and mind and strength and by the commandment to love your neighbor as yourself.

Most Christians are already aware of the prophetic or predictive element in at least some laws: we have come to think of Jesus as the ultimate temple, the ultimate Passover lamb, the ultimate high priest, the ultimate sacrifice of the Day of Atonement, and so forth. We follow the arguments of the New Testament writers to the effect that the Old Testament portrayal of these institutions and rites, though integral to the old covenant and rightly observed by those who were under that covenant, simultaneously pointed forward to, anticipated, and thus predicted, a reality greater than themselves—a reality Jesus himself *fulfilled*. The argument here is that something similar can be said, in general terms, of all the law and the prophets. For example, in the consummated kingdom we will no longer need a command to prohibit murder. This is not because murder will be tolerated, but because murder will be unthinkable (quite apart from the challenge of murdering someone with a resurrection body!); hate will be unthinkable; instead, we will love one another. Thus it is not as if the consummated kingdom *abolishes* the command to murder; rather, it *fulfills* it. The kingdom brings to pass the true direction in which the prohibition of murder points.

Moreover, although the consummated kingdom has not yet arrived, there is a sense in which the kingdom is already inaugurated; it has already begun; it is already partly realized. That leaves us with some terrible tensions, of course. The kingdom has come, but it is still coming; we have been transformed by the new birth, but we do not yet have resurrection bodies; we have been regenerated, but we have not yet experienced that perfect transformation that means we no longer sin; we hear the kingdom imperatives, but we recognize that this is still a cruel and broken world where the conflict between good and evil staggers on. That is the very stuff of New Testament eschatology, of New Testament ethics.

If what I have said about Jesus' words in Matthew's Gospel is right, however, we suddenly find ourselves close to what Jesus says in Mark. On Matthew's side, "All the Law and the Prophets hang on these two commandments" (Matt. 22:40), for these commandments constitute the direction in which the law and the prophets point, the coming of the good news of the kingdom. On Mark's side, "You are not far from the kingdom of God" (Mark 12:34)—for understanding and obeying these two commandments are very much bound up with what it means to be in the kingdom.

C. Some Theological and Practical Reflections

Perhaps the following points will draw some of the material of this lecture together.

First, we cannot fail to note that both of these commands *are commands*.[24] It is sometimes objected that love cannot be commanded: one falls in love, or one surges with love, or love grows cold, but the affections, it is said, cannot be commanded. Indeed, that is precisely why some have defended the false view that "agapic" love, Christian love, is the willed commitment to the other's good, irrespective of the emotions one might feel. The will can be commanded, it is argued; the affections cannot. That gives me scope for willing the good of the scoundrel whom I emotionally detest—a nice dodge, this. Love your neighbor and hate

---

[24]I use "commands" and "commandments" indistinguishably.

his guts. But we have already seen that such a view of "agapic" love is dismissed by the opening verses of 1 Corinthians 13, where Paul warns against the kind of willed philanthropy and even self-sacrifice that gives away all one's goods and consents to be burned at the stake but remains loveless. No, such a narrow view of love must not be allowed to prevail. We cannot get off the hook so easily. Scripture commands us in every facet of our being to do, to will, to trust, to love.

Our failure to respond wholly to the first and second commandments—that is, the fact that we do not love God with heart and soul and mind and strength and our neighbor as ourselves—is a function not of some alleged inherent incapacity of the affections to be commanded but of our moral weakness. This failure is a function of the fall. Just as in Paul the law functions, in part, to expose our lostness, our moral inability and culpability, and thus to multiply our explicit transgressions, so also here: these two great commands expose our lostness, our moral inability and culpability, and thus multiply our explicit transgressions.

Second, the first point becomes clearer when we recall that failure to love God with heart and soul and mind and strength is to dethrone God; it is to de-God God, to erect an idol in the place of God. For if we love something else more than God, the created thing more than the Creator, we have succumbed to the very heart of all idolatry. That is why any form of apostasy, any form of *not* loving God with heart and soul and mind and strength, is likened to adultery (e.g., Exod. 34:11-16; Lev. 20:4-6; Num. 15:38-40; Judg. 2:16-17; Hos. 1—3; Isa. 1:21; Jer. 2—3; Ezek. 16, 23):[25] it is to betray the love we owe to God, by loving another more. And that is why the prophet Hosea can (God help us!) portray God Almighty as a cuckolded lover: his people have disobeyed these two commands. It is not a comfortable thing to reflect on how frequently the fickleness of our own hearts, the hearts of the new covenant people of God, turn God again and again into the almighty cuckold.

Third, if in the preceding exposition I have rightly interpreted what loving God with our hearts (in the biblical sense of "hearts") and minds means, then serious Christians must recapture the Bible-reading habits of some earlier generations. No longer should we be happy with slogans

---

[25]See especially Raymond C. Ortlund, Jr., *Whoredom: God's Unfaithful Wife in Biblical Theology*, NSBT 2 (Leicester: InterVarsity Press, 1996).

such as "A verse a day keeps the devil away"; still less should we be happy with whatever spiritual nourishment we receive from public meetings while we ourselves do not transform our minds (Rom. 12:1) with the Word of God. Even within the church, there is rising biblical illiteracy. The impact of the cultural pressures upon us, not least from the media, is so devastatingly great that only a mind steeped in thinking God's thoughts after him will begin to withstand the onslaught.

What this demands of every believer who can read is devoted, reverent, disciplined reading and rereading of the Word of God, a reading discharged in an attitude of eager attentiveness. And what such reading presupposes is time. I am not trying to impose a new legalism. I am sadly aware that it is possible to read the Bible a great deal and merely become self-righteous or wallow in unbelief; but I doubt that it is possible to obey the first command without reading the Bible a great deal.

Earlier generations met the needs of illiterate believers with liturgy steeped in Scripture, lectionary cycles, festivals designed to repeat the great narratives that stand at the turning points in redemptive history. Nowadays most evangelical churches have abandoned these devices that helped shape former generations of people to think God's thoughts. Today even our few remaining festivals, our church-sponsored Christmas and Easter pageants, often have more to do with space raiders or yuppies or being nice at school than they do with biblical history. Choruses that help us celebrate do not necessarily teach us how to think. So with the demise of Bible reading, what teaches us how to think God's thoughts after him? How on earth shall we love him with heart and mind if we do not increasingly know him, know what he likes and what he loathes, know what he has disclosed, know what he commands and what he forbids?

Moreover, if loving God with heart and soul and mind and strength requires time and effort, so also does loving neighbors. Some folks coo charmingly that they love the whole world even while they give no sacrificial time to anyone other than their own set of friends. Any pagan can do that. Nor is the pressure of time a new thing. Here is Luther:

> I could almost say that I need two secretaries; I do hardly anything else all day long than write letters. I am monastery preacher; I am delegated

to read at table; I am expected to preach daily in the parish church; I am head of the monastery school; I am vicar of the monastery Order which means a prior eleven times over [because there were eleven cloisters in the district]; I am the officer responsible for the fish-pond; I act as substitute; I lecture on Paul and am studying the Psalms; and then all this correspondence which takes up the greater part of my time; I have scarcely any left for my private prayers, never to mention the special temptations of the flesh, the world, and the devil. All this shows what sort of a lazy fellow I am.[26]

So much more could be said about the first and second great commandments. I have barely scratched the surface. After that, there could be lengthy, meditative reflection on a host of related passages and themes. For instance: if Christians love, whether God or neighbors, it is in response to God's love (Col. 3:12-15; 1 Pet. 1:8; 1 John 4:11). Although Christian love is invariably the obligation of Christians, it is the fruit of the Spirit (Gal. 5:13). It is characterized by humility and gentleness (Eph. 4:1-2); in emulation of the Master, it eschews retaliation (1 Pet. 3:8-9). Inevitably self-restraint becomes a watchword (Rom. 14:13-15) as the Christian learns to love with heart and attitude no less than with action (1 Cor. 13).

But "love in hard places" is our theme. What is the first hard place? It is the hardest place of all, the place of love's origin—our own hearts and lives. There is a humorous cartoon of a preacher at his prayers. In the first panel, we find him on his knees, intoning before the Lord, "O God, smite my enemies for the wickedness of their conduct." In the second panel, he becomes more exuberant yet: "Bring down fiery judgment upon them, the just reward of their bitter hearts." By the third panel, he has become personal: "May flocks of vultures descend on the head of my most bitter foe." In the final panel, flocks of vultures are swarming all over him, and the preacher is left to pray, "Uh, let me rephrase that." In the immortal words of Pogo, "We have met the enemy, and it is us." Nothing but the gospel will soften up this hard place; no one but the Spirit can regenerate the human heart. And the softening job will not be complete until the consummation.

---

[26]From a letter by Martin Luther to his personal friend Lang, 1516.

2

LOVE AND ENEMIES,
BIG AND SMALL

I suppose that when we think about love in hard places, we naturally gravitate to the difficult demand of the Lord Jesus to love our enemies. Enemies come in various shapes and sizes. Before we reflect on the diversity of enemies, and therefore on the varieties of love we are called to display, we should think our way through what is perhaps the most important passage on the subject.

A. EXPOSITION OF MATTHEW 5:43-48

> ⁴³*You have heard that it was said, "Love your neighbor and hate your enemy." ⁴⁴But I tell you: Love your enemies and pray for those who persecute you, ⁴⁵that you may be sons of your Father in heaven. He causes his sun to rise on the evil and the good, and sends rain on the righteous and the unrighteous. ⁴⁶If you love those who love you, what reward will you get? Are not even the tax collectors doing that? ⁴⁷And if you greet only your brothers, what are you doing more than others? Do not even pagans do that? ⁴⁸Be perfect, therefore, as your heavenly Father is perfect.*

"You have heard that it was said . . . [b]ut I tell you": That formula occurs six times in Matthew 5, and because of the form, the occurrences are collectively called the six antitheses. In each case, Jesus exerts his authority. His aim, in part, is to correct a popular misunderstanding of the law. Sometimes he quotes only the Old Testament text (as in 5:38);

sometimes he quotes both the text and the interpretation he seeks to cor-rect (as here in 5:43). There are differences in the way Jesus deals with these Old Testament texts, and these differences have generated sub-stantial scholarly debate. As interesting as these are, I cannot pursue them here. I would only assert that in every instance, Jesus is concerned to show the true direction in which those texts point.

Although I cannot treat all the variations, it may clarify what I have to say about this command to love your enemy if I briefly consider two of the other five antitheses.

(1) *Oaths* (Matt. 5:33-37). The Old Testament did in fact tell the covenant people not to break their oaths. "Do not swear falsely by my name and so profane the name of your God. I am the LORD" (Lev. 19:12). "When a man makes a vow to the LORD or takes an oath to obli-gate himself by a pledge, he must not break his word but must do every-thing he said" (Num. 30:2; cf. Deut. 23:21). In fact, the Old Testament actually *commands* people to swear *by the Lord*: "Fear the LORD your God, serve him only and take your oaths in his name" (Deut. 6:13). Yet here is Jesus saying, "Do not swear at all" (Matt. 5:34). Isn't this a sim-ple contradiction of what the Old Testament mandates?

At a superficial level, of course, the answer must be yes. But when the Pentateuch commands God's covenant people to swear by the Lord, it was meant in part as a protection against idolatry. People swear by what they think is supreme, what they judge to be most sacred. Until recent times most American citizens, when they pledged in court to tell the truth, the whole truth, and nothing but the truth, placed their hands on the Bible because of the place of authority the Bible enjoyed in American tradition. In some variations, these citizens then uttered the words, "So help me God"—and once again, these words reflect a sacred tradition. Most Americans would not make a solemn oath in the name of God and add, "So help me Shiva," referring to one of the more vio-lent of the Hindu gods. Thus the command to swear by the Lord, by Yahweh, was an injunction to ensure that Yahweh was for the Israelite community their supreme good, their most sacred connection, the great God above whom there was no one greater.[1] It would be a singular mark

---

[1]Of course that is why, when God puts himself under an oath, he swears by himself, for there is none greater (Heb. 6:13).

of rebellion if the covenant people of God started taking their oaths in the name of one of the Baals, for instance.

But by Jesus' day, this business of taking oaths in various names had gotten a little out of hand. You can see this most clearly in Matthew 23:16-22. Some were saying that if anyone swears by the temple, it means nothing, and the oath is not binding; but if someone swears by the gold of the temple, the oath is binding. Or again, if someone swears by the temple's altar, the oath is not binding; but if someone swears by the sacrifice on the temple's altar, then the oath is binding. This approach is an attempt to assess the relative sacredness of various religious entities, but the effect is to introduce evasive lying. It's a bit like the kid who promises, "I didn't do it! I swear! Cross my heart and hope to die!" She then goes away and smugly tells her friend that the oath didn't count because she had her fingers crossed behind her back. Some said that if you swore by Jerusalem, the city of the Great King, you were not bound by your oath; but if you swore while facing Jerusalem, then you were bound by your oath.

Jesus rejects all the casuistry. "But I tell you, Do not swear at all: either by heaven, for it is God's throne; or by the earth, for it is his footstool; or by Jerusalem, for it is the city of the Great King. And do not swear by your head, for you cannot make even one hair white or black" (Matt. 5:34-36). The point is that everything that exists in God's universe is under God's sway. Therefore, to swear by any part of it, since you have no ultimate control over it yourself, is to swear by God. So stop the evasive lying. Better yet: don't swear at all. "Simply let your 'Yes' be 'Yes,' and your 'No,' 'No'; anything beyond this comes from the evil one" (5:37).

So at a superficial level, then, Jesus is formally contradicting the Old Testament. The Old Testament tells the people of God to swear by Yahweh; Jesus tells his followers not to swear by anyone or anything. Yet this is a superficial analysis. The direction in which the Old Testament Scriptures on this subject point is toward truth-telling—truth-telling in God's universe. By manipulating the inferences, some folk had transmuted Old Testament authority into justification for deceit. Jesus will not have it. Tell the truth: that is what actually "fulfills" this part of "the law and the prophets" (cf. 5:17-18). For that is what Jesus came to do. He did not come to abolish the law and the prophets but to "fulfill" them, i.e., to bring to pass everything to which they point, everything they predict.

But Jesus is not saying that there is something intrinsically evil in taking an oath in someone's name. After all, Paul can put himself under an oath (e.g., Rom. 9:1; 2 Cor. 1:23); God puts himself under an oath when he swears by himself (Heb. 6:13-18). But neither Paul nor God uses an oath for evasive lying. Nor would the absence of an oath mean that either Paul or God would be free to lie. Rather, the oath merely enhances their credibility among their hearers, who are so used to lying that an oath makes an utterance more solemn. In fact, Scripture tells us that that is exactly why God took an oath: he "wanted to make the unchanging nature of his purpose very clear to the heirs of what was promised" (Heb. 6:17). The problem was their unbelief, not any propensity on God's part toward deceit.

So the purpose of this antithesis on oaths, then, is to establish the true direction in which legislation on this subject points, viz. truth-telling. If that means a formal contradiction of the form of the old covenant legislation, so be it.

That brings us to the second antithesis to be considered.

(2) The *lex talionis*, the "eye for an eye" legislation (Matt. 5:38-42). The Old Testament law, "Eye for eye, and tooth for tooth," was established as part of the judicial system of the fledgling Israelite nation (Exod. 21:24; Lev. 24:20; Deut. 19:21). For certain kinds of crimes, it is, in fact, strictly just. The *lex talionis* cannot be applied in the case of many crimes—idolatry, for instance, or rape, or blasphemy—but in instances of, say, personal and intentional wounding of another, it is strictly just. Moreover, it has the advantage of making an ongoing feud unlikely. Justice, strict justice, has been served. And in the Old Testament context, this is the decision of the court. The famous riposte attributed to Gandhi—that the principle "eye for eye" means that pretty soon the whole world will be blind—is cute and memorable but frankly stupid. When enacted for specified crimes by a properly constituted judiciary, it has the effect of limiting and discouraging violence, ending feuds before they get started and inculcating the notion of strict justice.

Yet here is Jesus saying something quite different: "But I tell you, Do not resist an evil person. If someone strikes you on the right cheek, turn to him the other also. And if someone wants to sue you and take your tunic, let him have your cloak as well. If someone forces you to go one mile, go with him two miles. Give to the one who asks you, and do not turn away from the one who wants to borrow from you" (Matt. 5:39-42). What is to be made of this?

Judging from the examples that Jesus himself introduces, he is primarily responding to personal inferences that have been drawn from the *lex talionis* legislation. Apparently some Jews read that legislation and ripped it out of its judicial context. If someone does me an injury, they might say, Scripture itself gives me the right to pay the person back, eye for eye, tooth for tooth, injury for injury. So used, the legislation becomes justification for personal bitterness, sanction for personal revenge, divine permission for personal retaliation. At that point, Jesus insists on a better way. Absorb the blow, and offer your other cheek. If a Roman soldier impresses you to carry his bags or equipment for a mile (which was the soldier's legal right under Roman legislation, but from a Jewish perspective a form of grossly unjust exploitation), carry it for two miles instead of plotting revenge.

In the history of the Christian church, this passage and related texts have often been used to justify systematic pacifism. I think I understand its appeal as the ostensible "high ground" of morality. But I doubt that the pacifist has rightly understood what Jesus is saying. This passage no more abolishes all judicial sentencing, in the name of turning the other cheek, than the previous paragraph abolishes all taking of oaths, in the name of telling the truth. To think otherwise, I fear, is to pursue an exegetical tradition characterized by more than a little reductionism. Worse, this position fails to see how Jesus' instruction truly relates to the Old Testament passages to which he refers. For once again, Jesus rightly grasps the true direction in which the Old Testament legislation points.

The Old Testament legislation not only provides for strict justice; it envisages a rightly ordered society in which people get along and support one another without animus. Granted this is a broken and sinful world; legislation must be enacted to curb evil, satisfy the claims of justice, and discourage vendettas. But just as the Mosaic laws on oaths simultaneously enhanced the credibility of the speaker in a *fallen* world and held up the virtue of truth-telling as a good in itself, so also the

Mosaic *lex talionis* simultaneously enhanced strict justice, limiting vendettas in a *fallen* world, and held up the virtue of a rightly ordered society, people getting on with one another as a good in itself. Jesus perceives in both cases that the formal legislation points beyond the *fallen* world to an ultimate good.

That is why the chapter ends the way it does in verse 48: "Be perfect, therefore, as your heavenly Father is perfect." Almost certainly this is not a conclusion to verses 43-47 but to all six of the antitheses. In each case, Jesus says, the law not only exercises a regulative function within the Mosaic covenant, but it also points beyond that world to the perfection God demands, to the perfection that will be characteristic of the consummated kingdom. That is the direction in which the law points; that is the nature of the relationship between the Mosaic law—or, more broadly, "the Law [and] the Prophets" (5:17)—and the perfection of the consummated kingdom. The former points to the latter; the law and the prophets point to the kingdom. And that kingdom is already dawning; it is being inaugurated in the life and ministry and death and resurrection and exaltation of Jesus.

At this juncture we are likely to hear someone object: "This talk of the consummated kingdom is all very well, but we are painfully aware that this world remains fallen and broken. Evil still presides over every aspect of human existence." That is true, of course. But all that the objection succeeds in doing is pointing out one of the most persistent and characteristic tensions in the New Testament, namely the tension between the "already" and the "not yet," between the inaugurated kingdom and the consummated kingdom. There is a sense in which the followers of Jesus are to see themselves, as it were, as an outpost within time, within the time of fallenness, of the consummated kingdom still to come. Taken as a whole, the New Testament documents fully recognize the ongoing reality of evil even while they insist that this world is passing away (1 John 2:17) and that Satan is as furious as he is because he knows his time is short (Rev. 12:12). That is why we are to pray, "Your kingdom come" (Matt. 6:10). Inevitably, that means we live with certain tensions. But such tensions are the very stuff of New Testament ethics, precisely because they are the very stuff of New Testament eschatology. And Jesus fully recognizes the tensions. If he urges his followers to turn the other cheek when someone slaps them or to respond gently to a bullying Roman soldier, then Jesus is fully aware that the ethics of perfection must still at this point in history be worked out in a terribly broken and disordered world.

That brings us to the passage that is our immediate concern, namely Matthew 5:43-47. Jesus' hearers have heard that it was said, "Love your neighbor and hate your enemy" (5:43). Of course, there is no Old Testament passage that says just that. The first part, "Love your neighbor," is drawn from Leviticus 19:18. As we saw in the first lecture, Jesus incorporated that text into his double-love command. We do not need to repeat the examination of the Old Testament context in which it is found. But where did the second part, "and hate your enemy," come from?

One cannot be absolutely certain how the slogan "Love your neighbor and hate your enemy" developed, but it is not difficult to make some reasonable guesses. If the text says, "Love your *neighbor*," then surely, some might think, there is implicit sanction for *not* loving those who are *not* neighbors. That may not be logically sound, but it is understandable enough. And then it is only a small step to the conclusion that it is entirely appropriate to hate certain people, especially certain enemies. After all, doesn't the psalmist refer to his enemies and declare, "I have nothing but hatred for them" (Ps. 139:22)?

In fact, there is a long litany of texts that authorize a certain kind of hate. In 2 Chronicles 19:2 the prophet Jehu rebukes King Jehoshaphat for making alliances with the ungodly. He sharply asks him, "Should you help the wicked and love those who hate the LORD?" Jehu implies, of course, that the king should *not* love those who hate the Lord. In Psalm 35 David prays, "Contend, O LORD, with those who contend with me; fight against those who fight against me" (35:1)—which does not sound very much like turning the other cheek. There are scores of such passages. So is the slogan "Love your neighbor and hate your enemy" so very wrong?

Inevitably, the matter is more subtle than it first appears, just as it is with respect to the law on oaths or the *lex talionis*. When Jehu confronts Jehoshaphat, he rebukes him not for his personal attitude toward personal friends and personal enemies, but for his conduct as king: the covenant king does not have the right to make alliances with those on whom the Lord himself has pronounced judgment. Where David declares that he has nothing but hatred for certain people, the context is revealing: "Do I not hate those who hate you, O LORD, and abhor those who rise up against you?" he asks rhetorically. Then he concludes, "I have nothing but hatred for them; I count them my enemies" (Ps. 139:21-22). In the context, then, David seeks to align himself with God's perspective. He chooses to hate those whom God hates. He does not hate them because they are his enemies, but they are declared to be his enemies because he hates them, in imitation of God. And even in this he is careful not so much to seek vengeance himself as to ask God to slay the wicked (139:19). Indeed, this is part and parcel of the psalmist's commitment to think God's thoughts after him. This is the negative counterpoint to the positive rethinking of God's thoughts a little earlier in the psalm: "How precious to me are your thoughts, O God! How vast is the sum of them! Were I to count them, they would outnumber the grains of sand. When I awake, I am still with you" (139:17-18).[2]

It appears, then, that in addition to the special circumstances surrounding the responsibilities of a covenant king, the psalmists are interested in reflecting the example of God himself. God does not always, as it were, turn the other cheek. Moreover, as I argued in the previous book,[3] the Bible can simultaneously affirm God's wrath toward people and his love for them: it does not intimate that God's love and his judicial "hatred" are necessarily mutually exclusive. So why should love and hatred be exclusive in us? Even in a psalm of malediction such as Psalm 109, which is very rich in curses, the psalmist makes it clear that he *has* loved his enemies and prayed for them: "In return for my friendship [lit. 'love'] they accuse me, but I am a man of prayer. They repay me evil for good, and hatred for my friendship [lit. 'love']" (109:4-5).

The issue is rapidly becoming complex. Not surprisingly, a very wide range of attitudes toward enemies can be found in the Judaism roughly contemporaneous with the writing of the New Testament. In the document *Joseph and Aseneth*, Levi restrains the enraged Simeon by insisting that "it is not seemly for a godly man to repay evil for evil to

---

[2]See the useful discussion in John Piper, *"Love Your Enemies": Jesus' Love Command in the Synoptic Tradition and the Early Christian Paraenesis* (SNTSMS 38; Cambridge: Cambridge University Press, 1979), 33-34.

[3]D. A. Carson, *The Difficult Doctrine of the Love of God* (Wheaton, Ill.: Crossway, 2000), chap. 4.

his neighbor" (23:9). On the other hand, the *Manual of Discipline* from Qumran commands its sectarians "to love all that [God] has chosen and to hate all that he has despised . . . and that they may love all the sons of light . . . and that they may hate all the sons of darkness" (1:4, 9-10). Still, one should be careful not to infer too much from this passage. This may be saying little more than what some Old Testament passages say, since elsewhere in the *Manual of Discipline* the member of the community is to say, "To no man will I render the reward of evil, with goodness will I pursue each one; for judgment of all the living is with God, and he it is who will pay to each man his reward" (10:17-18).

We should not consider this stance exactly like Christian attitudes, of course, for the Qumran sectarians practiced a monastic-like separation that was grounded in racial distinction and what they judged to be their own covenantal obedience. Rabbinic debates went further. They disputed at length the meaning of "neighbor" and wondered whether it ever extended to Gentiles. There was no unanimity, but the preponderance of the voices developed an ethic from the Old Testament that seems to extrapolate from that side of the Old Testament represented by Psalms 69:21-28; 109; 139:19-22.[4]

All of these sources belong to reasonably learned circles. We have little direct access as to how such matters were handled by the ordinary person on the street, but it does not take much imagination to guess. If there are explicit injunctions to hate the outsiders in the writings of the learned, it is easy to see how such injunctions would likely be nurtured among ordinary folk.

The question to ask is this: Could it be that when Jesus says, "You have heard that it was said, 'Love your neighbor and hate your enemy,'" he intends to contradict not only the popular religion of the street and the imbalance of some religious contemporaries but the Old Testament balance itself? Certainly that has been suggested: the God of the New Testament, it is said, is a gentler, kinder God than the Old Testament Deity. But that simply makes no sense of the New Testament evidence. The God of the New Testament still abhors evil (Rom. 12:9). He is the God of both mercy and judgment, and on the last day he takes

---

[4]The evidence is neatly summarized in John Piper, *"Love Your Enemies,"* 47-49.

vengeance upon his enemies (e.g., Matt. 13:30; 25:46; Rom. 2:8; 12:19; Rev. 14; 20:9, 15). Even within the teaching of Jesus himself, not least in the Gospel of Matthew, there are scenes of blistering future judgment (read, for example, Matt. 23).

So it appears, then, that when Jesus excoriates the position, "Love your neighbor and hate your enemy," he is not criticizing the complex Old Testament balance between mercy and judgment, since he so largely maintains something similar. So do the writers of the New Testament, who were shaped directly or indirectly by Jesus. He is criticizing the unbalanced extrapolations from the Old Testament that use Old Testament passages and themes to justify personal hatred, in exactly the same way that he criticized use of the *lex talionis* to justify personal revenge or use of the laws on oaths to justify evasive lying.

These distinctions are important if we wish to understand what Jesus is actually saying. To absolutize what Jesus says about loving one's enemies is exegetically equivalent to absolutizing what he says about abolishing oaths or what he says about the *lex talionis*. It may have a certain initial appeal, but it is naive and sentimental and does not correspond to how Jesus himself acts and speaks of judgment and wrath.

That brings us back, then, to the passage itself. Over against the personal hatred that some people thought was warranted on the basis of their selective reading of Old Testament texts, Jesus mandates something else: "Love your enemies," he says, "and pray for those who persecute you" (Matt. 5:44). Here is a vision of love that is rich and costly: it extends even to enemies. It is manifested not least in prayer for enemies. We find it difficult to hate those for whom we pray; we find it difficult not to pray for those whom we love. In no one is this more strikingly manifest than in Jesus himself as he writhes on the cross and yet prays for his enemies, "Father, forgive them, for they do not know what they are doing" (Luke 23:34). If Jesus is our example as well as our Lord, what arrogance, bitterness, pain, or sloth could ever justify our failure to pray for our enemies?

In fact, the example that Jesus holds up for his followers in this instance is the Father himself. The importance of acting like God is made explicit in the first part of 5:45: You are to love your enemies, Jesus says, and pray for those who persecute you, "that you may be sons of your

Father in heaven." Here the notion of "sonship" is entirely functional. In a world where most sons ended up doing what their fathers did—bakers' sons became bakers—the parallels between fathers and sons were often striking. One of the characteristics of the son in this sort of world is that he acts like his father. If you lie and want to kill, the reason must be that your father is the devil himself, for the devil was a liar and a murderer from the beginning (John 8:44). Conversely, since God is the supreme peacemaker, then if you make peace, it is entirely appropriate that you be called a son of God (Matt. 5:9). So also here: if you love your enemies, then you are acting like God, and in this respect you are rightly called a son of God. After all, "[h]e causes his sun to rise on the evil and the good, and sends rain on the righteous and the unrighteous" (5:45b).

This is an appeal to God's providential love. Transparently, it is not an appeal to the love God displays in election, or to passages where God's love is explicitly conditional, or to intra-Trinitarian love (where there is no question of providing for the just and the unjust alike!). This is a straightforward appeal to God's universal, undifferentiated love in his providential provision for the righteous and the unrighteous alike. If God himself is so generous, should we not act similarly?

If this reading of the passage is correct, then while it is important not to lose the punch of the passage, it is also important not to infer too much. The inescapable fact is that in both Testaments God presents himself in many passages as the God of justice, the God of holy wrath. Jesus does not think that God's providential love is intrinsically contradictory to these complementary divine perfections. Again, other passages speak of God's conditional love or of his elective love: such texts could not legitimately be used to model the moral lesson Jesus draws here. Just as one cannot responsibly absolutize passages that speak of God's providential love and thereby domesticate or even eliminate other ways the Bible has of speaking of God's love, so also one cannot responsibly absolutize this passage's moral demand on Jesus' followers and eliminate other things we should be imitating in God. Elsewhere, for instance, we are told to be holy because he is holy (Lev. 11:44-45; 1 Pet. 1:15); again, in John 17 God's intra-Trinitarian love is held up as the controlling model for love among Christians, and this is certainly not considered an inferior sort of love because it is not directed toward enemies.

While it is important not to bleed too much from this text, it is no less important not to emasculate it. The sad fact is that in this twisted and broken world, most people love those who are like them and resent those who are different; they love those who admire them and resent those who criticize them. Jesus himself draws attention to the regular run of things: "If you love those who love you, what reward will you get? Are not even the tax collectors doing that? And if you greet only your brothers, what are you doing more than others? Do not even pagans do that?" (Matt. 5:46-47). Tax collectors were particularly despised in Jesus' day, not only because graft was endemic to the tax-farming system, but also because the higher echelons of tax collectors had contact with Roman overlords, which made them simultaneously ceremonially unclean and traitors to the ideal of Jewish independence. But even tax collectors had their friends—other tax collectors, for a start. Among Palestinian Jews of Jesus' day, pagans were almost universally viewed as morally inferior, but they too had their friends. If Jesus' followers adhered to the popular dictates of the day—"Love your neighbor and hate your enemy"—then they were no better than tax collectors or pagans.

The morality that Jesus demands is, finally, perfection—the perfection found in the Father himself: "Be perfect, therefore, as your heavenly Father is perfect." That is what will transpire in the consummated kingdom. And this standard is what is held up for Christians now in this twisted, selfish, broken world.

B. SOME RELATED PASSAGES

There are several other passages in the New Testament that contribute directly to the theme of loving one's enemies. Perhaps the most important three are these:

> [17]Do not repay anyone evil for evil. Be careful to do what is right in the eyes of everybody. [18]If it is possible, as far as it depends on you, live at peace with everyone. [19]Do not take revenge, my friends, but leave room for God's wrath, for it is written: "It is mine to avenge; I will repay," says the Lord. [20]On the contrary:

"If your enemy is hungry, feed him;
  if he is thirsty, give him something to drink.
In doing this, you will heap burning coals on his head."
21*Do not be overcome by evil, but overcome evil with good.*
  (Rom. 12:17-21)

Make sure that nobody pays back wrong for wrong, but always try to
be kind to each other and to everyone else. (1 Thess. 5:15)

9*Do not repay evil with evil or insult with insult, but with blessing,*
because to this you were called so that you may inherit a blessing.
10*For,*
"Whoever would love life
  and see good days
must keep his tongue from evil   ·
  and his lips from deceitful speech.
11*He must turn from evil and do good;*
  he must seek peace and pursue it.
12*For the eyes of the Lord are on the righteous*
  and his ears are attentive to their prayer,
but the face of the Lord is against those who do evil." (1 Pet. 3:9-12)

I cannot expound each of these passages in this lecture. Six observations, however, will carry the discussion forward.

First, the ethical exhortations of Romans 12 stand under the introductory exhortation in Romans 12:1-2: "I urge you, brothers, in view of God's mercy, to offer your bodies as living sacrifices, holy and pleasing to God—this is your spiritual act of worship. Do not conform any longer to the pattern of this world, but be transformed by the renewing of your mind. Then you will be able to test and approve what God's will is—his good, pleasing and perfect will." Here are some themes not dissimilar to several we have found in Matthew and Mark. For instance, the ethics of this chapter, diligently followed, will distance a person from "the pattern of this world," just as loving your enemy will distance you from the pattern of "tax collectors" and "pagans" in Matthew 5:43-47. The crucial means of your ongoing transformation is "the renewing of your mind," just as the greatest command demands that you love God with your "heart" (in the biblical sense) and your mind. This is the stuff of God-centeredness; otherwise put, it is "your spiritual act of worship." But the fresh element here is that Paul makes his exhortation by appealing to God's mercy: "I urge you, brothers," he writes, "in view of God's mercy." Transparently, the appeal is to the entire argument of the preceding eleven chapters. Paul is saying, in effect, that in view of God's mercies in his spectacular plan of redemption carefully laid out in Romans 1-11, Christians should live in a certain way.

Thus, if Matthew 5:43-47 urges us to love our enemies by appealing to God's providential love, Romans 12 urges us to love our enemies by appealing to God's mercies in redemption. After all, in redemption God has given us the supreme example of loving enemies: "God demonstrates his own love for us in this: While we were still sinners, Christ died for us" (Rom. 5:8). Similarly, the ethical appeal in 1 Peter 3:9-12 (above) finds itself under the explosion of praise in 1 Peter 1:3: it was in God's "great mercy" that he gave us new birth and thus empowered us to live in a certain way.

Second, the passage in 1 Peter goes so far as to say that Christians are *called* to a life in which we do not repay evil with evil, insult with insult, but rather with blessing. This is part of a still larger theme. Christians are *called* to follow Jesus—and if Jesus suffered reproach and hate, then his followers must surely expect the same, since a disciple is not above his master (John 15:18—16:4). Similarly, the apostle Paul tells the Philippians, "[I]t has been granted to you on behalf of Christ not only to believe on him, but also to suffer for him" (Phil. 1:29). We sometimes think that we Christians are *called* to faith, but if suffering and reproach occur, they merely happen, a sort of occupational hazard. But Jesus, Paul, and Peter unite in opposing this view: as surely as Christians have been called to faith, so surely also have we been called to suffering and even to non-retaliatory responses. Peter's words are nothing other than the outworking of Jesus' command that we love our enemies.

Third, this command, the command of enemy love—to bless those who persecute us—is very hard not only because it flies in the face of our built-in selfishness, but also because it seems to be terribly unfair, terribly unjust. Surely those who defy God, who blaspheme God, who hate his people, should not be treated with blessing but with punishment. After all, such punishment is meted out on them often enough in the Scriptures. When that happens, justice has been served. So must we not infer that justice is *not* being served when just punishment is *not* being meted out?

On this matter, the Romans passage is particularly helpful. According to Paul, one of the reasons why we are not to respond in kind, even when such response might formally be just, is that at the end of the day God himself will exact justice. In fact, we are to "leave room" for God's wrath (Rom. 12:19). The theological reason is that all sins are first of all sins against God himself (cf. Ps. 51:4). So the forgiveness of sin, or the punishment of sin, remains first and foremost within his purview. To arrogate such authority to the individual human being is a kind of idolatry: it is to take the place of God. When the state exercises justice, then, from a biblical perspective, it does so because it has been granted certain responsibilities *by God himself.* But because sin is primarily an offense against God, God alone is the One with the right to deal with it. The reason we are to "leave room" for God's wrath is because "it is written: 'It is mine to avenge; I will repay,' says the Lord" (12:19).

In fact, when the structure of this passage is examined closely, the argument is even stronger. Many contemporary commentators have argued that the metaphorical use of "you will heap burning coals on his head" means something like "you will drive them to feel ashamed of their actions" or the like. They say it would be incompatible with the theme of loving one's enemies if these "coals of fire" symbolized eschatological judgment. But live coals in the Old Testament invariably symbolize God's anger (2 Sam. 22:9, 13; Ps. 18:9, 13) or punishment of the wicked (Ps. 140:11) or an evil passion (Prov. 6:27-29). It is therefore intrinsically unlikely that Paul would be using "coals of fire" in a good sense to refer to human conscience. More importantly, Piper[5] reminds us of the structure of these verses:

> 19a Do not take revenge, my friends,
> 19b but leave room for God's wrath,
> 19c [because] it is written: "It is mine to avenge; I will repay,"
>   says the Lord.
> 20a On the contrary: "If your enemy is hungry, feed him;

---

[5]Ibid., 114-117.

20b if he is thirsty, give him something to drink.
20c [because] in doing this, you will heap burning coals on his head."[6]

The first set of three lines gives the negative injunction, what Christians are *not* to do; the second set of three lines gives the positive command, what Christians *must* do. The shift from the negative to the positive is introduced by the Greek word ἀλλά, rendered "On the contrary." In both sets the third line introduced by "because" provides the same motivating reason: It is God's prerogative to punish, and he will exercise that prerogative in due course.

Those who argue that this interpretation is untenable, because one cannot imagine that Paul is talking about final, eschatological judgment in the same context where he is talking about loving enemies, are guilty of the same misinterpretation as that pursued by pacifists in their reading of Matthew 5:43-47. They absolutize the command to enemy love without observing the contextual constraints, still less observing that both Jesus and Paul never abandon their firm conviction that God *does* bring in eschatological judgment at the end (e.g., Matt. 25:46; Rom. 2:6-8).

There is another small detail to think about if this understanding of the passage is correct. Paul addresses the Roman Christians and speaks directly to them in verse 20: "*you* will heap burning coals" on the head of the enemy. The argument, I think, presupposes an unexpressed conditional clause: "*if* the enemy is not moved by your forbearing love to genuine repentance." In other words, the Christian's love of the unbelieving enemy will in certain respects be like Christ's love for his enemies: either it brings about their conversion, or it multiplies their guilt. Paul understands this well. His own ministry is "the smell of death" to some people and "the fragrance of life" to others (2 Cor. 2:16). That is also why, when he is writing to the Philippians to tell them that they are *called* to suffer for Christ, Paul reminds them that their very steadfastness "is a sign [to the persecutors] that they will be destroyed, but that you will be saved" (Phil. 1:28).

On the short term, such persecution will be unfair, deeply unjust. So was the death of Jesus on the cross. But the injustice performed against

---

[6]Although I have largely followed the NIV, I have inserted the italicized *because* in order to reflect the Greek text more accurately and thus to bring out the parallelism.

Christians will lead to some persecutors becoming Christians, and all the injustice that these converts had perpetrated is precisely what Christ has borne. But the same injustice will lead to other people being hardened in their sin, their guilt painfully compounded. Then on the last day, God's justice will be done, and will be seen to be done. Christians do not restrict their moral horizons to immediate results; they make their ethical decisions from an eternal perspective.

Fourth, in the passage in 1 Peter, it is impossible not to notice the nexus of promise and hope. Christians are not to repay evil with evil, but with blessing, not only because we have been called to this, but also, Peter tells his readers, "so that you may inherit a blessing" (3:9). Indeed, the quoted Old Testament texts in the following three verses make the same point. That stance has already been laid out by the apostle Peter in the first chapter of this letter. Peter admits that his readers "may have had to suffer grief in all kinds of trials" (1 Pet. 1:6). But then he addresses them in these terms: "These [trials] have come so that your faith—of greater worth than gold, which perishes even though refined by fire—may be proved genuine and may result in praise, glory and honor when Jesus Christ is revealed" (1:7). In other words, trials come in various forms (in 1 Peter primarily from various kinds of persecution), and the faith of the believers is demonstrated by their distinctively Christian response—forbearance, joy, perseverance, passion for God's glory, and the anticipation of their own ultimate salvation when Jesus returns: "Though you have not seen him, you love him; and even though you do not see him now, you believe in him and are filled with an inexpressible and glorious joy, for you are receiving the goal of your faith, the salvation of your souls" (1:8-9). The thought is not dissimilar to what we find in 3:6-9: Christians display love for their enemies and return blessing for cursing so that they may inherit a blessing, in line with the promises of God in Scripture.

Fifth, in 1 Thessalonians 5:15 Paul tells his readers always to "try to be kind to each other and to everyone else." Transparently, there are two spheres: "each other" and "everyone else." The Christian's first circle of responsibility is the church, brothers and sisters in Christ. Then there is a further responsibility to be kind to outsiders, to as wide a circle as possible. That subtle distinction is very important and is mirrored in other parts of the New Testament. Elsewhere Paul can encourage Christians to do good to all people but especially to those who belong to the family of believers (Gal. 6:10). Some of the significance of this distinction I will draw out below (in Section D).

Sixth, oddly enough, the same distinction shows that Paul is realistic about problems *within* the church. If Christians are to be kind and not to pay back evil for evil, and to exercise this love and compassion *first of all to Christians*, what is presupposed is that some of the attacks and pain that any Christian will experience *will come from others in the church*. As wonderful as Christian fellowship and Christian love may be—and at their best they are beyond price, beyond words—both experience and Scripture tell us in frank terms that sometimes Christians face the worst pain from others within the family of faith. That is why, when he lists some of his most severe sufferings, the apostle can include "danger from false brothers" (2 Cor. 11:26). The same mark of raw realism is found in the Romans passage: live peaceably with all, Paul exhorts his readers, "as far as it depends on you" (Rom. 12:18). It takes little experience before we discover that sometimes peace is impossible.

Let me recap. We have found that the command to love our enemies is widely spread in the New Testament and surfaces in diverse and colorful ways. All of these diverse forms of expression are deeply challenging, but none is naive. There is even frank recognition that some of the Christian's enemies will be those closest to home. So it will be worth reflecting a little on the diversities of enemies before I bring this lecture to a close.

C. Little Enemies

When in this lecture's title I refer to "Enemies, Big and Small," obviously I am not thinking of their physical dimensions—bantam-weight enemies perhaps as opposed to three-hundred-pound enemies—but of the scale of their enmity. Not all Christians face persecuting enemies, but all Christians face little enemies. We encounter people whose personality we intensely dislike—an obstreperous deacon or warden or bishop; a truly revolting relative; an employee or employer who specializes in insensitivity, rudeness, and general arrogance; a business competitor more unscrupulous, not to say more profitable, than you are; the teenager whose boorishness is exceeded only by his or her unkemptness; the elderly duffers who persist in making the same querulous demands whenever you are in a hurry; the teachers who are so intoxicated by their own learning that they forget they are first of all called to teach students, not a subject; the students so impressed by their own ability or (if they come from certain cultures) so terrified by the shame of a low grade that they whine and wheedle for an "A" they have not earned; people with whom you have differed on some point of principle who take all differences in a deeply personal way and who nurture bitterness for decades, stroking their own self-righteousness and offended egos as they go; insecure little people who resent and try to tear down those who are even marginally more competent than they; the many who lust for power and call it principle; the arrogant who are convinced of their own brilliance and of the stupidity of everyone else. The list is easily enlarged. They are offensive, sometimes repulsive, especially when they belong to the same church. It often seems safest to leave by different doors, to cross the street when you see them approaching, or to find eminently sound reasons not to invite them to any of your social gatherings. And if, heaven forbid, you accidentally bump into such an enemy, the best defense is a spectacularly English civility, coupled with a retreat as hasty as elementary decency permits. After all, isn't "niceness" what is demanded?

The passage in the Sermon on the Mount already examined speaks rather pointedly to this situation. If we find our "friends" only among those we like and who like us, we are indifferentiable from first-century tax collectors and pagans. Both our neighborhood and the church will inevitably include their shares of imperfect, difficult people like you and me. In fact, the church will often collect more than its proportionate share of difficult folk, especially emotionally or intellectually needy folk, precisely because despite all its faults it is still the most caring and patient large institution around. There is a sense in which we should see in our awkward brothers and sisters a badge of honor. The dangers, however, become much greater (as do the rewards) when the church is richly multicultural, because the potential for misunderstandings rises significantly.

None of this is to deny that some offenses are so serious that they should not be overlooked. Some offenses are of the sort that Christians should follow the procedures set out in Matthew 18; in some cases, there should be excommunication. Moreover, in the New Testament there are many forms of mutual admonition short of excommunication. In the fifth lecture we shall consider some of the demands of love in such situations. But in many instances, what is required is simply forbearance driven by love. No one puts it more forcefully than Paul: "Therefore, as God's chosen people, holy and dearly loved, clothe yourselves with compassion, kindness, humility, gentleness and patience. Bear with each other and forgive whatever grievances you may have against one another. Forgive as the Lord forgave you. And over all these virtues put on love, which binds them all together in perfect unity" (Col. 3:12-14). To bear with one another and to forgive grievances presupposes that relationships will not always be smooth. Most of the time, what is required is not the confrontation of Matthew 18, but forbearance, forgiveness, compassion, kindness, humility, gentleness, or patience. Christians are to mourn with those who mourn and rejoice with those who rejoice (Rom. 12:15).

This action goes way beyond niceness. One thinks of Flannery O'Connor's biting and hilarious stories with their "nice" Christian ladies who have a domesticated Jesus who approves all they do and all they hold dear. They are spectacularly "nice"; they are also whitewashed tombs (Matt. 23:27). As Marilyn Chandler McEntyre puts it, their "sentimentality was a close kin to obscenity."[7] Forbearance and genuine tenderheartedness are much tougher than niceness, and sometimes (as we shall see in a later lecture) tough love is confrontational. Christian love, McEntyre writes, "may even demand that we be downright eccentric, at least if we are to believe O'Connor's word on the subject: 'You shall know the truth,' she warned, 'and the truth shall make you odd.'"[8] That, of course, is implicitly recognized by Jesus himself. If genuine love among his followers is their characteristic mark (John 13:34-35), then Jesus himself is saying that such love is not normal. It is odd.

That brings us to three reflections.

First, this loving of awkward people, first of all those within the household of faith but then also outsiders, is sometimes grounded not

---

[7]"Nice Is Not the Point," *Christianity Today* 44/13 (13 Nov. 2000), 104.
[8]Ibid.

on God's providential love (as in Matt. 5:43-47), but on a distinctively Christian appeal. The awkward people envisaged in Colossians 3:12-14 (quoted above) are to be loved and forgiven, but the basis is not divine providence: "Forgive as the Lord forgave you"—a frank appeal to the Christian's experience of grace. If, as we have seen in Romans, we are to "leave room for God's wrath," the appeal is not to divine providence so much as to eschatological expectation: we can live now with a certain amount of injustice because we know that justice will ultimately be done. Elsewhere we are to make every effort to maintain the unity of the Spirit in the bond of peace (Eph. 4:1-3)—a frankly Christian appeal. The passage that makes love the distinguishing mark of Jesus' followers carries an implicitly evangelistic motivation: by this mark everyone will know that we are Jesus' disciples. The sustained moral exhortation of Philippians 2:1-4—be like-minded, being one with others in spirit and purpose, doing nothing out of selfish ambition or vain conceit, walking in humility, considering others better than yourself, looking not only to your own interests but also to the interests of others—is ultimately grounded in the example of the redemptive work of Christ: "Your attitude should be the same as that of Christ Jesus" (2:5).[9] The glorious "Christ-hymn" follows: Christ Jesus humbled himself to become a human being, and humbled himself yet further to die the odious death of the cross, and in consequence God has exalted him to the highest place. Here, then, the motivational appeal is not to God's providential care but to the example of Jesus.

When I was a boy, I learned the lines:

> To live above with those you love,
> Undiluted glory;
> To live below with those you know,
> Quite another story.

But that verse is merely a wry way of getting at the fact that we Christians are passing through transformation on the way to consum-

[9]Another explanation of the relation between Philippians 2:1-4 and 2:5-11 is today urged in some commentaries. I am not persuaded it is right. The discussion need not be untangled here. See especially Peter T. O'Brien, *The Epistle to the Philippians: A Commentary on the Greek Text* (NIGTC; Grand Rapids: Eerdmans, 1991), esp. 253-271.

mation. In the new heaven and the new earth, we *will* love one another. And it is the most elementary Christian teaching that urges us to begin to live out *now* the values of the consummation that will be an inescapable part of our makeup *then*. Karl Barth was once asked the question: "Is it true that one day in heaven we will see again our loved ones?" He replied, "Not only the loved ones."[10]

Second, in practical terms this love for "little enemies" is sometimes (though certainly not always) more difficult than love for big enemies, for persecuting enemies. For when you face outright persecution, there may be something heroic about your stance. It is difficult, however, to find much that is heroic about getting two scrappy Christian leaders to work together (Phil. 4:2-3). And some people seem to be better at confrontation or at bearing up under persecution than they are at forbearing.

A few years ago a Christian brother took me aside and told me that he wanted a private word with me as I had offended him. We arranged a meeting. He told me that I had deeply offended him in three particulars. I was unaware of what I had done to cause him such distress. Eager to put things right, I asked him to elucidate. His first reason for being offended, he said, lay in something that had happened twenty-one years earlier. We had been talking about something or other in the theological world, and he quoted a few words from an author who had written in French. Without thinking, I had repeated the few French words after him because I had been brought up speaking French, and so I was unconsciously correcting his pronunciation. At the time he said nothing, but he had taken deep umbrage. "I want you to know, Don," he was now telling me, "that I have not spoken another word of French from that day to this."

I immediately apologized for having offended him, however unwittingly. But at the same time, I could not help thinking (1) that a bigger or more self-confident man would have either been grateful for the correction and improved his French or brushed off the correction; (2) that a bigger or more self-confident man, knowing my background (as this chap did), would have recognized the unself-conscious nature of my "correction," stemming from my own background; (3) that there was

---

[10]I have culled this often-repeated account from Miroslav Volf, "Love Your Heavenly Enemy," *Christianity Today* 44/12 (23 Oct. 2000), 94.

something profoundly evil about nurturing a resentment of this order for twenty-one years; and (4) in any case, even if I had been boorish in my remarks (and I certainly did not intend to be scoring points: after all, many other native speakers have corrected my German or Spanish or whatever, languages in which I was not reared and which I learned as an adult), it would have been the mark of Christian maturity if he had simply loved me, forgiven me. Love covers over a multitude of sins (1 Pet. 4:8), both real and imagined. Instead, twenty-one years after this event, he was back invoking Matthew 18. Better, no doubt, to be dealing with it rather late and in the wrong way than not to deal with it at all. But I suspect he had not learned the balance of Scripture very well.

It transpired that his other two complaints were of the same order of magnitude. It was all rather sad. But many a Christian has learned that there are forms of Christian rectitude that can be magnificently heroic in large issues and remarkably petty in small slights, real and imagined.

Third, I should make explicit something to which I have several times alluded. Jesus told his disciples, "As I have loved you, so you must love one another" (John 13:34)—which is again a distinctively Christian appeal, rather than an appeal to God's providential love. Then he adds, "By this all men will know that you are my disciples, if you love one another" (13:35). A few chapters on, when he is addressing his Father in prayer, Jesus says, "May they also be in us so that the world may believe that you have sent me" (17:21). In other words, there is a frankly evangelistic function to Christian love.

At this juncture, I can well imagine someone saying to me, "Wait a minute, Don. In this section you started off talking about Christians loving enemies, even if only 'little enemies.' Now you have sidled over to talking about Christians loving one another for the sake of communicating the gospel. What has this got to do with loving enemies? And besides, isn't Christian love for other Christians a bit, well, cliquish? Isn't this sort of love a much *lower* and *inferior* love to what Jesus is talking about when he speaks of loving enemies? After all, he says that tax collectors love tax collectors, and pagans love pagans, so why should it be surprising if Christians love Christians?"

The question is a good one and begs for separate consideration.

D. EXCURSUS: IS THE LOVE OF CHRISTIANS FOR CHRISTIANS AN INFERIOR LOVE?

Many would answer this question in the affirmative. For example, numerous contemporary commentaries on John's letters lay considerable stress on the observation that Christians are exhorted to love other Christians with similar beliefs, even while those whom John views as heterodox are being excluded. This stance, it is argued, is narrow, sectarian, doctrinaire; it is a long way removed from Jesus' insistence that his followers love their enemies. One commentator, for example, writes disparagingly of the "fierce intolerance" of 1 John. In a very recent essay, Wong tracks out what he takes to be the trajectory of development from Jesus' original command to his followers to love their enemies, to such passages as these in 1 John, and concludes that this is part of a pattern of "de-radicalization" of Jesus' teaching that takes place within the New Testament canon itself, to say nothing of the early patristic period.[11]

The technical questions about how to follow a "trajectory" cannot be probed here, as interesting as they are. But the charge itself depends on some deeply unbiblical presuppositions that need to be challenged. One of the deepest of these is that the love of Christians for Christians is intrinsically inferior to love for enemies. As usual with deep errors, there is a smidgeon of truth buried in the error, but it must not be allowed the clout it usually achieves.

Probably we should remind ourselves of a few of the many New Testament texts that encourage Christian love for Christians:

My command is this: Love each other as I have loved you (John 15:12).

This is my command: Love each other (John 15:17).

Be devoted to one another in brotherly love (Rom. 12:10).

Therefore, as God's chosen people, holy and dearly loved, clothe yourselves with compassion, kindness, humility, gentleness and patience. Bear with each other and forgive whatever grievances you may have against one another. Forgive as the Lord forgave you. And

---

[11]Eric K. C. Wong, "The De-radicalization of Jesus' Ethical Sayings in Romans," *Novum Testamentum* 43 (2001), 245-263.

over all these virtues put on love, which binds them all together in per-
fect unity (Col. 3:12-14).

Now about brotherly love we do not need to write to you, for you
yourselves have been taught by God to love each other. And in fact,
you do love all the brothers throughout Macedonia. Yet we urge you,
brothers, to do so more and more (1 Thess. 4:9-10).

Keep on loving each other as brothers (Heb. 13:1).

Now that you have purified yourselves by obeying the truth so that
you have sincere love for your brothers, love one another deeply, from
the heart (1 Pet. 1:22).

Above all, love each other deeply, because love covers over a mul-
titude of sins (1 Pet. 4:8).

This is the message you heard from the beginning: We should love
one another (1 John 3:11).

And this is his command: to believe in the name of his Son, Jesus
Christ, and to love one another as he commanded us (1 John 3:23).

I am not writing you a new command but one we have had from
the beginning. I ask that we love one another. And this is love: that we
walk in obedience to his commands. As you have heard from the begin-
ning, his command is that you walk in love (2 John 5-6).

We may see through some of the charges that are leveled against
Paul and John—and against Christians today—if we focus on five
things:
(1) Before we draw outsized conclusions from passages that talk
about Christians loving Christians (whether descriptive or prescriptive
passages), we should remind ourselves that the Bible offers not only different ways of talking about Christian love, but different ways of talking about the love of God,[12] and these different ways are not
hierarchialized. Are we prepared to argue, for instance, that God's intra-

---

[12]I reviewed them in the first chapter.

Trinitarian love—in particular, the explicitly mentioned love of the
Father for the Son and of the Son for the Father—is an inferior sort of
love because neither the Father nor the Son is an enemy to the other? Is
this intra-Trinitarian love inferior to God's love for us sinners, his love
exercised toward us even while we were his enemies (Rom. 5:8)? The
thought is outrageous. In any case, there is nothing in Scripture that warrants such hierarchialization. Most Christian thinkers would say that in
some ways, God's love for his enemies is an outflow of his very nature
as love (1 John 4:8-10), which nature is foundationally expressed in his
own being as God. So if the different ways the Bible speaks about the
love of God are not hierarchialized, why should the different ways the
Bible speaks of Christian love be hierarchialized?

(2) More to the point, in one crucial chapter in John's Gospel, God's
intra-Trinitarian love is set forth as the model and standard of Christians
loving Christians. "I have made you known to them," Jesus tells his
Father, "and will continue to make you known in order that the love you
have for me may be in them and that I myself may be in them" (John
17:26). It is very difficult to depreciate the love of Christians for
Christians, indeed the unity that Jesus mandates among Christians,
without simultaneously depreciating God's intra-Trinitarian love and the
very unity of the Godhead.

(3) According to 1 John, the obligation of Christians to love one
another is not some late development at the tail end of a wretched trajectory, a trajectory that betrays a degeneration from love of enemy to
love of Christians. The command to Christians to love fellow Christians
is an "old one" (1 John 2:7), i.e., it goes back to the very beginning of
Christianity. It goes back to the explicit teaching of Jesus himself (John
13:34-35). Repeatedly, therefore, we are told things like this: "This is
the message you heard from the beginning: We should love one
another" (1 John 3:11). In other words, this command is as old as the
command to love enemies: both go back to Jesus. The differences
should not be seen as different spots along a trajectory of development
or of degeneration, but as different ways the Bible has of speaking of
Christian love, depending on the context and the existential priorities
of the historical setting.

(4) I suspect that one of the reasons why there are so many exhor-

tations in the New Testament for Christians to love other Christians is because this is not an easy thing to do. Many fellow Christians will appear to be, at least initially or to the immature, "little enemies." To put the matter differently, if Christians love Christians, it is not exactly the same thing as what Jesus has in mind when he speaks rather dismissively of tax collectors loving tax collectors and pagans loving pagans. What he means in these latter cases is that most people have their own little circle of "in" people, their own list of compatible people, their friends. Christian love, as we saw in the first part of this lecture, must go beyond that to include those outside this small group. The objects of our love must include those who are *not* "in": it must include enemies.

Ideally, however, the church itself is not made up of natural "friends." It is made up of natural enemies. What binds us together is not common education, common race, common income levels, common politics, common nationality, common accents, common jobs, or anything else of that sort. Christians come together, not because they form a natural collocation, but because they have all been saved by Jesus Christ and owe him a common allegiance. In the light of this common allegiance, in the light of the fact that they have all been loved by Jesus himself, they commit themselves to doing what he says—and he commands them to love one another. In this light, they are a band of natural enemies who love one another for Jesus' sake.

That is the only reason why John 13:34-35 makes sense: "A new command I give you: Love one another. As I have loved you, so you must love one another. By this all men will know that you are my disciples, if you love one another." If Christian love for other Christians were nothing more than the shared affection of mutually compatible people, it would be indistinguishable from pagan love for pagans or from tax collectors' love for tax collectors. The reason why Christian love will stand out and bear witness to Jesus is that it is a display, for Jesus' sake, of mutual love among social incompatibles. That is also why we must work at it, why we must beware of the erosion of love. And that is also why it entirely misses the point to suppose that the love of Christians for Christians is something inferior to love for enemies. The categories are all wrong; indeed, very often from the perspective of social differences, the love of Christians for Christians is nothing other than the love of Christians for enemies.

(5) Neither God's intra-Trinitarian love nor the love of Christians for other Christians is ever permitted in Scripture to dilute or diminish the fundamental truths of the gospel. When 1 John excludes certain people from the fellowship of the church, it is not because of personal animus but because of stances that, in the New Testament, must face discipline if the church is to continue to be the church. The people this epistle excludes deny that Jesus is the Son of God, certainly do not think that men and women may be reconciled to God exclusively on the basis of Jesus as the "atoning sacrifice" for our sins (2:2), and flagrantly fly in the face of Jesus' commands. It is not that John is venting against people whose personalities clash with his own. The gospel itself is at stake, and John sees no incompatibility between, on the one hand, the love of Christians for Christians, and, on the other, church discipline. To malign this as "fierce intolerance" presupposes, without warrant, that a liberal, sentimental view of "love" must prevail. But that is not even true of God: the God of the Bible, for all the diversity of ways in which his love may be displayed and extolled, is invariably the God whose wrath remains on those who reject the Son (John 3:36).

Another way of putting this is to recognize that the Bible itself recognizes that unity is not an *intrinsic* good. There is good unity, and there is bad unity. Bad unity occurs in Genesis 11 when rebellious humankind unites to build a tower to heaven to defy God. God's response is to introduce *dis*unity, viz. the multiplication of languages and the carving up of the race, precisely to foil the evil purposes of this godless unity. Bad unity occurs when the two "beasts" of Revelation 13 seek to impose a uniform authority, in defiance of God, over "every tribe, people, language and nation" (13:7). Good unity occurs around the throne of God, which is surrounded by people bought by the blood of the Lamb of God, people drawn "from every tribe and language and people and nation" (Rev. 5:9). Good unity is found among the disciples of Jesus, those for whom he prays (John 17:20ff.): "May they be brought to complete unity to let the world know that you sent me and have loved them even as you have loved me" (17:23).

Correspondingly, there is both good and bad division. The same

Jesus who prayed that his disciples might be one also said, rather shockingly, "Do you think I came to bring peace on earth? No, I tell you, but division. From now on there will be five in one family divided against each other, three against two and two against three" (Luke 12:51-52). But there can be evil division, the subject of apostolic warning: "I urge you, brothers, to watch out for those who cause divisions" (Rom. 16:17).

It must be said with pain and regret that the ecumenical movement's effort to hijack John 17 is deeply injurious to accurate understanding of the text. This movement presupposes that (1) the unity to be desired is primarily ecclesiastical and organizational; (2) that in such unity people may entertain thoroughly disparate understandings of what the gospel is; and (3) this unity has not been achieved, with the result that the prayer of Jesus is deeply frustrated, and this is the principal reason why more people do not become Christians today.

But, in fact, (1) the unity to be achieved is first and foremost relational, displayed in Christians loving other Christians, the echo and extension of God's intra-Trinitarian love; (2) as the Gospel of John shows and all the Johannine writings attest, this unity is a gospel unity, and those who deny the fundamentals of the gospel that John lays out are everywhere regarded as outside the locus of this fold; (3) in the context of all of John's writings, and of the New Testament documents as a whole, one finds a deep conviction that, however flawed the church is, the unity for which Jesus prayed is nevertheless real, deep, and partially realized this side of the consummation. Despite substantial differences over important issues, genuine believers reach across cultural, linguistic, organizational, denominational, racial, and economic barriers, and by their love they promote the gospel of Jesus Christ.

This is not to suggest even for a second that the church does not have many sins of which to repent. Nor is it to deny that there are countless devoted believers within the ecumenical movement who do not abandon a deeply confessional commitment to the gospel or to deny that evangelicals are sometimes prone to needless division. It is simply to say that not all unity is good; unity is not an intrinsic good. In some circumstances it may be a deep evil. In the biblical mandates for Christians to love (whether this love is directed toward other Christians or toward unbelievers), there is nothing that sanctions evil or views the denial of the gospel as a peccadillo to be embraced within the church.

In short, the charges of those who accuse 1 John of "fierce intolerance" fail because they are driven by contemporary presuppositions fundamentally at odds with those of the biblical writers.

E. BIG ENEMIES—I.E., PERSECUTING ENEMIES

Jesus said, "Blessed are those who are persecuted because of righteousness, for theirs is the kingdom of heaven. Blessed are you when people insult you, persecute you and falsely say all kinds of evil against you because of me. Rejoice and be glad, because great is your reward in heaven, for in the same way they persecuted the prophets who were before you" (Matt. 5:10-12).

We will do well to observe several things.

(1) The kind of persecution that Jesus envisages in this passage is prompted by the "righteousness" of those who are being persecuted; it is, Jesus says, "because of me." In other words, these people are being persecuted because they are Jesus' followers, with the conduct to match. That partly accounts for the shift in person. In line with the preceding beatitudes, this theme of persecution begins in the third person: "Blessed are those who are persecuted . . ." (v. 10). But when Jesus elaborates this thought, he chooses to address his own followers more intimately in the second person: "Blessed are *you*, when people insult *you*," etc. (vv. 11-12).

This has happened often enough, of course. Christians are persecuted simply because they are Christians. Very often, however, the motives of the persecutors are mixed. When Mao Tse-Tung (or Zedong, as his name is now spelled) was busily killing countless thousands of Christians, he was also killing a still larger number of Buddhists. The Soviet empire cracked down on Christians; it also cracked down on Jehovah's Witnesses and Mormons and those it saw as revisionist Czarists. In the Sudan, the odious persecution of Christians in the south by the national government in Khartoum is motivated by an abominable mix of Muslim fanaticism, tribalism, lust for power, and greed (75 percent of the oil is in the south).

(2) According to Jesus, persecution does not have to be violent. It does not necessarily end in a prison cell or in a grave. Jesus lumps together insults and slander with persecution: "Blessed are you when people insult you, persecute you and falsely say all kinds of evil against you because of me." In most Western countries, Christians do not face much violent persecution. But we are learning to face a lot more sneering condescension, intellectual dismissal, and worse. There was a time in the West when it was considered honorable to go into the ministry. In many circles such a vocation is now associated with bigotry, ignorance, and an antiquated modernism. And who knows what the future will bring forth?

Missiologists and demographers tell us that during the past century, there were more Christian martyrs in the world than in the previous nineteen centuries combined. The cruelty and slaughter going on in the southern Sudan and among the Karel people of Burma are violent and ugly. As I write this, news is coming in of a group of motorcycle gunmen killing sixteen people in a church in India. Over three hundred churches have been burned by Muslim extremists in northern Nigeria during the past three years. Earlier generations used to read *Foxe's Book of Martyrs*. Perhaps today one should begin by reading volumes that document current sufferings.[13] In some places carefully compiled Internet reports provide the most reliable information.

(3) According to Jesus, persecution marks out his followers as belonging to a certain sector in the stream of redemptive history. His persecuted disciples follow in the train of the prophets who were persecuted before them. Elsewhere, Jesus insists that his followers should expect opposition and violence, since that is what he himself faced, and his servants must not think of themselves as above their Master (John 15:18—16:4). Small wonder, then, that when the apostles received their first flogging after Jesus' resurrection, they rejoiced "because they had been counted worthy of suffering disgrace for the Name" (Acts 5:41).

(4) In the light of the fact that the passage we studied at the beginning of this lecture—Matthew 5:43-47 with its exhortation to pray for enemies—is found here in Matthew 5, i.e., in the same chapter that tells

---

[13]E.g., Don Cormack, *Killing Fields, Living Fields* (London: Monarch Books, 1997), on the Cambodian church.

Jesus' followers to expect persecution and even to rejoice in it, we must infer that the enemies for whom we should pray include persecuting enemies. After all, that is what Jesus did on the cross (Luke 23:34, "Father, forgive them, for they do not know what they are doing"), and in this he is followed by the first Christian martyr, Stephen (Acts 7:60). Perhaps the New Testament book that examines the Christian response to persecution most persistently is 1 Peter: see especially 3:9-17a; 4:1-5, 12-19.

Three further reflections will maintain before us some of the subtleties of Christian response to persecution.

First, we should not think of physical persecution as necessarily worse than emotional or intellectual persecution. There are degrees of both, and people sometimes crumple under both.

Physical persecution can stiffen the backbone of a church and can have the effect of purifying it. On the other hand, sustained and really violent persecution can simply wipe out all the churches of a region, as in Albania under the Communists. It is not always true that "the blood of the martyrs is the seed of the church." Where this statement is true is usually in the lag times when persecution abates. Then the church begins to grow and multiply. When the persecution is not universal, sustained, and determined, when the church survives, at the very least persecution helps Christians to see what their priorities are and can foster a deeply spiritual faithfulness grounded in the ever-present prospect of eternity.

Emotional and intellectual persecution, coupled perhaps with subtle exclusions that keep Christians out of certain jobs or economic sectors, can in theory strengthen believers, but in practice it very often seduces them. For the sake of gaining plaudits, it is easy to trim one's theology or to keep silent about the bits that we know will cause umbrage, in the hope of gaining the approval we crave. Alternatively, some believers will fight back with a nasty anti-intellectualism, a "circle-the-wagons" mentality that is neither loving nor evangelistic but merely defensive. Ironically, Christians who adopt these postures become just as scurrilously condescending as those who are attacking them. These Christians have become compromised by the very people who dismiss them. So I wonder if these forms of persecution are not more dangerous on the long haul to the life and well-being of the church than the more violent forms of persecution.

Second, it should be obvious that Western culture is in certain respects returning to the empirical pluralism and multiculturalism that was everywhere present in the Roman Empire in the first century. Imperial Rome encouraged religious diversity, for it knew that religious wars could be terrible. For this reason, it was a capital offense to desecrate a temple, any temple. The diversity we are increasingly experiencing, even if it is coming about for mixed reasons, is making it easier and easier for us to understand the New Testament documents, for we are living in situations more closely analogous to New Testament times than our parents lived in.

On the other hand, there is one huge difference between our pluralism and the pluralism of the Roman Empire—or, more precisely, there is one huge difference that we should reflect on here. In the first century, religious pluralism was the given, and as the church began to make its inroads into the Empire, the church was perceived to be (even when it was resented and hated) the reforming party, the party at the front end, the compassionate party, the principled party. Today, however, because the culture is distancing itself from the Judeo-Christian heritage, the church is perceived to be the obsolete party, the mere traditionalists, the obscurantists, the whiners, the naysayers, the uptight, the backward-looking. To recognize this distinction immediately prompts us to think afresh about what our strategies should be in evangelism.

Third, from the perspective of these lectures, the most important thing to recognize is the link between Matthew 5:10-12 and Matthew 5:43-47. We should not only expect persecution, be prepared for it when it comes, discern its various forms, anticipate the nature of its diverse threats, and even see ourselves in a grand tradition that began with the Old Testament prophets and continues around the world to this very day, but we should love our enemies, our persecutors, and pray for them.

F. "Other" Enemies

The quotation marks in this heading are crucial to understanding the topic. By "other" enemies I do not mean "other enemies." The expression "other enemies" would simply refer to enemies other than the ones mentioned in the earlier parts of this lecture. But I am referring to people who are enemies because they are "other": they belong to a different race, a different party, a different country, or a different socioeconomic group—in short, to a different "tribe."

Miroslav Volf has recently written a hugely interesting book called *Exclusion and Embrace*.[14] He argues that many of the factors that shape our self-identity implicitly class other people as "not us," as "others," and therefore as somehow excluded. I am white; if you are not white, you are not like me; therefore, you are "other"; therefore, you belong to a different tribe; you do not belong with me. Of course, the same thing would be true if I began, "I am black. . . ." I can then add in other propositions: "I am male," "I am English-speaking," "I am middle-aged," "I am Canadian," and so forth. It does not take much exposure to many regional conflicts to sense the depth of mutual hatred, the unyielding nature of the profound mutual suspicions generated by the mutual exclusions of self-identity and "other"-identity: Israelis/Palestinians, Hutus/Tutsis, Serbians/Croats, Protestant Paras and Catholic IRA, and on and on. Each side really loathes the other; each believes the worst of the other; each has its own interpretation of their shared history; each feels that the only adequate response to violence is retaliatory violence. So deep are the suspicions that if the leaders are somehow forced to the negotiating and bargaining table, it will take a splinter group no more than a few bombs or a few rounds of sniper fire to bring all the peace processes to an unseemly end.

Volf argues that the distinctively Christian mode of existence is to embrace the "other," regardless of how different, regardless of the wrongs that the "other" has committed. There is no way forward, Volf argues, unless there is forgiveness.

On many fronts, Christians surely want to voice their hearty "Amen!" to this argument. Yet we have already begun to see that biblical passages mandating Christian love are diverse in their emphasis (as are passages that talk of God's love), and that it is easy to distort what the Bible says by absolutizing one facet of this rich diversity. We have already seen, at least in a preliminary way, that Christian love for Christians does not exclude church discipline; that God's love for the just

[14]*Exclusion and Embrace: A Theological Exploration of Identity, Otherness, and Reconciliation* (Nashville: Abingdon, 1996).

and the unjust does not exclude the final judgment; that Christian love for Christians may in some instances be a subset of love for enemies. We have begun to learn that it is as dangerous to absolutize one of the ways the Bible talks about Christian love as to absolutize one of the ways the Bible talks about God's love.

Disputed matters can easily become more pressing yet. So far we have not reflected very much on political or national enemies or on the responsibilities of the state. Should we forgive Osama bin Laden? Why or why not? Who should do the forgiving? Should we forgive him and then bring him to justice? Or does forgiving him mean that we should absorb the hatred ourselves? Or do we say that the state has the authority to retaliate, but Christians do not? If so, does that mean Christians should be pacifists and refuse to join the armed services of any state? If Osama bin Laden is an "enemy," what does it mean to love our "enemies" and pray for them? Is this an example of an "other" enemy, where the differences have to do with competing "tribes" that reflect diverging views on race, language, religion, morals, form of government, and foreign policy?

I am not sure that we shall be able to think through these issues very clearly until we extend our reflections from the diverse ways the Bible speaks of love to the diverse ways the Bible speaks of forgiveness. And then we shall have to struggle with the relationships between "just war" theory and the various biblical commands to love. None of this is easy. At the very least we are learning that contemporary sentimental appeals to love are woefully inadequate. Love always does its most impressive work in the hard places.

3

LOVE AND FORGIVENESS: THINKING ABOUT BASICS

The biblical passages that call on God's people to love—to love God, to love fellow believers, to love neighbors, to love enemies—simultaneously accomplish three things. (1) They penetrate our defenses and show us how selfish and loveless we can be. (2) They prompt us to reflect on the fact that the one Bible not only talks about Christian love in a variety of ways but also talks about God's love in a variety of ways, inevitably inviting us to reflect on the relationships between the two. (3) They disclose the subtlety and wisdom of the biblical texts. In so doing, they warn us against an easy proof-texting that makes one passage or theme, without adequate reflection on the context or on complementary or even competing biblical mandates, control the entire structure of Christian ethics.

Necessarily tied to these themes is the subject of forgiveness. The love that is demanded in many of the hardest cases, if it is more than merely gritty altruism, inevitably demands some form of forgiveness. For the hardest cases are those where the party that is so hard to love has either committed something evil or has been thought to commit something evil. It is not surprising, therefore, that the New Testament writers themselves sometimes link love and forgiveness. "Bear with each other and forgive whatever grievances you may have against one another. Forgive as the Lord forgave you. And over all these virtues put on love, which binds them all together in perfect unity" (Col. 3:13-14).

Should a woman forgive the man who brutally raped her? If so, when? On the spot? Two years later? Only when he repents? Should a man forgive the father who abused him? While he is abusing him? Only later? Only if he repents? Should the survivors of the Holocaust forgive the Nazis? Should they have done so during the Holocaust? May the friends of Holocaust victims forgive the perpetrators for sins and crimes performed against their friends and relatives? Is that within their purview, since the sins and crimes were not against them but against their friends and relatives? If we *should* forgive Osama bin Laden, does that mean we are not to go after him militarily? Suppose we know that he is planning another attack. Should we simply absorb it on the other cheek, as it were? And who is this "we" that makes the decision? Those who are actually killed and maimed in the attack, the nation as a whole, or the government that represents the whole nation? What do love and forgiveness demand if while walking home on dark streets, you see four toughs brutalizing a woman? Should you try to stop them? Or forgive them on the spot? Or wait until they are finished and then forgive them for what they have done? Supposing, instead, you see four planes brutalizing several thousand people? Suppose you are a passenger on a plane racing over Pennsylvania toward Washington D.C., clearly bent on destruction and even genocide. Do your pacifist principles prevent you from trying to wrest control of the plane from the terrorists since it is highly likely that some will die in the assault, and possibly the entire planeload of passengers?

Transparently, the issues are complex. Not that long ago on television we heard a soldier protest, "You must understand . . . it was our *revenge!*" The soldier was a Serb captured by the Kosovo Liberation Army. His words were broadcast in a television interview, nicely translated for the benefit of English-speaking peoples. He admitted that his unit had been involved in brutal acts of ethnic cleansing. Certainly he was frightened to be in the hands of his enemies, but he did not appear to be ashamed: "You must understand . . . it was our *revenge!*"

That is the trouble with revenge, of course: it does not feel like a sin. It feels like justice. Many of us have become inured to the distinction because we have watched so many movies or read so many books in which *revenge*, especially revenge that is adamantly pursued when the proper authorities either cannot or will not pursue justice, is itself *just*. It matters little if the hero is Clint Eastwood in a spaghetti western or a Dirty Harry film, or Bruce Lee in a martial arts flick, or Rambo getting even in Vietnam. In every case, we enjoy a cathartic release because we are made to feel the violence is *just* and therefore that the revenge is justified. When the right is on your side, revenge, no matter how violent, is a pleasure. It is *just*.

Yet before we mock these films too sternly, even too self-righteously, we must at least ask if in the situations they set up, society would be better served if there were *no* revenge, if there were no "justice," regardless of how rough. Is the American bombing of Afghanistan an act of vengeance or an act of justice? Are there times when vengeance and justice are one? Or does it depend, at least in part, on whether the action is undertaken by an individual or by a government? But cannot governments be corrupt?

In what follows, I want to reason my way to some conclusions in two very different ethical areas. My conclusions are not particularly startling or profound, but I try to reach them while keeping in mind what the Bible says about love—and the exercise of getting there may be a help to some. Before thinking through those two areas, however, I must say a little more about forgiveness.

SOME DIMENSIONS OF FORGIVENESS

The Bible talks about forgiveness in several different ways. Before surveying some of them, however, it is important to recognize the distinction between forgiveness and reconciliation. The latter presupposes the former; the former does not entail the latter. In other words, although forgiveness may bring about reconciliation, it may not. It is possible for one party to forgive another from the heart while the other party remains hardened in self-righteous bitterness.[1] To put the matter another way: in some contexts, forgiveness is bound up with reconcil-

---

[1]Thus I reject the definition of forgiveness given by D. W. Augsburger, "Forgiveness," in *New Dictionary of Christian Ethics and Pastoral Theology*, ed. David J. Atkinson, David F. Field, Arthur Holmes, and Oliver O'Donovan (Leicester: InterVarsity Press, 1995), 389: "Forgiveness is the mutual recognition that repentance of either or both parties is genuine and that right relationships have been restored or achieved." As we shall see, there are some kinds of forgiveness in which there is neither repentance nor mutual recognition of repentance.

iation, but in other contexts forgiveness reflects the stance of the one who forgives, even though no reconciliation with the other party has taken place.

(1) God Forgives

When God discloses something of the afterglow of his glory to Moses (Exod. 34), he first hides Moses in a cleft of a rock and intones before him, "The LORD, the LORD, the compassionate and gracious God, slow to anger, abounding in love and faithfulness, maintaining love to thousands, and forgiving wickedness, rebellion and sin. Yet he does not leave the guilty unpunished; he punishes the children and their children for the sin of the fathers to the third and fourth generation" (Exod. 34:6-7).

Here three principal emphases are permitted to exist in tension. *First*, God is compassionate, slow to anger, gracious, abounding in love and faithfulness. Despite false stereotypes, the God of the Old Testament is not short-tempered and violent. The biblical writers always present him as slow to anger. *Second*, the supreme way his compassion and love and faithfulness manifest themselves is in "forgiving wickedness, rebellion and sin"—which of course explain his anger. *Third*, even though he forgives so lavishly, "he does not leave the guilty unpunished." Indeed, some of his punishments extend across generations, for sin is most commonly socially complex.

But how the *second* and the *third* points cohere is not made clear. Does the passage mean that God forgives some sins and punishes others? Or that while he forgives, there may nevertheless be some temporal punishments to pay? Or that "the guilty" refers to those who do not learn their lessons when they are forgiven? We would have to probe such questions by recourse to other passages, for this one does not sort them out. The least that must be said, however—and it is an important point—is that once again God is not portrayed as pollyannaish in his forgiveness. God forgives; God punishes. He is just; he is compassionate.

When we examine God and his forgiveness in the Old Testament, we must not restrict ourselves to certain word-groups, but word-groups are a place to start. The root *kpr* most commonly carries the notion of atonement; when it means "to forgive," God is always the subject, and it is hard to avoid the conclusion that atonement is made. A second root, *slh*, has more or less the same range of meaning as our word *forgive*, and it too has only God as the subject. It is repeatedly connected with the sacrificial system. A third root, *nśʾ*, commonly means "to lift" or "to carry"; when it means "to forgive," the subject can be either God or human beings—but this word-group can be used not only for the forgiveness of sin but also for the bearing of the penalty of sin (Num. 14:33-34; Ezek. 14:10).

What this evidence suggests, then, is that forgiveness is not something that should be taken for granted; it is not bound up with the nature of things. After all, many passages speak of God *not* pardoning certain offenses (e.g., Deut. 29:20; 2 Kings 24:4; Jer. 5:7; Lam. 3:42). When forgiveness is granted, it is a mark of God's mercy—and very commonly it is explicitly or implicitly connected with sacrifices, sacrifices that God himself has prescribed and promised to accept.

God is (lit.) "a God of pardons" (Neh. 9:17; NIV "a forgiving God"). "The Lord our God is merciful and forgiving" (Dan. 9:9). But never is God's forgiveness something to be presumed upon: "If you, O LORD, kept a record of sins, O Lord, who could stand? But with you there is forgiveness; *therefore you are feared*" (Ps. 130:3-4, emphasis mine). When he does forgive his people, he makes a thorough job of it: "as far as the east is from the west, so far has he removed our transgressions from us" (Ps. 103:12). God "blots out" the transgressions of his people for his own sake and remembers their sin no more (Isa. 43:25; cf. Jer. 31:34). "Who is a God like you, who pardons sin and forgives the transgression of the remnant of his inheritance? You do not stay angry forever but delight to show mercy. You will again have compassion on us; you will tread our sins underfoot and hurl all our iniquities into the depths of the sea" (Mic. 7:18-19).

In the New Testament, John the Baptist opens the narrative by preaching "a baptism of repentance for the forgiveness of sins" (Mark 1:4). The link between forgiveness and repentance is not uncommon. The early church preached that God exalted Jesus to his own right hand as Prince and Savior "that he might give repentance and forgiveness of sins to Israel" (Acts 5:31). Not uncommonly forgiveness is linked to the ultimate sacrifice, the sacrifice to which all other sacrifices point, the sacrifice of the Lord Jesus on the cross. According to Matthew 26:28, when Jesus instituted the Lord's Table, he said, "This is my blood of the covenant, which is poured out for many for the forgiveness of sins." After his resurrection, Jesus taught his disciples that the Christ had to suffer and rise from the dead on the third day, "and repentance and forgiveness of sins will be preached in his name to all nations, beginning at Jerusalem" (Luke 24:47). Paul writes, "In him we have redemption through his blood, the forgiveness of sins" (Eph. 1:7).

Even when there are more general references to Jesus, and not explicitly to his cross or death or blood, we are to understand that Jesus and his death and resurrection cannot be separated. So the words, "I want you to know that through Jesus the forgiveness of sins is proclaimed to you" (Acts 13:38) properly means "through Jesus, the messianic King and Suffering Servant, the one who died and rose again, the forgiveness of sins is proclaimed to you" (as the previous verses suggest). For in the New Testament story-line, forgiveness rests finally on the atoning work of Christ. It is the blood of Jesus, God's Son, that "purifies us from all sin" (1 John 1:7). Precisely because God honors the new covenant terms sealed with the blood of his Son, John declares him to be "faithful and just," and therefore he "will forgive us our sins and purify us from all unrighteousness" (1 John 1:9).

Of the many related themes that might usefully be introduced at this point, I mention only two.

(1) In the striking account of the healing of the paralytic who is lowered by four of his chums through the roof, Jesus, on seeing their faith, says to the paralyzed man, "Son, your sins are forgiven" (Mark 2:5). This sets off a debate with some "teachers of the law," who think that Jesus is usurping a prerogative that belongs to God alone. The course of that debate I need not trace here, but its culmination is stunning. When he finally heals the paralytic, Jesus casts the miracle as evidence that he *does in fact* have the right to forgive sins: "But that you may know that the Son of Man has authority on earth to forgive sins . . ."—and then he performs the miracle.

Who has the right to forgive the offenses of another? This side of the Holocaust, the question has been raised in plaintive terms. Only the victims of the Holocaust have the right to forgive the perpetrators, argues Simon Wiesenthal;[2] and since they are all dead, no forgiveness is possible. It is not merely impertinent for others to think they can forgive such crimes; it is immoral, odious. How would the victim of a vicious rape feel if I went up to the perpetrator and declared that I forgave him? Would she not scream out that I do not have the right?

That is why, in the ultimate sense, *only* God has the right to forgive sins, all sins—for all sins have first and foremost been committed against him, as David himself recognized (Ps. 51:4). This is not to deny that many others may be abused, violated, offended; it is to say that in the ultimate sense, what gives sin its deepest odium, its most heinous hue, is that it offends the God who made us and who stands as our Judge. That is why he and he alone has this ultimate right to forgive sins. The way Jesus was speaking, in the case of the paralytic, shows that he thought of himself as having exactly the same prerogatives as God in this matter—and his opponents understood the implications. In a derivative way, of course, Christians absolve others of their sins, even when those sins have not been committed against the Christians themselves, by the proclamation of the gospel (John 20:23). But in that case, we are simply acting as God's agents in declaring what God himself has already declared in the gospel.

(2) Thoughtful Christians can never forget Jesus' haunting prayer on the cross, offered up with respect to the men who were torturing him in crucifixion: "Father, forgive them, for they do not know what they are doing" (Luke 23:34). The prayer is often used as a kind of generalized incentive to Christians to forgive everyone under every circumstance, but that reading is surely incorrect. Several observations may clarify some of the things we should learn from the prayer.

First, when Jesus says that they do not know what they are doing, he does not mean that their ignorance is so absolute that they are innocent. For if they were innocent, there would be nothing to forgive. He must mean, rather, that they are relatively ignorant and therefore relatively innocent. They have acted barbarically, and they may have heard that the court proceedings were a farce, but that is still different from

---

[2]Simon Wiesenthal, *The Sunflower: On the Possibilities and Limits of Forgiveness* (New York: Schocken, 1976).

engineering the rigged trial, and it is vastly different from knowing exactly who it was that they were executing.

Second, Jesus does not say or pray this with respect to everyone who was involved in his betrayal and execution. Regarding Judas Iscariot, for instance, Jesus gave him various warnings but finally pronounced, "It would be better for him if he had not been born" (Mark 14:21). Jesus himself could tell parables that show that some people face eternal judgment at the end while others enjoy eternal life (e.g., Matt. 25:46). In other words, this prayer is not so all-explaining that it can be used to overthrow other things that Jesus said and did.

Third, the manner in which Jesus' Father answered this prayer is not transparent. Perhaps these soldiers later became believers; perhaps the Father showed his forbearance and forgiveness by not wiping them out on the spot. We simply do not know.

Fourth, when Jesus utters this prayer, he certainly does not do so because these men have already repented of the degree of evil in which they were complicit. And that means, *fifth*, that the most important thing about this prayer is not the precise way in which it was answered or the precise degree of guilt that the men incurred and for which they needed forgiveness, but the way it discloses Jesus' heart.

(2) Christians Must Forgive

Perhaps the most important evidence that Jesus' followers must forgive is found in the prayer the Lord Jesus himself taught us to pray: "Forgive us our debts, as we also have forgiven our debtors" (Matt. 6:12)—where sin is seen as a debt. The parallel in Luke is no less forthright: "Forgive us our sins, for we also forgive everyone who sins against us" (Luke 11:4). In case we miss the message, Jesus himself in Matthew's account offers an explanatory expansion: "For if you forgive men when they sin against you, your heavenly Father will also forgive you. But if you do not forgive men their sins, your Father will not forgive your sins" (Matt. 6:14-15). The same point is made explicit elsewhere: "Forgive, and you will be forgiven" (Luke 6:37). The parable of the unmerciful servant (Matt. 18:21-35) is astonishingly effective at making the same point. The one servant is initially forgiven a stupendous amount, but because he will not forgive a fellow servant a trivial amount, his master turns him over "to the jailers to be tortured" (18:34). In case we miss the lesson, Jesus makes it explicit: "This is how my heavenly Father will treat each of you unless you forgive your brother from your heart" (18:35).[3]

These passages must neither be explained away nor misinterpreted. On the one hand, they must stand in all their stark demand: there is no forgiveness for those who do not forgive. On the other hand, in the light of all that the New Testament writers say about grace and change of heart, it would be obtuse to understand these passages as if they were suggesting that a person could *earn* forgiveness by forgiving others. The point is more subtle. It is that people disqualify themselves from being forgiven if they are so hardened in their own bitterness that they cannot or will not forgive others. In such cases, they display no brokenness, no contrition, no recognition of the great value of forgiveness, no understanding of their own complicity in sin, no repentance.

A great deal of contemporary study of forgiveness emphasizes the psychological benefits of this virtue.[4] Not for a moment would I suggest that such studies are valueless. But they often lead us slightly astray. They are full of discussion about our suffering, the importance of being released from bitterness, the advantages of the psychological unshackling that the virtue of forgiveness can bring, and much more.

There is a great measure of truth in what they say. A woman in her thirties who is freezing up in her relationship with her husband may need to forgive the father who repeatedly abused her sexually when she was fourteen or fifteen. Part of getting to that point may be tied up with looking the evil straight in the face, seeing it for what it is, and then forgiving the man who did it.

---

[3]The attempt of Samuel P. Lamerson, "The Parable of the Unforgiving Servant in Its First-Century Jewish Milieu: The Relationship Between Exile and Forgiveness in the Gospel of Matthew" (Ph.D. dissertation; Deerfield: Trinity Evangelical Divinity School, 2001), to connect this parable to the exile theme is unconvincing. He thinks the parable shows that "God's offer of forgiveness, extended through Jesus, realizes the exilic hope of final forgiveness" and that "whoever fought against the forgiveness offered to sinners through Jesus also fought against an end to the exile" (Abstract). In my view, the exile theme is far more minor than some contemporary scholars think. If so, then the connections ostensibly built on it cannot be more convincing than the prop itself. But it would add little to our examination of the present theme to probe the matter here.

[4]E.g., Margaret Grammatky Alter, "The Unnatural Act of Forgiveness," *Christianity Today* 41/7 (16 June 1997), 28-30; Gary Thomas, "The Forgiveness Factor," *Christianity Today* 44/1 (10 January 2000), 38-45; Everett L. Worthington, Jr., ed., *Dimensions of Forgiveness: Psychological Research and Theological Perspectives* (Philadelphia/London: Templeton Foundation Press, 1998).

But the fact remains that the *psychological* benefits do not receive primary stress in Scripture, where the emphasis is on the *eternal* benefits of being right with God. And in the light of some texts (e.g., the parable of the unmerciful servant referred to above), there is enormous personal and eternal danger in *not* forgiving others. For nothing, nothing at all, is more important than being assured of the forgiveness of God. On this point, the psychological works are almost silent or commonly presuppose, quite wrongly, that the forgiveness of God is the unconditional "given" to which the human forgiveness should attach itself for the sake of psychological well-being. This badly skews the biblical emphases. In the Christian way, those who know they are forgiven are the same people who forgive. One of the marks of growing spirituality in a Christian, Whitney argues, is that he or she is becoming a "quicker forgiver."[5]

(3) The Different Flavors to Forgiveness

Flavors may not be quite the right word. What I mean is that in the Bible the forgiveness that we exercise toward others has at least three axes on which we find ourselves. Where we are on those axes affects the "flavor" of the forgiveness we extend. There are commonalities in all genuine forgiveness, of course. The person who forgives refuses to demonize the wrongdoer and recognizes the wrongdoer's common humanity; the person who forgives quietly surrenders vengeance, the right to get even. The person who forgives may actually wish the wrongdoer well. But despite the commonalities, different biblical contexts depict various kinds of forgiveness with different "flavors."

First, there are different motives that go into the act of forgiving. As we have already seen, one of the motives is to maintain the spirit of contrition and brokenness that means that we ourselves may enjoy forgiveness (Matt. 6:14-15). Another is the fact that we have already been forgiven: ". . . forgiving each other, just as in Christ God forgave you" (Eph. 4:32). The idea is not simply that we have been forgiven, and therefore we ought to forgive, but that *God himself*, in Christ, has for-

---

[5]Donald S. Whitney, *Ten Questions to Diagnose Your Spiritual Health* (Colorado Springs: NavPress, 2001), 111-120.

given us, and therefore our debt is incalculable. No matter how much wretched evil has been done against us, it is little compared with the offense we have thrown in the face of God. Yet God in Christ has forgiven us. If we know anything of the release of this forgiveness, if we have glimpsed anything of the magnitude of the debt we owe to God, our forgiveness of others will not seem to be such a large leap.

But there are other motives, and none is more important than love. Even the verse just quoted doubtless presupposes that motive: "Be kind and compassionate to one another, forgiving each other, just as in Christ God forgave you." Forgiveness and love are linked in several crucial passages (e.g., Col. 3:13-14). Love, after all, "keeps no record of wrongs" (1 Cor. 13:5)—surely an evocative way of saying that love forgives completely and thoroughly.

Second, sometimes the forgiveness of which the New Testament speaks presupposes repentance on the part of the offender and sometimes not. As an example of the former, consider the astonishing teaching of Jesus: "If your brother sins, rebuke him, and if he repents, forgive him. If he sins against you seven times in a day, and seven times comes back to you and says, 'I repent,' forgive him" (Luke 17:3-4). This is not an invitation to be naive about your brother's inconsistency; it does not mean that he should be trusted as if he had no track record of untrustworthiness. What is at issue is a person's sheer willingness to forgive. Some brothers, hot-tempered perhaps, are constantly putting their foot in it, but they soon return in mortified repentance. Why should we not extend forgiveness again and again? After all, again and again God extends forgiveness to us. But the interesting thing about this utterance of Jesus is that he presupposes that the repentance of the offending brother is part of the package.

In other passages, however, as we have seen, forgiveness appears to be more closely allied with forbearance: "Therefore, as God's chosen people, holy and dearly loved, clothe yourselves with compassion, kindness, humility, gentleness and patience. Bear with each other and forgive whatever grievances you may have against one another. Forgive as the Lord forgave you. And over all these virtues put on love, which binds them all together in perfect unity" (Col. 3:12-14). One thinks immediately of the prayer of the dying Stephen: "Lord, do not hold this sin against them" (Acts 7:60)—which certainly is not offered in the wake of any observable repentance!

The difference in result between forgiveness that responds to repentance and forgiveness independent of the repentance of the offending party is, of course, that the former pattern issues in reconciliation while the latter does not. But in both cases what is presupposed is that the believer forgives the offender. Transparently, reconciliation is a good thing if it can be achieved, but the goal of reconciliation should not become a cloak for nursing bitterness because it cannot be achieved.

Third, despite all the emphasis on personal forgiveness, the Bible can reserve an important place for punishment without forgiveness. There are several circumstances where this theme surges to the fore.

(a) The state is given the power of the sword; the civil magistrate "is God's servant, an agent of wrath to bring punishment on the wrongdoer" (Rom. 13:4). Ideally, such magistrates hold terror only "for those who do wrong" (Rom. 13:3). There is no suggestion that the state or the magistrate simply "forgive" the wrongdoer, *even though these verses occur immediately after the insistence at the end of Romans 12 that Christians are not to follow the path of vengeance but to leave vengeance to the Lord.* That contextual connection alone is enough to raise suspicions that Romans 12:17-20 should not be used to defend pacifism. If the state has the power of the sword, then of course this brings up the possibility that the wrongdoer may commit his crime against a Christian, who, as a Christian, will surely arrive sooner or later at the importance of forgiving the offender, while the state is supposed to exercise the sword. In other words, the state cannot afford the same luxury; it cannot display the same virtue of forgiveness. The state's virtue is maintained insofar as it pursues justice. By implication, if the state's magistrate is a Christian, that Christian better remember which virtue takes precedence in his or her role as servant of the state.

(b) Numerous passages anticipate that God will bring down final and irrevocable judgment at the end. Some passages make simple disjunctions (e.g., between the sheep and the goats, and their respective destinations, Matt. 25:46). Others picture the "day of the Lord" as an occasion of sudden, unanticipated destruction (e.g., 1 Thess. 5:3). Still others deploy staggeringly frightening images (e.g., Rev. 14:6-20). For our purposes, the point on which to reflect is that forgiveness is not so absolute a virtue that other virtues—in this case, the certainty and implacability of God's ultimate judgment against the unrepentant—may be overridden, with strange speculations about hell existing but being empty. There is no convincing evidence that the Bible holds out hope that in the end forgiveness will be extended to everyone without exception.

(c) In Revelation 6:9-10 we find Christian martyrs, those who are "under the altar" in John's vision and "who had been slain because of the word of God and the testimony they had maintained," calling out in a loud voice, "How long, Sovereign Lord, holy and true, until you judge the inhabitants of the earth and avenge our blood?" Each is then given a white robe and told to wait a little longer until the number of martyrs is complete. Where is Christian forgiveness in this vignette? Clearly, it isn't there. But before we become too critical, we should remember that all parties in the book of Revelation know that the final judgment is not only inevitable but just. These martyred believers are not, after all, looking to exact personal vengeance: they remember the biblical instruction that vengeance belongs to the Lord (e.g., Rom. 12:17-20), which is why they address their prayer to him. They know full well that the Lord's irrevocable vengeance is on its way; they know that justice will be done, and will be seen to be done. Their prayer is that it might come sooner rather than later.

After all, Christians have been taught by the Bible, both Old and New Testaments, that God is a God of justice. And justice demands that those who are not finally found under the forgiveness paid for by Christ's death face the just recompense of their defiance of God. That, too, is part of the picture when we pray as Jesus taught us: "Your kingdom come, your will be done on earth as it is in heaven" (Matt. 6:10).

The preceding Scriptures suggest that Christians experience an unavoidable tension. On the one hand, they are called to abandon bitterness, to be forbearing, to have a forgiving stance even where the repentance of the offending party is conspicuous by its absence; on the other hand, their God-centered passion for justice, their concern for God's glory, ensure that the awful odium of sin is not glossed over. The

former stance without the latter quickly dissolves into a mushy sentimentality that forgets how vile sin is; the latter stance without the former easily hardens into rigid recriminations, self-righteous wrath,
unbending retaliation.

(d) This tension between the demand for forgiveness and the passion for justice is found not only in the martyrs under the altar who
await the end of history, but in an apostle or a pastor charged with
protecting the flock of God. Thus Paul can label certain people "false
apostles" (2 Cor. 11:13-15) and insist that it is the church's obligation
to expel them—just as he expected the church to expel the member
who was caught up in moral debauchery (1 Cor. 5:13). In the same
line, he himself has exercised his apostolic authority by handing
Hymenaeus and Alexander over to Satan so that they might learn not
to blaspheme (1 Tim. 1:20)—perhaps the same Alexander whom
(Paul is confident) the Lord will repay for all the damage he has done
(2 Tim. 4:14). And when Jude calls down his "Woe!" on certain people (Jude 11), he is, after all, doing no more than his infinitely more
famous half-brother, the Lord Jesus (e.g., Matt. 23). How does forgiveness fit into these settings?

This subject is so important that I shall probe it at greater length in
the next lecture. But here I must say at least this. Quite apart from the
competing demands of forgiveness and justice, one must reckon with
the competing *objects* of love. In the West, we often focus so much of our
attention on the individual that we tend to overlook the corporate body.
Would Paul be displaying transparent love *for the Corinthian congregation* if he did not warn them about the extraordinary dangers they
were facing if they did not exercise discipline? That point lies close to
the surface in all of the severe passages just quoted. Paul knew full well
that a rotten apple can spoil the whole barrel; a little yeast affects the
entire batch of dough (1 Cor. 5:6). Jesus knew full well that one of the
effects of the teaching of the Pharisees was that it imposed heavy loads
on the shoulders of the people (Matt. 23:4). Transparently, Jude was
writing to call the faithful to persevering obedience so that they would
not be snookered by the false teachers whose influence was multiplying.
In other words, Jude displayed his deep love for his readers by warning

them against certain false teachers. Would he have been a truly loving pastor if he had *not* so warned them?

What this suggests, then, is that moral indignation, even moral outrage, may on occasion be proof of love—love for the victim, love for the church of God, love for the truth, love for God and his glory. *Not* to be outraged may in such cases be evidence, not of gentleness and love, *but of a failure of love.*

This is where our motives can become thoroughly confused, not to say corrupted. For the line between moral outrage for the sake of God and his people, and immoral outrage because I am on the opposite side of a debate, is painfully thin. On the issue I may even be right; in my heart I may be terribly wrong, precisely because I am less motivated by a passion for the glory of God and the good of his people than for vindication in a wretched squabble with a few individuals. What should be obvious by now, however, is, *first*, that to quote passages on justice in order to justify the nurtured bitterness of personal injury is for the Christian inexcusable; and, *second*, that to plead for endless "forgiveness" when the interest of the state demands justice or when love for God and his people is hopelessly absent is, far from being a Christian virtue, merely a cloaked indifference to moral integrity and biblical fidelity.

I have barely probed the periphery of forgiveness. But perhaps enough has been said to warrant some introductory reflection on two hard cases.

4

LOVE AND FORGIVENESS:
TWO HARD CASES

As important as it is to think through what the Bible says about love and forgiveness—the purpose of the preceding lecture—it is scarcely less important to work out such themes in tough cases. The two that I discuss here are far from being the only tough cases. It may be better, however, to deal with only two and probe them at slightly greater length than to choose, say, ten tough cases and handle all of them cursorily. While the discussions that follow are in some ways mere introductions, they are an excuse to "think out loud" so as to demonstrate the kinds of theological themes and the kind of theological reflection that go into serious attempts to relate some of the Bible's complex, interlocking themes to some of today's complex, interlocking problems.

A. HARD CASE ONE: RACISM

Racism has many faces. Just how many faces depends a fair bit on definition. If the "race" in "racism" is given a broad and technical definition, then "racism" does not include, for instance, the rivalry and exclusions that regularly occur between the Chinese and the Japanese. Any mutual animus between Chinese and Japanese, some argue, is not an instance of "racism" since both parties belong to the same "race." Rather, it is a matter of ethnic conflict. In Africa the genocide in Rwanda is not a matter of racism (the argument continues), but a function of tribalism or merely a power struggle, since Hutus and Tutsis (for instance) belong to the same race—as do the Mau Mau and the Kikuyu.

But genocide is genocide, whether Nazis are slaughtering Jews or Hutus are slaughtering Tutsis (or vice versa). To preserve technical niceties over the term "racism" rather misses the ugly reality. Nowadays "racism" carries connotations of evil. If the term can be relegated away from a particular display of the same fundamental evil, there is political advantage since there is no similar term (such as "ethnicism") that carries the same load of evil. In some ways, therefore, it is better to adopt the habit of Miroslav Volf, who sidesteps these problems of definition by talking about "exclusion."[1] There is nevertheless a slight disadvantage with "exclusion": the term does not carry the shame and opprobrium of "racism." So I will continue to use the term "racism," but when I use it, I am referring to *all* patterns of exclusion of others grounded *in race or ethnicity*. This does not include *all* patterns of rejection of the "other," which I briefly mentioned in the second lecture.[2] For example, under this definition, treating some groups as "other" because of political views or economic difference is not itself racist. Here I am restricting myself to racism as a subcategory of the exclusion of the "other," a subcategory that turns on differences of race or ethnicity (even if other features such as religion or economics usually also play a role).

Under this definition, the phenomenon of racism is disturbingly rampant. Quite apart from the black-and-white variety engendered in the West by the tragic history of slavery, racism surfaces all over the world. Most Chinese parents would not want their daughter, for instance, to marry a European-American lad; most Japanese think that Koreans are a step down. The list is endless. Add the tribal conflicts in Africa, of which the genocide in Rwanda is merely the most notorious recent example; add the

---

[1]See especially his book, *Exclusion and Embrace: A Theological Exploration of Identity, Otherness, and Reconciliation* (Nashville: Abingdon, 1996).

[2]It appears to me that Douglas R. Sharp, "'There is no longer . . .': Razing the Idol of Race," *Ex Auditu* 15 (1999), 103-117, allows his rhetoric to get away from him when he assigns to "racism" all definitions of "other" that somehow emphasize "difference," regardless of whether or not they are grounded in race or ethnicity. Under his definitions, differences grounded in economic disparities, or in distinctions between management and workers, or in religious belief systems, or anything else, fall under the one word *racism*. That there can be detrimental exclusions in almost any domain, that the challenge of loving the "other" remains with us until the end of the age, is indisputable. Whether *racism* as a term should be applied quite so broadly is another issue. To use it that way may unwittingly draw attention away from the peculiar forms of exclusion of "other" that are grounded in race and ethnicity.

myth of Aryan supremacy that demanded not only *Lebensraum*, precipitating World War II, but issued in the Holocaust; add the slaughter of a
million and a half Armenians at the beginning of the twentieth century;
add the Russian slaughter of Ukrainians and widespread non-Russian
Slavic distrust of Russians; add the horrors of apartheid, now abolished
in law but a long way from being totally overcome; add the treatment of
Aboriginals by Australian Caucasians; add the treatment of "Indians" in
the Americas (North, Central, and South) by Canadians, Americans,
Brazilians, and the Hispanic countries. The list is endless. In some ways,
all of these examples of racism are subsets of the perception of "other"
enemies that I briefly treated at the end of the second lecture.

My focus here will necessarily be narrow. I am not going to address
the entire sweep of what might fall under the rubric "racism," but focus
on one small subset of the problem that has a peculiar bearing on
Christians. It has been argued that in America the most segregated hour
of the week is 11:00 A.M. on Sunday morning. I am not sure if that is
true, but it may well be. This claim results in repeated calls for reconciliation, repentance, hard love, forgiveness, forbearance, sacrificial love,
renouncing the past, and much more. Some of these calls are spot on;
some of them, one fears, descend to the level of demagoguery and
manipulation. In this section I cannot possibly address complex patterns
of racism among Christians as those patterns are manifest in different
parts of the world. Instead, I want to focus especially on the North
American context and think out loud about some of the ways racism displays itself in the church. In particular, this means thinking about the
ways in which the demands for love and forgiveness need to be applied.
In short, it means thinking about the urgent need for love in hard places.

I shall organize what I have to say into five points.

(1) I begin with some brief historical reflections. I am indebted to
some recent books on race and slavery that have taught me a good deal.
Among the best researched of these are some works by Thomas Sowell.[3]
He points out that until the nineteenth century, slavery in one form or
another had been part of every major civilization. Various Chinese

---

[3]See his *Migrations and Cultures: A World View* (New York: Basic Books, 1996), and especially his
Race and Culture: A World View (New York: Basic Books, 1994), not least chap. 7, "Race and
Slavery."

dynasties had slaves; Indians had slaves; the dominant African tribes had slaves (substantial numbers of slaves sold to the Western world and to the Persian Gulf were sold by other Africans); the Israelites had slaves; the Egyptians, Hittites, Assyrians, Babylonians, Persians, Greeks, and Romans all had slaves. The major "barbarian" tribes of Europe had slaves. The Arab world had slaves. So there is a sense in which, from the vantage of history until about two centuries ago, the phenomenon of slavery was not itself viewed as shocking.

When Sowell hunts down the deciding element in the moves toward the abolition of slavery, he fastens primary attention on the impact of the Evangelical Awakening. Not only John Wesley himself, but also many of the leading converts of that God-given movement, including the Countess of Huntingdon, William Wilberforce, and the Earl of Shaftesbury, invested enormous energy in navigating the abolition of slavery through the British Parliament. Once it was passed, British gun-boats (doubtless with other motives as well) largely halted the trade across the Atlantic. It is estimated that about eleven million Africans were shipped to the Americas (though substantial numbers failed to reach the other side, owing to the horrific conditions slaves had to endure in the boats). At the same time, about fourteen million Africans were shipped up the Persian Gulf or across the Sahara into the Arab and Egyptian worlds under traveling conditions more horrific yet.[4] British gunboats eventually shut down most of that trade as well once the Ottoman Empire formally banned slavery and thereby gave the British navy the legal pretense to proceed.[5] Interestingly enough, there has arisen considerable guilt-literature regarding slavery in the Western world; it is difficult to find much that is similar in the Arab world.

I must hasten to add that Christians, especially in America, must not pat themselves on the back too quickly for the beneficial social results

---

[4]See, *inter alia*, Ralph A. Austen, "The Trans-Saharan Slave Trade: A Tentative Census," in *Uncommon Market: Essays in the Economic History of the Atlantic Slave Trade*, ed. Henry A. Gemery and Jan S. Hogendorn (New York: Academic Press, 1979), 68-69; Reginald Coupland, *The Exploitation of East Africa 1856-1890: The Slave Trade and the Scramble* (Evanston, Ill.: Northwestern University Press, 1967), 148; nicely summarized in Thomas Sowell, *Race and Culture*, esp. 188, 208.

[5]Eventually other European powers joined in the ban, enforcing it both at home and in their colonial domains, prompting Thomas Sowell (*Race and Culture*, 222) to write, "More specifically, it was European imperialism which stamped out slavery over most of the world. The last nation to abolish slavery officially was Mauritania, on 5 July, 1980, though the practice continued after the ban—as it still does in several parts of the world today."

of the Evangelical Awakening so far as slavery is concerned. For the fact of the matter is that the part of the country where evangelical confessionalism was strongest, in the South, was the place where slavery was hardest to dislodge. In the end it took the Civil War (though that war was about more than slavery), America's bloodiest.

Not all forms of slavery are alike, however. Inevitably cultures that enslave others are dominant, and a fair bit of slavery, historically speaking, has issued from military might. Some has been conscripted forced labor (e.g., for the building of the Egyptian pyramids); some of it has been fed by religious persecution (e.g., the slaughter and enslavement of the Huguenots); very often there are mixed motives (e.g., the current savage bloodshed and slavery in the southern Sudan, which is fed by tribalism, religion [Muslim versus Christian], and oil interests). In some cultures, economics must not be discounted. In the Roman Empire, for example, there were no bankruptcy laws—ancient equivalents to Chapter 11 and Chapter 13 in the U.S. and similar legislation in other countries. When a family fell into arrears, selling one or more members of the family to the creditor was often the only way out. A well-to-do relative or neighbor could redeem these slaves, but doubtless that did not happen as often as many slaves might have liked.

These realities meant that slavery in the Roman Empire was a bit different from that in the West. In the West, none of the slavery was the result of free people selling themselves into slavery because they were bankrupt. More important, in the Roman world there were slaves from many different races and cultures: slaves could be British, from the Italian peninsula, Jewish, African, and so on. But there were also free individuals from all those heritages, and some of these were learned or influential. That meant that there was little identification between slavery and one particular race.[6] By contrast, in the West from the beginning almost all blacks were slaves, and certainly only blacks were slaves.[7] That meant that even after legal emancipation, the psychological asso-

---

[6]The point is rightly made, though somewhat overstated, by Frank M. Snowden, Jr., in his book *Before Color Prejudice: The Ancient View of Blacks* (Cambridge: Harvard University Press, 1983).

[7]Although this is true, strictly speaking, we do well to recall other groups of people who for a considerable period of time were indentured workers treated little better than slaves. One thinks, for instance, of the tens of thousands of Chinese "coolies" who labored to build American railroads.

ciation of slavery and black skin has lingered on for a long time *both in the minds of whites and in the minds of blacks.*

This history has also contributed to the public perception, including the Christian perception, of where the problem lies when it comes to the desirability of integrating Christian churches. For without giving it much thought, when we think of integrated churches, we primarily think of black/white integration, and we usually assume the deepest barriers are on the white side, the majority side. But the issues are complicated. Without for a moment wanting to play down the commonness of white prejudice, we must reflect as well on the many Korean churches here, the many Chinese churches, the many Latino and Vietnamese churches, and so forth. In all of these cases, very often the Christians who are least desirous of integrating with others are from the *minority* side: many Koreans and Chinese and Vietnamese and Latinos want to preserve something of their own culture and race and heritage. Some of the problems come, as we shall see, in the second and third generation. And similarly, it is not too surprising that many African-Americans would *prefer* to worship in African-American churches, even while they may feel that the point of exclusion is entirely or almost entirely on the European-American side.

The issues become still more complicated when two other factors are borne in mind. *First,* many minority churches argue today that the church is the only social institution that preserves the meeting of minorities as minorities, and it is this social construction that permits a group to raise up leaders to represent it. Many of the earliest African-American civil rights leaders were clergy—an eloquent testimony to the significance of churches in preserving a social identity.

Second, there has been a shift from the agenda of the 1960s to the agenda of the 1990s and beyond. In the 1960s the call was for equality, inclusion, integration; in the 1990s and now in the new millennium, the call is for multiculturalism, respect for diversity, the importance of preserving distinct communities.[8] Inevitably, therefore, "otherness" is more

---

[8]This change has drawn a great deal of comment. Popular sociology often refers to the first model, usually now with a good deal of disparagement, as the "melting-pot model": all the ingredients lose their individual identities in the stew. The primary alternative often calls forth a "salad-bowl image": each ingredient keeps its distinctive taste and yet contributes to the integrated flavor of the entire dish. Images aside, commentators increasingly recognize that the latter model can easily generate unseemly one-upmanship and foster discord and isolationism. Seeking a mediating pattern, some have tried to carve

difficult to assess. It might be a reflection of the desire to preserve something good, not least among minorities themselves; equally, it might be a reflection of xenophobia, resentment, exclusion. The human heart being what it is, in most cases both of these motives will surface simultaneously.

If in North America we talk about the integration of the local church, however, the shape of that discussion, given our history and demographics, will necessarily focus first of all on the black/white divide, even if it must extend far beyond that divide. It will be determined, at least in part, by the demographics of a particular neighborhood.

(2) I think we need more public discussion of the fact that racism, as defined here, usually comes from *both* sides of any race divide. Many African-Americans do not accept this. They think that racism is the sin of the powerful, the sin of the overlord; they think of racism as the sum of racial prejudice plus power. By definition, then, they cannot be racists since they do not have the power. I do not see how thoughtful Christians, black or white, can accept such a definition.

True, *slavery* is the sin of the powerful, not the weak; and very often racism follows the same pattern. But if racism is defined in terms of exclusion, then racism occurs wherever anyone is dismissed or disowned or demeaned or stereotyped for no other reason than his or her race or ethnicity. Doubtless many white racists think that African-Americans are intrinsically prone to violence, not too bright, and more of the same; but many an African-American finds it hard to imagine that "Whitey" can ever be trusted or should ever be given the benefit of the doubt. It may be useful to draw an analogy. If materialism is the exclusive sin of the rich, then only rich people can be materialistic. But if materialism is the passionate love of material goods, such that God himself is deposed, then poor people may be as horribly materialistic as the rich.

Because I am white, I am sure it is difficult for some African-Americans to hear such plain home truths from me; indeed, I have had African-American students at the seminary where I teach gently and ruefully tell me that although they are sure what I am saying is the truth, it

out a special domain of integration in the public sphere: see, for instance, Clarence Walhout, "Literature, Christianity, and the Public Sphere," *Christian Scholar's Review* 29 (1999), 361-373. Discussions are ongoing, but in my view public and private spheres are not so easily sealed off from each other.

is very hard for them to accept it from me. All the more honor to them, then, for trying.

Moreover, some leaders on *both* sides of any racial divide love to play the race card to keep themselves in power. George Wallace used to do it all the time, flagrantly and repeatedly, until he had a change of heart; not a few of our contemporaries follow the early George Wallace, not the later George Wallace. That early Wallace stance was profoundly repulsive, deeply evil.

Because of the many legal sanctions now in place, some forget the bitter degradation of the Jim Crow culture. The *attitudes* wedded to the Jim Crow culture have not everywhere been expunged. I suspect that most European-Americans have very little understanding of the cumulative destructive power of the little degradations that almost all African-Americans, especially older African-Americans, have experienced—to say nothing of the less common but still too frequent threats, racial profiling, and frankly illegal (to say nothing of immoral) injustices they have suffered.

On the other hand, the Reverend Al Sharpton constantly plays the race card on the African-American side, and he is far from being the only one. The instant appeal to "racism" when young thugs are expelled from a school, regardless of color or ethnicity, succeeds only in reducing the credibility of the ranters. The best way to diminish racist demagoguery is for European-Americans to expose and dismiss European-American demagogues and for African-Americans to expose and dismiss African-American demagogues.

Because of the background of racism in America, it is easy to discern racism where it does not exist. I recall an African—i.e., a citizen of an African country, not an African-American—telling me of his painful, belittling experiences when he was trying to secure his "green card" at a major U.S. immigration point. Initially he was convinced that what he had experienced was raw racism. But I could not help encouraging him to loosen up a little, for I had had identical—indeed, as we compared notes, even worse—experiences when my wife and I applied for our "green cards" at the same center a few years earlier. The association of rudeness with racism is entirely understandable, of course, but there is plenty of rudeness to go around even where there is little racism.

Once again if we are interested in integrated local Christian churches, it is high time that we recognize that the challenge extends beyond the black/white divide and that the attitudinal problems are on both sides of most divides. Many a Korean-American church (to take but one example) is run by first-generation Korean Christians who are most comfortable with the way things are done back home. That means that "otherness" is hard for them, especially if part of the issue is language, part of the issue is preserving Korean culture (and even Korean forms of "spirituality"), part of the issue is a Confucian preservation of hierarchy and order, and part of the issue is their desire that their children marry other Koreans. Sometimes these churches keep calling senior pastors fresh from Korea, thus renewing the strong linguistic and cultural links with "home." This practice may have the effect sooner or later of repelling second- and third-generation Korean-American Christians, whose command of Korean may not be all that good anymore and, more importantly, whose cultural adaptation means they no longer live in the world of their parents. Those same parents can easily see these developments as cultural or even personal betrayal, or the fruit of degenerative and corrupt moral influence. Some of this judgment, of course, may be right! But some of it, quite frankly, is racist. To add to the complexity, some in the third generation, by now profoundly Americanized, choose to *revert* to their Korean roots, and in consequence tend to shun other American "friends." At what point is this an expression of racism?

Lest anyone should think that I am picking on Koreans, I hasten to add that most of our major influxes of immigrants have faced similar problems. They are at different points in the transition, depending on how long ago the major influx for that group took place. I am old enough to remember not a few German Baptist churches facing similar problems as the number of German-speakers declined in their congregations, and their children became more assimilated. In some ways, of course, their assimilation was smoother because Germans are (mostly!) white; in other ways, their assimilation faced peculiar difficulties associated with the hatreds aroused by World War II.

(3) Now I must look at this from the other end. Consider some local churches that are remarkably integrated. I am thinking of one in the San

Francisco Bay area, for example, that has three full-time pastors. One pastor is Latino (he was born in Mexico), and he is married to a Japanese-American wife (second generation). Another is Anglo, married to an African-American woman; a third is also Anglo, married to a Vietnamese-American. And, frankly, their interesting diversity reflects the demographic diversity of the church they serve.

I am also thinking of another church, this one on the East Coast, in one of the boroughs of New York City. The last time I was there, I personally talked to people from more than thirty countries. Better yet, there was very little evidence of stereotyping. South of the Mason-Dixon line, most people who sit down and eat in restaurants in many neighborhoods are white; most who serve are black. But at this church I met an African-American who had just gotten out of Rikers on a drug charge and another African-American who was an influential physician. I met a white chap of Italian descent, recently converted, and with family ties to the Mafia; I met another white chap (I have no idea of his descent) who is a high-level executive in a large banking firm. Add to this the mix of Japanese, Koreans, Chinese, Latinos, Europeans, and on and on. As far as I could tell, this church was very much a reflection of the demographics of the borough.

Does this mean that these two churches are more spiritual than their more monolithic counterparts in the Midwest? I doubt it. I was overjoyed to visit them. But both churches reflected the demographics of their respective areas, and in those parts of the country there is a lot more "mixing" already going on in the culture. Some of this, doubtless, is a very good thing: it can ease tensions, add rich diversity to a church, and prove to be a witness to others.

On the other hand, one suspects that some of the mixing is achieved in the culture at large, as well as in the local church, by the "flattening" of cultural or racial distinctives. Japanese and Mexicans may intermarry in California because in some circles (though certainly not all), the preservation of distinctively Japanese and Mexican heritages seems less urgent, less important. The enrichment of the common pool is sometimes at the expense of preserving the distinctiveness of the separate inherited cultures. However much we may admire the peace, we would be less than candid if we did not admit that *something* is being lost by this bargain. In other words, thoughtful Christians will surely hesitate before they adopt without reservation some Christianized version of the "melting pot" model. There is something lost in each of the contributing subcultures, as well as something gained in the new mix, by the "flattening" that has made the mix more socially acceptable.

Moreover, precisely because these changes are demonstrably taking place in the broader culture, it is less than transparent that the churches are at the front end of such change. In some cases, at least, they are simply going along with the trajectory of the broader culture. Where that is the case, it is hard to see that a more integrated church is necessarily more spiritual than a less integrated church in a less integrated part of the country. Small wonder that in the Midwest a mixed-race couple may well feel it advisable to live in one of the suburbs where there is a good mix of their respective races so that their children have mixed exposure in the schools. Meanwhile, the latest census shows that the mix is spreading from the coasts across the country. Iowa is becoming a desirable place for Latinos and other immigrants. Granted the demographic trends, churches that are trying to think these things through should be planning ahead for what the demographics of their area will be like in six months, a year, five years—and while they evaluate their Christian responsibilities in the light of Scripture, they had better take note of such trends.

Not for a moment am I suggesting that no racism operates in our churches. Moreover, to have a truly integrated church (reflecting the demographic profile of the neighborhood in which it is found) takes hard work, very substantial forbearance, self-sacrificing winsomeness, patience—in a word, love. But the issues are complex, and the relationships between the culture and the local church have many layers. There is an urgent need for fresh biblical and theological reflection on many of these questions.

(4) We must press a little further, not only to become aware of churches that have achieved more integration than usual, but to think through how highly diverse patterns in various parts of the world may inform our own theological reflection. In other words, one of the things that would help us, I suspect, in addition to exegetical and theological meditation on the love and forgiveness themes being treated in this series of lectures, is consideration of churches where the patterns are rather dif-

ferent. These different patterns have no normative value in themselves, of course, but they might open our eyes to different ways of doing things.

Thankfully, there are now some helpful books that expose us to various fruitful models of multiethnic ministry within this country.[9] We might also cast a glance abroad. For example, a church I know in Australia has over the past quarter-century developed about eighteen or nineteen "congregations" within the one "church," and almost half of them are ethnic. The senior minister has sought out young converts of distinctive ethnic backgrounds at the nearby university and helped to train them and put them through theological college. Thus a student with roots in Greece was soon evangelizing the considerable Greek-speaking population in the area, and a Greek-speaking congregation was started. In similar fashion, Cantonese, Mandarin, Korean, and other congregations were started. Is this zeal somehow a betrayal of the New Testament goal to build one church?

Before deciding, one must remember that there are other New Testament goals—goals which, like the passion for unity, are motivated by love. In particular, consider the passion for evangelism, the concern to win people from every tribe and people and nation. Very frequently this is most effectively and strategically done in the language and culture of the targeted group. In this particular church, the elders/leaders of the diverse congregations work together, strategize together, and pray together as a team. The children of ethnic parents may well end up in one of the more Anglo congregations. The rising mix in that particular part of Sydney means that interracial marriages are becoming more common.

Clearly there is a tension here—a tension between building *one* church that displays Christian love, and the Christian love that reaches out to people in all their diversity. That tension is already found in the pages of the New Testament. The same apostle Paul who refused in Jerusalem to permit Titus to be circumcised because he thought that the heart of the gospel was at stake (Gal. 2:1-5), and who was passionately committed to the unity of the church (e.g., Eph. 4:1-3), was quite prepared to circumcise Timothy because he wanted to knock down any

---

[9]See especially Manuel Ortiz, *One New People: Models for Developing a Multiethnic Church* (Downers Grove, Ill.: InterVarsity Press, 1996).

obstruction to the promulgation of the gospel in Jewish circles (Acts 16:3).[10] To a cynical outsider, this might look like cheap compromise, raw pragmatism, or an unprincipled desire to please different people (see the charge leveled against Paul in Galatians 1:10). In fact, competing principles are at stake, competing goals, both rightly driven ideally by Christian love. But it is Christian love in service of the Christian gospel, well understood and articulated.

There are plenty of other models. São Paulo is a city of enormous interest in this regard because of its staggering mix of races and cultures and some of the ecclesiastical patterns that are beginning to develop. When such patterns are carefully thought through *in the light of the biblical mandates*, the path of love, which includes not only love for the "other" expressed *within* the church, but also strategic effectiveness in evangelism to see people from diverse backgrounds converted, may look a little different in different parts of the country, in different parts of the world, in different cultures and subcultures.

None of this should be an excuse for doing nothing, for remaining stagnant in one's own comfort zones, for moral lethargy. The point is that globalization, like many a cultural development, can have both good and bad effects. It can breed a sad "flattening" of rich cultural diversity. That flattening in turn can breed a number of defensive postures in which everything in "my" culture assumes an unwarranted importance, and globalization is nothing but a threat. But a global perspective can also expose us to different points of view, to different ways of tackling things, to different models. *Provided these are set within the nonnegotiables of the gospel*, they can only enrich us, teach us humility, expand our horizons, and help us to worship all the more knowledgeably and fervently the God who so loves diversity that he promises to gather men and women from every tongue and tribe and people and nation.

(5) All this suggests, in turn, that we need to engage in some mature *theological* reflection. Precisely because the issues are so complex (a complexity on which I have barely touched), all the greater

---

[10]There are, of course, additional factors in this example since the "cultural" barrier of the circumcision law is deeply tied to the Old Testament Scriptures that both Paul and his non-Christian Jewish contemporaries shared. In other words, a different interpretation of canonical Scripture is at stake, not a cultural item unmentioned in Scripture.

urgency attends the need for Christians to think biblically and theologically. Otherwise we will be driven by faddishness, slogans, or mere pragmatics.

Here are a few of the theological foci that must control Christian reflection.

First, we must not pit justice against forgiveness but humbly attend both demands.

A few years ago one of my colleagues was lecturing at an evening class made up entirely of African-American students. All of them held down jobs during the day; in the evening they were trying to get some Bible and theology to enable them better to serve their local churches. My colleague was lecturing on the night that the TV networks first showed the beating of Rodney King by the L.A. police. The students were seething with rage. My colleague encouraged them to talk about their own experiences of suffering racism. All of them had bitter stories to tell. This cauldron of barely suppressed anger simmered for almost an hour. Then my colleague asked the question, "What theological principles should we be thinking about as we face up to racism?" Everyone in the class almost exploded with the answer: "Justice! Justice!"

My colleague then asked, "And what biblical passages do you have in mind?" No one could mention a single one. Certainly no one mentioned forgiveness, and no one mentioned the cross.

On the other hand, many a white church in a mixed-race community is full of people who honestly think they are above racism and yet who have never once fully tried to understand what it would be like for a black family to come into their church. "Of course they're welcome," these fine folk might protest. "Anyone is welcome here." But all it takes is for one member to say something really insensitive, and all of the courage it took to walk in the door dissolves in disgust and a sense of victimization. Would a white member who indulged in such condescending malice face church discipline? Would the black newcomers be invited to white homes and treated as peers? And if there are economic disparities as well, would there be any reflection on the fact that some white/black economic disparity is a function of years of discrimination that, morally speaking, *ought* to be vehemently opposed by concerned

Christians?[11] Moreover, if the black couple visiting the white church has a teenage boy who asks a white girl out on a date, what will be the response? And if such white believers were brought into a room and asked what the fundamental *theological* issues should be that govern their reflection on such matters, would they with one voice instantly and vehemently insist, "Justice! Justice!"?

I don't know what they would answer. I suspect that there would be such diversity of opinion that unanimity would be impossible. I imagine that very few would begin with the cross.

And do not all these issues become all the more complicated when white Christians are berated or berate themselves for segregation with respect to African-American churches, and then justify the "rights" of Chinese-Americans to have their "own" churches and to exert communal pressures to prevent one of their daughters from dating a white lad?

I doubt that we shall improve much in Christian circles until the parties with the most power reflect a lot more than in the past on matters of justice, and the parties most victimized reflect a lot more than in the past on forgiveness.[12] Perhaps the former need to get down on their knees and read Amos; the latter need to get down on their knees and read 1 Peter. All of us need to return to the cross. For the cross teaches us that if all we ask for is justice, we are all damned; it teaches us that God himself is passionately interested in forgiveness and its price. That is why we cannot expect such responses from large swaths of the secu-

---

[11]I must add in passing that the latest statistics show that when stable black family incomes are compared with stable white family incomes, and when a fudge factor is introduced to allow for the fact that more black families live in the South than in the North (where incomes are higher—though often expenses are, too), there is no statistical difference between the two groups. Of course, there is still a large difference between black mean income and white mean income because these figures are based on individuals, and there are far more single parents among blacks than among whites—which itself owes a great deal to complex and sometimes profoundly reprehensible social pressures.

[12]One of the most moving stories I know in this regard is the account of Ruby Bridges, the six-year-old African-American girl who in 1960 for an entire academic year was protected when she entered and exited a white school after court-ordered integration. Under pressure from the jeering white adults who screamed hate-filled abuse at her every day, she was observed one day to be talking—her lips were moving. "I wasn't talking to them," she explained. "I was praying for them." The story has been told many times (see her own account at www.rubybridges.net/story). "Usually I prayed in the car on the way to school, but that day I'd forgotten until I was in the crowd. *Please be with me*, I'd asked God, *and be with those people too. Forgive them because they don't know what they're doing.*" Ruby's account faithfully reflects on the hatred and fear of people, both black and white, who wanted the Bridges to stop their action; and on the help they received, from both black and white, and not least from her white teacher, Mrs. Barbara Henry, who poured herself into her one first-year pupil, Ruby, all that year and who was let go by the school at the end of that year.

lar society, whose categories for redressing social evils, real and perceived, lie elsewhere. Among Christians to expect anything less is to betray the faith.

Both justice and forgiveness cry out for more examination even if there is little space for it here.

On the side of justice: Most discussions recognize the distinction between retributive justice and distributional justice—the justice that punishes the miscreant and the justice that tackles structural evils that control and manipulate the weak. Amos is certainly concerned with both. If Christians in power are concerned with issues of justice, they had better not sacrifice either pole. We may, of course, gropingly disagree, for example, on what the wisest and most effective changes in structure should be. Should we levy more taxes and entrust the government with the responsibility to redistribute wealth and change the social structures by legislation? Or have many of these experiments in fact generated a large and dependent underclass, making it a wiser course to reform economic injustices by other means? But whatever our disagreements on the pragmatic outworkings of justice, the passion for justice must characterize all who claim to serve a just God. None of this will be easy work. But love demands that we try—and we had better be more interested in effective results than in the slogans of the party faithful.

On the side of forgiveness: We have already seen that the most desirable forms of forgiveness are those that are tied to genuine reconciliation, but that Christians bear a responsibility and a privilege to forgive enemies even when the enemy is unwilling to be reconciled or remains unaware of the depth of the offense that he or she has caused. None of this forgiveness will be easy. But whatever our disagreements about the relationships between forgiveness that is carefully nurtured in one's heart and mind and the practical outworkings of such forgiveness, the passion to forgive must characterize all who claim to serve a forgiving God.

Second, we must reflect on both creation and the fall. Creation tells us that the human race was made *imago Dei*, in the image of God (Gen. 1:27). From the first man and woman came every nation of human beings (Acts 17:26). If there is but one God, he is God of all, recognized or unrecognized, known or unknown, and salvation comes from him alone (Rom. 3:29-30). God invested in the first human pair a genetic potential for astonishing diversity—in exactly the same way that God invested in original dogs the genetic potential for astonishing diversity. Apparently God delights in diversity; we should, too.

The fall did not introduce mere sins; it introduced the "fallenness" that is endemic to every human being. God is no longer at the center of every one of us; each of us wants to be at the center, to have a domesticated God (in other words, a false god, an idol). Such idolatry means that we seek to control not only our own lives but in some measure the lives of all who touch us. This massive de-godding of God, this odious idolatry, works out in countless sins of every description. It includes oppression on the one hand and nurtured resentments on the other— and both feed into what we call racism. Idolatry means we are so self-ish most of the time that most of us do not automatically think in terms of sacrificial service. If idolatry produces tyrants whose chief lust is to control, it also produces populist demagogues whose chief lust is to con-trol—and both of them will entertain mixed motives, confusing their genuine desire to do good among their own people with their transpar-ent lust for power. Because almost all sin has social ramifications, the biases, hatreds, resentments, nurtured feelings of inferiority and superi-ority, anger, fear, sense of entitlement—all are passed on in corrosive ways to new generations.

These two poles, creation and the fall, must be thought about together. There is more than a little danger that we will try to reverse the effects of racism by talking endlessly about human rights, about human dignity, about inherent human freedom. Great insight lies in all of these themes. If they are cut free from other biblical teaching, how-ever, they tend to foster the lust for human autonomy that lies at the very heart of the fall. The desire to be free from God can also produce a Nietzsche, a Stalin, a Hitler, a Mao Zedong, a Pol Pot. The heart of the Christian message is not that human beings are made in the image of God and therefore must be set free to be autonomous. The heart of the Christian message is that although human beings, made in the image of God, created by him and for him, have catapulted themselves into a squalid revolution with disastrous consequences, God himself has taken action to reconcile them to himself. When they become rec-onciled to God, they are set free in principle from sin—not in order to become completely autonomous, but to return to the God who made them and who owns them.

That is why the Bible can repeatedly depict believers as being slaves of God, slaves of Christ.[13] The first human pair before the fall were slaves of God in the very best sense. He owned them. Doubtless they were to do his bidding, but that bidding was always immaculately wise and good. They thought their rebellion would bring them freedom, would make them like God himself, but it merely brought them into a new slavery, a slavery as different from the initial slavery as darkness is from light. Our freedom from this infinitely odious slavery—slavery to self, to sin, to Satan—is achieved not by becoming utterly autonomous, but by being restored to the first slavery. We are Christ's; we were made by him and for him (Col. 1:15-20); we are his not only by creation but by redemption. We have been bought with a price, and we are not our own (1 Cor. 6:20).

What is this but another way of saying that the salvation granted in the gospel restores us to the place where we begin to cherish what it means to love God with heart and soul and mind and strength and our neighbors as ourselves?

Third, never should we forget the centrality of the cross or the power of the gospel. I am referring not only to the importance of forgiveness in the Christian message (for I have said enough about that for the moment), but I am referring also to the fact that the New Testament documents teach us that the death and resurrection of Jesus secured for his people *all* the blessings of the gospel—all the way up to and including the resurrection existence of the new heaven and the new earth. Although the consummation of those blessings still lies in the future, already we enjoy more than judicial pardon and the experience of forgiveness. The cross not only cancels sin, but it breaks sin's power. As the hymn writer puts it, "He breaks the power of canceled sin / He sets the prisoner free."

That is why a passage such as Ephesians 2 not only assures us that

---

[13]The book to read is Murray J. Harris, *Slave of Christ: A New Testament Metaphor for Total Devotion to Christ*, NSBT 8 (Leicester: InterVarsity Press, 1999)—who gives lists of passages, noting that our common English translations use "servants" on occasion where the right translation is "slaves." For example, "slave(s)" should be used in all of the following passages: Acts 2:18; 4:29; 16:17; Rom. 1:1; Gal. 1:10; Eph. 6:6; Phil. 1:1; 1 Pet. 2:16; Rev. 2:20; 7:3; 19:2, 5.

we have been saved by grace through faith (2:7), but that God has "made us alive with Christ even when we were dead in transgressions" (2:5). Indeed, "we are God's workmanship, created in Christ Jesus to do good works, which God prepared in advance for us to do" (2:10). The ensuing verses work out the "Therefore" of verse 11: because Christ Jesus himself is our "peace"—not only our peace with God but the "peace" that brings together Jews and Gentiles in a new humanity, holding together as one people, having "access to God by one Spirit" (2:18)—Christians cannot think of their salvation in exclusively legal or individualistic terms. We constitute a new humanity, the humanity of the last times, for by the cross God put to death the hostility that engulfed us (2:16). To be satisfied with anything less than this high vision is to betray the gospel.

That is also why Paul's letter to Philemon demands that Christians transcend the categories of justice and forgiveness. True, Paul wants Philemon to forgive Onesimus, the runaway slave who had stolen some of his master's property. Indeed Paul offered to pay back the property loss himself (v. 19). But the thrust of his appeal to Philemon is that he ought to accept the converted Onesimus as "a dear brother," "a brother in the Lord" (v. 16). "So if you consider me a partner," Paul writes to Philemon, "welcome him as you would welcome me" (v. 17). The gospel extends to these fundamentally *relational* categories, which go beyond matters of justice and forgiveness narrowly conceived. And once again, to be satisfied with anything less than this high vision is to betray the gospel.

Fourth, this transformation is not accomplished all at once. The eschatological dimension to our salvation means that the perfection toward which we press and for which we are responsible is not going to be perfectly achieved until the dawning of the new heaven and the new earth.

The practical consequences are considerable. On the one hand, we must never appeal to the consummation that is not yet attainable in order to justify moral lethargy now. On the other hand, we must exercise forbearance and forgiveness toward fellow believers who are still far from perfect, for not only are we, too, in the same state, but we must all give an account to our heavenly Father, whose judgment on the final day will be just.

On the one hand, Christ has died and risen again; we have been justified and regenerated; there is no excuse for sin. Moreover, because of these great realities, Christians have a new perspective: we are no longer to view anyone from a worldly point of view (2 Cor. 5:16). We are already new creatures; the old has gone, the new has come. "All this is from God, who reconciled us to himself through Christ and gave us the ministry of reconciliation: that God was reconciling the world to himself in Christ, not counting men's sins against them. And he has committed to us the message of reconciliation . . . : Be reconciled to God" (2 Cor. 5:18-20).[14]

On the other hand, Christ has not yet returned; God has not finished with us yet. The perfection toward which we press ought to be an incentive to slip the shackles of the vision of those whose horizons are more limited. At the same time, however, we neither promise nor expect any utopia to arrive before then. Neither Marxist visions of the "new man" nor the hopes of liberal democracies, still less the naiveté of liberal education theory (have some people forgotten how good German universities were on the eve of World War II?), can cure the evil ingrained in all of us.

So we must struggle on, never satisfied with what we have achieved (cf. Phil. 3:12-13), and yet quietly realistic and never embittered about the tensions we face as we live between the "already" and the "not yet."

Fifth, the church is the only institution that will survive this world and continue to exist in all of its perfected splendor in the next. That means that the church is supposed to be an outpost in time of what it will one day be in eternity. We are part of the cultures in which we find ourselves; we exist in time, in this fallen order, in this *created* and fallen order. But we also belong to the heavenly realms (see esp. Eph. 1:3, 20; 2:6; 3:10; 6:12), and we hunger for what we will become. The gospel does not only declare us forgiven. It forges for us a new reality in which we already participate, the new reality of the dawning of the new age, the coming of the kingdom, the formation of the new humanity. And though we are not yet what we will be, and to our shame we are not even what we should be, yet by the grace of God we are not what we were, and by that same grace we learn to live with eternity's values in view.

---

[14]In contemporary Christian literature, it is far too common to interpret Paul's "ministry of reconciliation" as if it were peacemaking on the largest scale. Doubtless the Scriptures lay on believers such large-scale peacemaking, but Paul's focus in this passage is on the reconciliation between God and his image-bearers who are wretchedly alienated from him. In a word, his focus is on evangelism.

Our dual citizenship means that we simultaneously reflect our own cultures and are called to be light and salt in these cultures. We belong; yet we do not belong. This means we must return to Scripture again and again in every generation to think through what elements of our culture are to be cherished, or at least not opposed, and what elements are evil and in need of reformation or overthrow. Truth to tell, very often the two are so intertwined that separation is not always easy. We must embrace both of our citizenships. Only when they overtly conflict do we give absolute precedence to our heavenly citizenship. We belong to two cities, and even if one of them is passing away, at the moment we cannot escape this duality. Christian discipleship necessarily works itself out in this tension. The same Christians who have been taught to pray, "Your will be done on earth as it is in heaven," also cry, "Even so, come, Lord Jesus."

The foregoing is the biblical and theological matrix in which we who call ourselves Christians must work out the deep antagonisms toward the "other"—especially the antagonism and exclusion reflected in racism in all its forms. At a bare minimum, we must become "quicker forgivers" and passionate about justice, especially for those with the least access to distributive justice. While we must be the first to treat all human beings with dignity and respect, we must disavow those forms of multiculturalism that insist that all cultures and belief systems are equally valid and equally valuable in every respect—for how can anyone with a passion for the "good news" view it as a mark of love to withhold it from others on the ground that everyone's religion and everyone's culture is as good as any other's? Was the subculture of the Nazis morally equivalent to the subculture of Mother Theresa? Is the religion that advances self-denial for the sake of others and that insists that all human beings are made in the image of God the equivalent of the religion that burns widows on their husbands' funeral pyres?

While happy to cherish many forms of cultural and ethnic diversity, we who are Christians must be constantly on guard against all forms of cultural and ethnic pride (especially in our own hearts) that mark out others as intrinsically inferior. Where it is judged good and right (for the sake of maintaining some cultural diversity? for the sake of reaching out into well-defined ethnic subgroups in the culture? for the sake of training up minority leaders?) that some cultural and ethnic difference be preserved within a congregation, that difference must be embedded in a profound commitment to Christ and the gospel that seeks out and finds many little ways of expressing Christian oneness across the racial, ethnic, and other barriers. And although the ways in which we will live out the gospel mandate of becoming one new humanity may take somewhat different shapes in different subcultures, we must be doing *something* to realize that gospel goal; certainly we must not be perceived to be knee-jerk reactionaries who are dragged into racial reconciliation kicking and screaming, bringing up the end of the pack, the last to be persuaded. For we constitute a new humanity under the Lord who insisted, "By this all men will know that you are my disciples, if you love one another" (John 13:35).

B. HARD CASE TWO: OSAMA BIN LADEN

By the time this manuscript appears as a book, Osama bin Laden may have been captured or killed. In one sense, I am using him only as a cipher for many different kinds of political and military or even terrorist "enemies." I suppose I might have chosen Hitler or Pol Pot except for two things: Osama bin Laden is current, and the threat that he and his friends represent marks in certain respects a new stage in warfare that demands serious reflection.

Some weeks ago I was lecturing and preaching in Geneva, Switzerland. The pastor of one of the churches there told me about a conversation he had had the week before with a high-level UN official. That official told the pastor he would attend church the Sunday that the pastor announced that his sermon title would be "Why Christians Must Love Osama bin Laden." About the same time I heard of a prayer meeting that was held within a few days of the horrible violence of September 11, in which a woman prayed words to this effect: "Lord, bless Osama bin Laden. Pour out your blessing upon him. You have commanded us to pray for our enemies, and so we pray that you will bless him." Was this the right thing to pray?

To gain some contrast, it is worth reporting that a few days after the destruction of the World Trade Center and the Pentagon, one enraged citizen phoned in to a "talk radio" program and fumed, "I'd go in and nuke them. I'd nuke them all. Then I'd make Christians out of them." One marvels at the sequence. More to the point, certain esteemed journalists have written editorial pieces on the virtue of pure hate. For them, hate is an entirely appropriate response to the massive violence of September 11. And before we gather our robes of self-righteousness around ourselves and declare it is not so, how much do such articulations of hate differ from what the psalmist says? "Do I not hate those who hate you, O LORD, and abhor those who rise up against you? I have nothing but hatred for them; I count them my enemies" (Ps. 139:21-22).

So how should Christians think about terrorists, Osama bin Laden, and mortal enemies in a time of war?

In what follows, I presuppose the exegeses and distinctions I have drawn in the previous lectures. My aim now is to build on these and add some more material to illustrate how the Christian responsibility to love one's enemies might bear on these horribly difficult moral quandaries. I shall offer six points.

(1) It may be helpful, first of all, to reflect on pacifism and "just war" theory in the light of the biblical commands to love and forgive. I shall begin by distinguishing three positions.

First, some people hold to a sentimental pacifism, a squishy pacifism. It is not intellectually rigorous, and it is spectacularly naive about evil. It is well exemplified in the recent writings of Susan Sontag in *The New Yorker*, the speeches of Noam Chomsky and Oliver Stone, the opinions of Alice Walker in *Village Voice* (on Osama bin Laden: "What would happen to him if he could be brought to understand the preciousness of the lives he has destroyed? I firmly believe the only punishment that works is love. . . . What would happen to his cool armor if he could be reminded of all the good, nonviolent things he has done?"). That is the fruit of a massive inability to think that evil can ever be caused by something more than poverty or ignorance. Quite apart from biblical and theological reasons for accepting the existence of evil, this moral myopia is historically blind: it cannot explain the Third Reich, Pol Pot, or Genghis Khan. But since most readers of these pages will not need persuading on this point, I leave it to one side.

Second, rigorous pacifism, historically grounded, is often tied in the

West to certain Anabaptist and related traditions. People in these traditions hold that passages like the ones I have examined in the first two
lectures really do mandate consistent pacifism. For them, however difficult the decision, pacifism is a matter of Christian discipleship. But
these pacifists can be subdivided into two smaller groups. One group
says, in effect, that pacifism is the only morally right course, and all governments as well as all individuals should follow it. The military should
be disbanded; all we need are police forces (though why the state has
the right to maintain the sword in one domain and not the other is not
entirely clear). If as a result nations are overrun by evil powers, so be it:
that is still morally preferable to killing people.[15]

The other group acknowledges that the Bible assigns the sword to
the state. So Christians should never serve in any position in any government that would assign them the obligation, in the name of the state,
to wield the sword. In other words, because of their pacifist convictions,
Christians must withdraw from political life, unless it is at so low a level
that their pacifist convictions cannot be threatened. To put this in "two
kingdoms" language: Christians belong so exclusively to the kingdom
of God that they must on many fronts renounce allegiance to the kingdoms of this world. This is not because the kingdoms of this world do
not have a legitimate place: God has given the sword to the state. But
Christians no longer belong to such kingdoms; or, if it can be said that
they belong to both the kingdom of God and to the kingdoms of this
world, these two realms clash so frequently in their value systems that
thoughtful and consistent Christians must never rise high enough in the
earthly kingdom to jeopardize their absolute allegiance to the heavenly
kingdom, which demands pacifism.

I suppose that just about everyone acknowledges that Christians
belong in some sense both to this age and to the age to come. But where
are the lines to be drawn? In the pacifist tradition, the explicit teaching
of the New Testament, as pacifists understand it, sees war as something

---

[15]These pacifists often argue that violence is an intrinsic evil, and it is therefore always inappropriate to
use violence, an intrinsic evil, to combat some other evil. Just war theorists would reply that a distinction must be made between violence and force. Violence, they would say, is disordered, unautho-
rized force that aims to injure, destroy, abuse, elicit terror. Force, rightly authorized within the
constraints of just war theory (on which see below), aims to secure justice, defend the innocent, and
is deployed to ward off or rectify some far greater malady.

in which no informed disciple of Jesus should ever engage. It is one of those domains where Christians must simply reply, "We must obey God rather than human beings." On this understanding of Scripture, of course, such Christians must also, to be consistent, abjure any right to tell the state how to conduct its war. But at the end of the day, the cogency of this position turns in no small part on how a handful of New Testament texts are understood.

I have said enough in the earlier lectures to indicate some of the reasons why I do not find this position exegetically or theologically convincing; I need not repeat those arguments here.[16]

Third, just war theory has predominated in the West, at least since the time of Augustine,[17] and it has gone through several adaptations that need not detain us.[18] Just war theory attempts to limit both the reasons for resorting to war (*ius ad bellum*) and the actual conduct of war (*ius in bello*), constraining both by what justice allows. Ideally, it gives priority to reconciliation and seeks to prevent conflict from descending into unrestrained vengeance. The principles of just war theory have been articulated in several ways, but most of the principles fall into the two obvious divisions.[19] First, several rules govern going to war: (1) The only just cause for going to war is defense against violent aggression. (2) The

---

[16]In addition to the exegetical discussions scattered through the preceding chapters, it is worth pointing out as well that some of the demands that Christians disown violence in their personal relationships assume the maintenance of justice by governmental force as the social matrix (e.g., Matt. 5:41); that in his preaching, John the Baptist was prepared to command soldiers to be content with their wages and to forbid them from using their power to extort money (Luke 3:14), but he was not prepared to command them to become pacifists; and that two of the most remarkable of the early followers of Jesus were centurions (Matt. 8:5-13; Acts 10—11), and no demand was put on them to renounce arms.

[17]Despite what is sometimes said, Augustine was not the only church father who defended the use of force. Clement of Alexandria, Eusebius, and Ambrose (to name three others) did as well.

[18]The standard literature includes, among the most important shapers of just war theory, Thomas Aquinas, Francisco de Vitoria, John Calvin, Francisco de Suarez, Hugo Grotius, John Locke, and, with respect to modern warfare, Paul Ramsey. Just war theory was increasingly secularized between the sixteenth and the eighteenth centuries. With the collapse of a moral basis to international legal order and the rising dominance of the sovereign nation-state, the possibility of total war became ever stronger, culminating in World War I. The horror of modern warfare in that cataclysm issued in the League of Nations (and later the United Nations Security Council), the Geneva Conventions, and other attempts to limit the worst horrors. But if World War II saw neither side using gas (as both sides did in World War I), it also gave us the atomic bomb and the Holocaust. Out of this cauldron emerged stronger notions of "human rights," "crimes against humanity," and "war crimes." But Amos inveighed against war crimes three-quarters of a millennium before Christ.

[19]For convenience I here summarize the points laid out by Arthur F. Holmes, "Just-war Theory," in *New Dictionary of Christian Ethics and Pastoral Theology*, ed. David J. Atkinson, David F. Field, Arthur Holmes, and Oliver O'Donovan (Leicester: InterVarsity Press, 1995), 521-523.

only just intention is to restore a just peace—just, that is, to friend and foe alike. (3) Military force must be the last resort after negotiations and other efforts (e.g., mediation) have been tried and have failed. (4) The decision to engage in such a just war must be made by the highest governmental authority. Second, several rules govern the conduct of war: (5) The war must be for limited ends, i.e., to repel aggression and redress injustice. (6) The means of a just war must be limited by proportionality to the offense. (7) There must be no intentional and direct attack on noncombatants. (8) War should not be prolonged where there is no reasonable hope of success within these limits.

One may well begin to wonder, at this point, what any of this has to do with love. Isn't this nothing more than a lot of casuistry to defend the violence of war?

Not really. For the best defenses of just war theory have pointed out that several of the "rules" that govern either going to war or the actual conduct of war are in fact motivated by love.[20] When just, war can be a form of love.[21] Consider the relatively "easy" cases. Where an enemy is perpetrating its horrible holocaust, is it not an act of love that intervenes, even militarily, to prevent that holocaust if a nation has the power to do so? And is not restraint in such cases a display, not of loving pacifism, but of lack of love—of the unwillingness to sacrifice anything for the sake of others? Indeed, such a war may be, according to Calvin, a Godlike act, since God himself restrains evil out of love for his creatures. This is not to say that we fallen human beings can manage to conduct just war perfectly, without sin, the way God conducts himself without sin; it is to say that failure to do the good that is in our power to do may reflect not only a want of courage, but a lack of love. Cole concludes:

> The most noteworthy aspect of the moral approach to warfare in Aquinas and Calvin is that it teaches—contrary to today's prevailing views—that a failure to engage in a just war is a failure of virtue, a failure to act well. An odd corollary of this conclusion is that it is a greater evil for Christians to fail to wage a just war than it is for unbelievers.

---

[20]Most recently see the able exposition of this theme by Darrell Cole, "Good Wars," *First Things* 116 (Oct. 2001), 27-31.

[21]That was the argument of Aquinas, who, interestingly enough, discusses just war theory not in his section on justice, but in his section on charity—more specifically, in his section on the love of God (*Summa Theologiae* II-II.40).

When an unbeliever fails to go to war, the cause may be a lack of courage, prudence, or justice. He may be a coward or simply indifferent to evil. These are failures of natural moral virtue. When Christians (at least in the tradition of Aquinas and Calvin) fail to engage in just war, it may involve all of these natural failures as well, but it will also, and more significantly, involve a failure of charity. The Christian who fails to use force to aid his neighbor when prudence dictates that force is the best way to render that aid is an uncharitable Christian. Hence, Christians who willingly and knowingly refuse to engage in a just war do a vicious thing: they fail to show love toward their neighbor as well as toward God.[22]

Observe, too, how many of the "rules" of a just war presuppose the love mandate. In the second, the only just intention aims at restoring just peace *to friend and foe alike*; in the third, the use of force is a last resort; in the first, it is justified only in defense against violent aggression. Thus it cannot be deployed out of a demand for mere revenge, which is forbidden by the sixth entry, which stipulates proportionality in the response. These constitute some of the reasons why ethicists distinguish between *Christian* just war theory, which frankly appeals to love, and the earlier form of just war theory defended by Cicero (c. 106-43 B.C.), which was based on justice without love.

Clearly, this appeal to love and justice focuses primary attention on the victims, not the perpetrators. If someone asks, "How does the Allied response in World War II show love for Hitler?" the first answer must be, "Do we not first of all have an obligation to show love for Hitler's victims, present and (potentially) future? In principle, may not the Allied response show love for Czechs, Poles, Hungarians, Jews, Gypsies, and so forth?"

Similarly with Osama bin Laden. If someone were to ask, "How are you showing love for Osama bin Laden? Is he not an 'enemy' who must be loved?" then quite apart from earlier discussions about what the double-love command and the "love your enemy" passages and the forgiveness passages *mean*, we must also first ask, "How do we show love for the victims in the World Trade Center and for those who were bereaved by their deaths? How do we show love for the next wave of

---

[22]Cole, "Good Wars," 31.

victims, granted Osama's avowed intentions?" To identify Hitler or Osama bin Laden or Pol Pot with the "enemy" to be loved, without consideration of these related questions, is to fall into the pacifist error; my reasons for being unpersuaded by such arguments have already been given. But focusing on the enemy and forgetting the victims is a typically sentimental, liberal-humanist error. (There is more to be said about the Christian attitude to an Osama bin Laden himself, of course, but I shall reserve a few comments for the end of this lecture.)

(2) On the other hand, all war, even just war, is never more than rough justice. Even the just war is prosecuted by sinners, and so injustices will occur. The point is implicitly recognized even in the Old Testament. David can praise God for strengthening him for war, but one of the reasons why David is not permitted to build the temple is that all his life he has been a man of war. Even in World War II, perhaps the clearest recent example of a large-scale "good versus evil" conflict, the Allies committed some dreadful evils that break the boundaries set by just war theory. In response to the destruction of Coventry, we took out cities such as Dresden. In response to the bombing of London, we flattened Berlin. We firebombed Tokyo. These were not instances of going after military targets while regretting the collateral damage; they were attacks aimed at destroying the lives and homes and well-being of noncombatants. In terms of just war theory, such actions were utterly without excuse. The western Allies were far more restrained in victory than were the Russians on the eastern front, and after the war they financed the Marshall Plan, but inevitably some American troops engaged in rape and pillage. Certainly Americans treated captured Japanese troops much better than Japanese troops treated captured Americans (the Japanese had not signed the Geneva Conventions and made no effort to abide by its limitations), but there are known instances of Americans slaughtering Japanese soldiers who had surrendered.

When the assault on Afghanistan and the pursuit of Osama bin Laden were first announced, the mission was given the name "Infinite Justice." That was more than a little worrisome, for it sounded more like "Mean-spirited Revenge." By the time President Bush addressed both houses of Congress, he used the expression "Patient Justice." Today the mission is called "Enduring Freedom." I am thankful beyond words for these changes.[23] If we appeal to infinite justice, we will all stand condemned; we will all be damned. For war, even a just war, even a "good" war in which the rules of just war theory are as scrupulously observed as can be reasonably expected, will never bring about more than rough justice, simply because sinners are involved. They unavoidably bring their mixed motives, their differing levels of commitment to just war theory, their own lusts and greed.

Yet it does not follow that the notion of just war is thereby vitiated, as if all sides in every conflict are equally guilty and equally innocent, and therefore the only moral stance is pacifism. Hitler, for instance, had to be stopped. Moreover, to adopt the view that any injustice performed by those defending just war theory overthrows just war theory is to argue that any sin performed while pursuing good aims taints those aims. On this principle, we should not allow teaching because some teachers are child abusers, and no teacher is perfect; we should not give to the poor because mixed motives may be involved, and sometimes alms-giving is corrupted by politics. In short, this second point—that even just wars provide nothing more than rough justice—cannot overturn the first point: granted that this is a fallen and broken world and that sometimes aggressive violence must be stopped by principled force, war may be the *right* thing to do, the *moral* thing, the *loving* thing—even if, God help us, war is hellish and inevitably casts up some injustices on all sides.

It follows that I am less than convinced by two other positions that have received wide circulation.

The *first* of these has been ably set forth by Desmond Tutu. He describes the "victim hearings" set up in South Africa, largely at his instigation, once apartheid had legally ended and Nelson Mandela had become president of the Republic.[24] Much of what took place, as far as I can tell, was helpful and healing. On the one hand were the bands of thugs, often drawn from the police and military, who were quietly encouraged by the white regime to get on with their illegal reprisals, their

---

[23]The reasons for the changes have not, so far as I know, been made officially public. But the press have said that the abandonment of "Infinite Justice" arose out of the protest of Muslim allies, who insisted that only Allah can provide infinite justice.

[24]Desmond Mpilo Tutu, *No Future Without Forgiveness* (New York: Doubleday, 1999).

selected torture, their state-sanctioned terror; on the other hand were rebels, often sponsored by the ANC, who believed that violence and destruction were the only means of overturning the injustice intrinsic to apartheid, and who acted on those beliefs. What was the way forward? Should both sides be prosecuted equally? Only the white side, now that the blacks were in power?

The "victim hearings" offered a way forward. Under the auspices of the TRC (Truth and Reconciliation Commission), victims were encouraged to bring their charges, often in visceral terms, and those charged, if they owned up to their crimes, would under certain conditions be forgiven. The person applying for such amnesty had to meet four conditions: (1) the act for which amnesty was required had to have occurred between 1960, the year of the Sharpeville massacre, and 1994, when Mandela was inaugurated as president; (2) the act had to have been politically motivated. Perpetrators did not qualify for amnesty if they killed because of greed or some other motive, but only for, or on behalf of, a political organization, whether the former apartheid state or recognized liberation movements such as the ANC; (3) the applicant had to make full disclosure of the relevant facts of the event or events for which amnesty was being sought; and (4) even then the rubric of proportionality had to be observed—that the means were proportional to the objective.[25] Tutu argues that justice was served because there had to be an acceptance of responsibility. Victims could speak, accuse, and object, but if the TRC ruled that the perpetrator had met the conditions, the perpetrator was pardoned, and the victim had no further recourse. These victim hearings, Tutu argues, constituted an important step in a relatively peaceful transition from a repressive regime to a full democracy.

I am too far removed from the scene to gauge how effective these victim hearings were, but they may well have been politically expedient. Whether it would have been possible to prosecute people who had committed violent and illegal actions on both sides in an even-handed way, without inciting more violence, may well be doubted. Of course, the victims were the ones on both sides who paid the price, since the state imposed nothing, merely (through the TRC) pronouncing amnesty.

---

[25]These four points are a summary of Tutu, ibid., p. 50.

Strictly speaking, justice was not served: merely "accepting responsibility" does not mean that justice has been accomplished. But I suspect that this approach succeeded politically because there was a great deal of violence done by *both* sides, and these hearings helped the fledgling nation get past the violence and move on without resorting to further waves of recrimination and violence.

If Tutu's book merely described these procedures and justified them, for the purposes of these pages I would have little quarrel with it. But Tutu sets up the victim hearings as a "third way," an alternative to both Nuremberg and "national amnesia" (to national or international trials on the one hand and simply forgetting about all the violence and injustice on the other, pretending they didn't happen). In the context of South Africa, granted that politics is the art of the possible, this may well have been a good way forward. But by bringing up Nuremberg the way he does, Tutu is in fact presenting his "victim hearings" as a superior "third way" to both a court system and to "national amnesia." He does not recognize that the situations that precipitated Nuremberg and his victim hearings were massively different. One of the primary reasons why the victim hearings worked as well as they did was because in the context of apartheid, injustice and violence were found on *both* sides. The state acted illegally and immorally; so did the ANC. And these were conflicts *within one state*: I have not addressed the complex issues relating to civil war, still less revolutionary war. But at Nuremberg where was the equivalent and reciprocal injustice? How had the Jews in country after country across Europe offered violence against the Nazis? In what way would the "victim hearings" be reciprocal? And in what sense was the blood-letting of World War II a civil war or a revolutionary war?

My objection to Tutu's book, then, has little to do with what was set up in South Africa under the TRC. It has to do with Tutu's effort to cast his victim hearings in an a-historical, a-temporal way against Nuremberg, as if he has found a morally superior way that applies to every international conflict or atrocity. In fact he has not explored the differences under which *war may be the only good way forward, the only loving recourse*, and along with war the holding of people to account for grievous injustice.

The *second* position from which I must distance myself is set out in the closing pages of the book by Miroslav Volf, to which I have already referred.[26] Those who have followed my argument so far will know how deeply indebted to Volf I am, not least in his treatment of exclusion and "otherness" as more encompassing categories than "racism." I have learned much from him and invariably read what he says with deep profit. But the last two paragraphs of his book summarize a position he adopts from which I must regretfully dissent:

> It may be that consistent nonretaliation and nonviolence will be impossible in the world of violence. Tyrants may need to be taken down from their thrones and the madmen stopped from sowing desolation. Dietrich Bonhoeffer's decision to take part in an attempt to assassinate Hitler is a well-known and persuasive example of such thinking. It may also be that measures which involve preparation for the use of violent means will have to be taken to prevent tyrants and madmen from ascending to power in the first place or to keep the plethora of ordinary kinds of perpetrators that walk our streets from doing their violent work. It may be that in a world suffused with violence the issue is not simply "violence versus peace" but rather "what forms of violence could be tolerated to overcome a social 'peace' that coercively maintained itself through the condoned violence of injustice."[27] But if one decides to put on soldier's gear instead of carrying one's cross, one should not seek legitimation in the religion that worships the crucified Messiah. For there, the blessing is given not to the violent but to the meek (Matt. 5:5).
>
> There are Christians who have a hard time resisting the temptation to seek religious legitimation for their (understandable) need to take up the sword. If they give in to this temptation, they should forego all attempts to exonerate their version of Christian faith from complicity in fomenting violence. Of course, they can specify that religious symbols should be used to legitimate and inspire only *just* wars. But show me one warring party that does not think its war is just! Simple logic tells us that at least half of them *must* be wrong. It could be, however, that simple logic does not apply to the chaotic world of wars. Then all would be right, which is to say that all would be wrong, which is to

---

[26]*Exclusion and Embrace: A Theological Exploration of Identity, Otherness, and Reconciliation* (Nashville: Abingdon, 1996).

[27]At this point, Volf is citing Marjorie Hewitt Suchocki, *The Fall to Violence: Original Sin in Relational Theology* (New York: Continuum, 1995), 117.

say that terror would reign—in the name of the gods who can no longer
be distinguished from the devils.[28]

This fine, emotionally charged rhetoric easily sweeps readers along
without allowing them to see what the issues are. Throughout the book,
when Volf refers to some of the same biblical texts that I have treated,
not once does he engage in careful, contextually constrained exegesis.
The texts are simply cited as if anyone can see that they support the position that Volf is expounding at the time. Very often I cannot see it. Since
Volf acknowledges that force must sometimes be used to stop what he
calls "tyrants" and "madmen," then by his own reasoning whenever
such action is undertaken, it must either be undertaken by unbelievers
(one of the pacifist positions I listed above), or, if Christians do engage
the enemy (as Bonhoeffer did), then, according to Volf, they "should not
seek legitimation in the religion that worships the crucified Messiah."

But that crucified Messiah is also the exalted Lord who metes out
punishment at the end. While the God and Father of this crucified
Messiah insists that vengeance is his (Rom. 12:17-20), he also assigns
the sword to the state (Rom. 13:1-7). In other words, the crucified
Messiah is also the Lord of history who demands justice. And it may be
an act of self-sacrifice, willing self-sacrifice even to the point of death,
that engages in a just war to prevent massive, violent injustice. In such
sacrifice there is at least a pale echo of Jesus' self-sacrifice. It shares nothing of his perfection, and it is not in the same way redemptive; it is but
following Jesus at a distance, as some of the Reformers put it. But it is
at least that, and Volf's dismissal is neither exegetically grounded nor
theologically astute, regardless of how persuasive the rhetoric.[29]

(3) Several other factors are often thrown into the debate about how
we should respond to Osama bin Laden and other terrorists. I shall
argue that these factors are not well conceived, but even if they were,
they are almost irrelevant to the moral issues.

---

[28]Volf, *Exclusion and Embrace*, 306.

[29]A volume of essays has been promised by Chalice Press in early 2002 that will offer more reflection
on September 11 and its aftermath. At this writing, that volume has not yet appeared, and I have not
seen the contributing manuscripts. The list of contributors, which includes Miroslav Volf, suggests
that some at least will be closely aligned with Volf. See John L. Berquist, ed., *Strike Terror No More:
Theology, Ethics, and the New War* (St. Louis: Chalice Press, 2002). Certainly this new type of war
demands fresh, careful theological reflection.

Most of the additional factors can be reduced to three charges leveled against the United States. *First*, many Europeans (though not, by and large, the British) charge that the United States lacks sophistication in its foreign policy, and if it would listen a little more closely to the accumulated wisdom of centuries of European statesmanship, this horrible eruption might not have happened. *Second*, by its multinational giant corporations the United States has long exploited the poor, and by its long military arm it has rained down terror on people no less innocent than those in the World Trade Center—such as the people in Iraq and Afghanistan. *Third*, the United States has long embraced a foreign policy that is tilted so one-sidedly toward Israel and has been so insensitive to the world of Islam that it has brought this terror on itself—or, at the very least, the terror attack would have been much less likely if the United States had been more even-handed.

The charges are not well conceived. On the *first* charge, I am not persuaded that sophistication in foreign policy is something that can be passed on from generation to generation, like genes. Just because European civilization is older than its American counterpart does not mean it is wiser. Do we have to remind ourselves, for instance, of the Anglo-French fiasco in the Suez Canal half a century ago? Or remember that the two twentieth-century world wars were not caused by failures in American statesmanship? Or recall that the French and English rammed through the Treaty of Versailles at the end of World War I against the will of President Woodrow Wilson and thus constructed one of the major grievances that made Germany more open to a Hitler? Not for a moment am I suggesting that American policy has always been wise. The point, rather, is that there is plenty of praise and plenty of blame to attach to both sides of the Atlantic.

We should also recall that the European stance toward the United States, often condescending, has become more condescending than ever now that Europe relies less heavily on the United States for protection against the Russian bear. With the progress of the European Union, one understands how many in Europe try to forge their continental identity by contrasting themselves with the only remaining "superpower." It's all a bit childish, really—nothing more than politics as usual. And recall, too, that several European nations—including Germany, France, Spain, and to a lesser extent the UK—have very sizable Muslim populations, which inevitably affects the outlooks of their governments, at least as much as the Jewish lobby influences American politics. Add to this that during the past ten years several major European governments have taken a leftward turn, while America with the election of George W. Bush has taken a rightward turn, and the differences in perspective become palpable.

The *second* charge is no better conceived. It maintains that by its giant multinational corporations the United States has long exploited the poor, and by its long military arm it has rained down terror on people no less innocent than those in the World Trade Center—such as the people in Iraq and Afghanistan. The implication is that in some respects America is simply getting what it deserves. But multinational corporations provide jobs and raise economies even if some of them are exploitative. As with people, so with corporations: some have an excellent track record, and some have a miserable track record.[30]

As for the "terrorist" bombing of Afghanistan (a staple of the Muslim press), just war theory makes two distinctions that must constantly be reiterated. It does not deny that innocent noncombatants may be killed in a war but forbids that they should ever be targeted—as was blatantly the case in the attack on the World Trade Center. Moreover, just war theory insists that actions in the cause of justice be taken by the highest governmental levels, not by self-appointed liberators (a point I shall explore further). In other words, most Western uses of "terrorist" and "terrorism" presuppose a certain kind of stealth warrior with either no connection or only loose connection between the alleged terrorists and any government.

By contrast, Muslim use of "terrorist" and "terrorism" is narrowly psychological: where terror has been induced, there we find terrorists and terrorism. By this standard, all acts of war without exception are acts of terrorism. Psychologically, that may be so, but it does not help us to think clearly about one of the distinctions on which just war theory insists: any war, to be just, must be the result of a decision taken by the highest level of government. By itself, of course, that does not make any action right, for then the Holocaust would have to be judged right, for no other reason than that it was put into effect by the decision of the highest level of government.

---

[30]See the penetrating article by Alec Hill, "Let Justice Flow Like a River," *Crux* 37/2 (June 2001), 2-12.

But the Holocaust, however abominable, is not usefully labeled an act of terrorism or a series of acts of terrorism, for precisely the same reason.

As for this particular conflict, must we also remind people that before September 11 America was the largest supplier of humanitarian aid to Afghanistan—with not one penny of aid coming from a rich Muslim country like Saudi Arabia?

The *third* charge—that the United States has long embraced a foreign policy tilted so one-sidedly toward Israel and has been so insensitive to the world of Islam that it has brought this terror on itself—is no less badly conceived, even if we concur that America has not always got this matter right or that Israel has sometimes committed indefensible acts of violence. There are several reasons why the charge is badly conceived. The most violent Muslim opponents, such as Hezbollah, Islamic Jihad, and al-Qaeda, have gone on record saying that what they want is the obliteration of Israel. As long as America stands as guarantor of Israel, the most violent voices in the Muslim world will charge the United States with tilting toward Israel. In fact, one can make a case for the view that by *forcing* the leaders of Israel and the Palestinians to the peace table and forcing concessions from both sides, the United States has precipitated the bloodshed from the extremists who know all too well that their actions will likely stall and perhaps halt all negotiations.

Leaders cannot afford to get too far ahead of their people. Doubtless America could have squeezed Israel harder to stop building houses on the West Bank. But it is not altogether clear that if America had done this, and Israel had complied, terrorist attacks would have ceased. Moreover, although it is true that America has supported Israel, America has also supported Muslim regimes in Turkey, Pakistan, and Egypt—and, in its earlier form, the Taliban itself in Afghanistan. It is hard to believe that America is on an anti-Islam crusade when it has proved hospitable to its own five million or so Muslims.

Nor will it do to say that the chief problem is that America has propped up oppressive Muslim regimes and now is reaping the wrath of disgruntled Muslim citizens. That theory is nothing but the myth-making of Western liberalism. For the current terrorists think that most Muslim regimes, including the most despotic of them, are themselves too liberal. Saudi Arabia is not trusted by them because the Saudis want

American bases on their soil. The former Shah of Iran, Mohammed Reza Pahlavi, was not brought down by proto-democrats but by Muslim fundamentalists. President Anwar el-Sadat of Egypt was assassinated in 1981 by members of the Egyptian Islamic Rhad group.

In fact, the issues are much bigger and have to do with Islam itself. One of the most percipient commentators is Samuel P. Huntington.[31] In 1993 in an essay titled "The Clash of Civilizations?" published in *Foreign Policy*, Huntington argued that for all the talk of "globalization" there is very little common culture outside the confines of a small, highly educated elite. In fact, global media could actually serve to highlight differences and encourage opposing parties to make a play for the media spotlight. Huntington suggested that in the next century the fundamental sources of conflict would not be primarily ideological or economic but cultural. The principal sources of conflict, he argued, will be between nations and groups of nations that belong to different civilizations.

Huntington's article called forth a storm of protest. Unrepentant, he enlarged on his ideas in an important book published four years later.[32] This side of September 11, he seems almost prescient. The West, he argues, generates ideologies; the East generates religions. Communism, after all, was essentially a Western ideology. More importantly, on the scale of Western history, communism was a fleeting specter, a seventy-year event—nothing compared with the struggle between the West and Islam that has been going on for more than a millennium. "The dangerous clashes of the future are likely to arise from the interaction of Western arrogance, Islamic intolerance, and Sinic [Chinese] assertiveness."[33] Conflict will arise from a clash of civilizations. It is typical of Western sentimentalism to hold that people from other civilizations, if they had the opportunity, would want the same things we want. In some ways this is a generous conceit—but it is simply untrue.

Of the thirty-eight countries in which most Muslims live, not one permits free and open religious conversion. No less importantly, when a nation is on the edge of the Muslim habitat, there are almost always

---

[31]For an excellent summary of his developing views and seminal publications, see Robert D. Kaplan, "Looking the World in the Eye," *The Atlantic Monthly* 288/5 (Dec. 2001), 68-82.
[32]Samuel P. Huntington, *The Clash of Civilizations and the Remaking of World Order* (New York: Simon and Schuster, 1997).
[33]Ibid., 183.

problems with neighbors, problems of violence and oppression. One thinks, for example, of the slaughter of an estimated eight thousand Christians and the displacement of a further half million since January 1999 on the Maluku island chain in eastern Indonesia. The shootings and arson have been carried out by the extremist Indonesian Muslim group Islamic Jihad, supported by radicals from Afghanistan with ostensible connections with Osama bin Laden. One thinks of the systematic extirpation of Christian churches in northern Nigeria.

Confident assertions to the contrary, the word *Islam* does not mean "peace" but "submission." Under Islam's domain, Christians may convert freely to Islam but never the reverse. Christians rightly blame themselves for the Crusades and are blamed by Muslims; there is no concomitant Muslim self-blame and almost no Christian blaming of Muslims for earlier taking over parts of eastern and southern Europe by military force, not to mention Palestine itself, thus precipitating the Crusader attempt to take some of it back by force. True, during the First Crusade the slaughter in Jerusalem was abominable, ruthless genocide. It was also nicely matched by the Saracen violence at Antioch and Acre. Before the First Crusade began, Palestine had been the scene of savage conflict between the Turkish Seljuks (Sunni Muslim) and the Arab Fatimid dynasty (Shi'ite Muslim), with massacres committed by both sides. Still earlier, the Fatimid caliph Al-Hakim (ruled 996-1021) persecuted both Jews and Christians with appalling violence.

None of this justifies the Crusader violence, not for one moment. But one does become weary of endless justification of current Muslim attitudes toward the West grounded in Crusader violence almost a millennium ago, when the fuller account of who did what to whom is conveniently forgotten.[34] Little thought has been given to the fact that the earliest Christian expansion (Christianity's first three centuries) was entirely through preaching and acts of self-denying service and not infrequently martyrdom. Islam's earliest expansion (Islam's first three centuries) was almost entirely through conquest.

Many Islamic scholars today, not least the intellectuals who interact

---

[34]Gene Edward Veith has rightly pointed out that Muslims are constantly fed on their carefully selected "history," reminding themselves of every Christian offense, real and imagined, fostering a sense of outraged injustice, feeding the fury of vendetta. By contrast, most Christians do not know enough about

with the Western tradition, insist that the Qur'an's references to *jihad* are properly understood metaphorically (e.g., *Sura* 9:5). That may or may not be the case; I leave it to Islamic scholars to give their judgments on such thorny issues of interpretation of the Qur'an. What cannot be denied, however, is that expansion by conquest and retention by totalitarian control have, with few exceptions, characterized Islam across the centuries.

Similar use of force has not been typical of Christian expansion; moreover, where Christianity has stooped to that indefensible level, later Christian tradition has been the first to distance itself from its past and repent of its sins. I have not yet encountered serious Muslim writings that repent of its military expansion into Europe during the eighth and ninth centuries or of its violence against contemporary Christians in Nigeria and the Southern Sudan. Why do some people find it easier to condemn the West for some serious evils committed almost a millennium ago, and frequently repented of, than to condemn similar evils committed by Islam three centuries earlier and still being committed on a wide scale, and never repented of? And who is protesting when the Saudis chop off the hand of a pickpocket?

Distinctions currently being offered between Islam, "which overflows with peace and tolerance," and Islamicism—alleged to be a violent, intolerant, fundamentalistic, and indefensible usurpation of true Islam—may be politically expedient but are at best a kind exaggeration. In reality, these distinctions have to fudge too much history to be accepted at face value and are at worst deceitful propaganda.[35]

Numerous commentators (and not just Huntington) are now point-

their own history to mount a response. See his "Memory Loss," in *World* for November 17, 2001, p. 14. Worse, some Western publications, equally ignorant of history, pick up on Muslim historical reconstructions and repeat them, feeding the Western propensity for self-blame without having a good grasp of the facts.

[35]Samuel P. Huntington, *Clash*, 258, has tabulated two further sets of figures that deserve pondering. "In the 1980s Muslim countries had military force ratios (that is, the number of military personnel per 1000 population) and military effort indices (force ratio adjusted for a country's wealth) significantly higher than those for other countries. Christian countries, in contrast, had force ratios and military effort indices significantly lower than those for other countries. The average force ratios and military effort ratios of Muslim countries were roughly twice those of Christian countries." Further, throughout most of the twentieth century, "While Muslim states resorted to violence in 53.5 percent of their crises, violence was used by the United Kingdom in only 11.5 percent, by the United States in 17.9 percent, and by the Soviet Union in 28.5 percent of the crises in which they were involved. Among the major powers only China's violence propensity exceeded that of the Muslim states: it employed violence in 76.9 percent of its crises. Muslim bellicosity and violence are late-twentieth-century facts which neither Muslims nor non-Muslims can deny."

ing out rightly that what is at issue is a clash of civilizations. The things for which the West prides itself—including democracy, more or less vibrant economies, capitalism, technological innovation, freedom of speech and of the press, religious freedom, and much more—are the very things that much of Muslim civilization sees as barbaric, immoral, God-defying, contemptible, and signs of inward weakness. Moreover, much of the Muslim world, with its controlled press, has learned to think of itself as victimized by the ostensibly Christian West. These are the brute realities that explain the video pictures of tens of thousands of people dancing in the street for joy at the sight of thousands being killed on September 11. It is why, in the wake of September 11, there are numerous Muslim blanket denunciations of terrorism in general (which then includes whatever the United States has done in Afghanistan), but very few Muslim leaders could sign the simple declaration proposed by the Universal Press Syndicate: "We, political leaders of the community of Islamic nations, reject such terrorism as was practiced on September 11, 2001. The men who took this action in the name of Allah were impostors who profaned the word of the prophet." As Buckley rightly comments, "No more would need to be said, but that Declaration of Islamic Doctrine on Modern Terrorism, with names and titles of world leaders, should appear everywhere—in parliaments, mosques, subway stations. And airports."[36]

One need not agree with all of this analysis[37] to perceive that the initial charge against the West in general and America in particular is simply too glib. Nor is this argument an attempt to paint the world in terms of "good guys" and "bad guys," with the bad guys always being the "other" guys—far from it (as we shall see!). Experience on the ground in many Muslim countries has thrown up countless Muslims who have

[36]William F. Buckley, Jr., "On the Right," *National Review* 53/22 (19 Nov. 2001), 63.

[37]For instance, many of the penetrating essays of Fareed Zakaria adopt a rather different stance. See, for instance, his "Special Report" in *Newsweek* (15 Oct. 2001), 22ff. Zakaria minimizes the "clash of civilizations" theory—a little too glibly, in my view—and argues that the problem is localized in the forms of Islam found in the Middle East. He ties the animus in the Islamic world in the Middle East to specific developments in their own history during the last thirty years: totalitarian leaders, failed ideas, the suppression of freedom, and populist religious fanatics adept in demagoguery. Out of the resulting sense of humiliation and despair have bubbled the deepest resentments against those who seem to be in power. At very least, these are immediate and contributing factors. But there are deep worldview issues as to *why* modernity has failed in most Muslim nations, *why* Islam has not produced a heritage of democracy but has generated controlling regimes (it is no accident that the Muslim nation that is perhaps the most democratic, Turkey, is one of the most secularized). I am far from certain that the larger worldview issues can be entirely ignored while small-scale political developments are judged completely determinative.

expressed the most profound regret and sorrow at the violence of September 11. All I am arguing at this juncture is that, whatever America's sins and political miscalculations, the charges against her are not well conceived but are driven by a sad blend of a profound ignorance of history and unbending ideologies.

The conflict seems to be shaping up in part because globalization is seen as a threat. This side of the cold war, many Western commentators, themselves deeply secular in their outlook, have promised peace, prosperity, multiplying democracies, and more and more market economies precisely because this is what people around the world (we are told) really want. Doubtless some do, not least the partially secularized cultural elites of many countries. But countless millions utterly reject the American form of freedom of religion because it is perceived to elevate materialism and immorality over God, while most Muslims insist that the demands of Islam go beyond and often against the goals of mere nationalism, and certainly beyond and against the goals of any state that threatens Islam's insistence that there must never be a separation between government and confessional Islam. From this perspective, the movement of globalization is often seen by Muslims as another ploy to extend Western secularism, whose long-term effect will be to rob Islam of its vitality. Traditionally, Islam has at least limited tolerance for "people of the Book" (viz. Jews and Christians); they have none for secularism. And that is precisely what increasingly prevails in the West.[38]

In short, the charges against America, to the effect that it has supported Israel too strongly and therefore invited on itself the attack of September 11,[39] fail to penetrate very deeply.

But my argument with respect to these charges against the West is

---

[38]"The underlying problem for the West is not Islamic fundamentalism. It is Islam, a different civilization whose people are convinced of the superiority of their culture and are obsessed with the inferiority of their power. The problem for Islam is not the CIA or the U. S. Department of Defense. It is the West, a different civilization whose people are convinced of the universality of their culture and believe that their superior, if declining, power imposes on them the obligation to extend that culture throughout the world. These are the basic ingredients that fuel conflict between Islam and the West" (Samuel P. Huntington, *Clash*, 217-218).

[39]As one person put it to me, the destruction of the WTC should be seen as a side effect of Israeli destruction of Palestinian homes. Not for an instant should we overlook Israeli displacement of Palestinians. But this sort of analysis, conducted by both sides ("If only the Israelis would . . ." or "If only the Palestinians would . . ."), is not only profoundly reductionistic, but is habitually one-sided—whereas the reality is that the cycle of attack and counterattack in a confined space over decades produces a vendetta mentality that itself becomes part of the problem. Those who attempt to intervene are invariably accused by both sides of supporting the other side.

finally deeper. *Even if all of them are in some measure true, they are largely irrelevant.* Perhaps the easiest way to demonstrate the point, in the first instance, is by an historical analogy. Let us concede that one of the contributing factors in the rise of Hitler, and therefore of World War II and the Holocaust, was the Treaty of Versailles (1919). Let us also further imagine that if Britain and France had stepped in when Hitler took over the Rhineland, they would have stopped him before he became too powerful. Does that mean that the rise of Hitler was fundamentally the fault of the nations who became the Allies? Or, more to the point, does it mean that because the Allied nations were culpably responsible for these bad decisions that contributed to the rise of Hitler and all that followed, therefore those same Western nations had no justification for taking up arms against Hitler?

Most of us would surely disown such inferences. Hitler had to be stopped *regardless of the influences that contributed to his rise.* Even if maximum weight is assigned to each of those malign decisions, Hitler did not have to take the path he did. And even if we infer (after the fact!) that his path, once those and similar decisions had been taken, was inevitable (which is not the standard view),[40] it still would not mitigate the impregnable fact: he had to be stopped[41]—out of love for his victims as much as out of righteousness.

The relevance of this historical analogy should be clear. We may usefully think about things that America and other Western nations might have done differently in the Muslim world and assign various degrees

---

[40]See especially Ron Rosenbaum, *Explaining Hitler: The Search for the Origins of His Evil* (San Francisco: HarperCollins, 1999).

[41]Some who are so quick to assign blame should reflect on possible alternative histories. Suppose, for example, that Britain and France had stopped Hitler when he rolled into the Rhineland. That would have been the courageous and (in retrospect!) far-sighted thing to do. But if they had tried to do so, it might have turned bloody before they succeeded. Then such was the mood at the time that they might have been blamed for the conflict. Suppose, nevertheless, that Hitler had been stopped, with the result that the Austrian *Anschluss* never took place, nor the rape of Czechoslovakia, nor the assault on Poland, nor the Blitzkrieg across France, and so forth. So we are spared World War II. On the other hand, Hitler might then have poured his energy and money into those scientists who were working on atomic weapons. Without the onset of war, it is far from clear that Roosevelt would have authorized the Manhattan Project. And Hitler would not (under this reconstruction) have lost so many of his scientists. But once he, and he alone, had atomic bombs, will anyone demur at the suggestion that he would have taken over the world? My point is not that France and Britain were right, after all, not to attempt to stop Hitler at the Ruhr, but that there are so many intangible and unpredictable elements to historical unfolding that it is somewhat naive to contrast the bad outcomes of the actual decisions with imagined good outcomes of theoretical alternatives, without recognizing that with a few more leaps of the imagination it is possible to conjure up bad outcomes for many decisions.

of blame for this or that decision or action. But the fact remains that al-Qaeda has to be stopped. Terrorism with the potential for mass destruction depends on two things—the will and the means. Osama bin Laden has shown he has the will; we know he and his followers are working to find the means. Regardless, then, of the contributing causes to the rise of al-Qaeda, Osama bin Laden has to be stopped. It is a righteous thing to do; more, it is the loving thing—for if he is not stopped, the almost certain outcome sooner or later will be countless deaths.

(4) Historically, wars have changed their form from time to time, generating fresh discussion about just war theory. It is time to begin this process again.

All wars have commonalities and differences, of course, but it is fairly easy to spot some of the most distinctive turning points. The Boer War and, on a larger scale, World War I marked the onset of truly mechanized war. This is not to say that there were not "mechanisms" earlier, of course. It is to say that the invention of such things as high-powered howitzers changed the nature of artillery fire, while the development of highly efficient machine guns made cavalry charges obsolete. Napoleon's troops camped out in the fields in tents or in the open air; by the beginning of the twentieth century, only soldiers a long way from the front could be so relaxed. But if machine guns and heavy artillery made trenches necessary, by the end of World War I the invention of tanks rendered obsolete the kind of trench warfare that had slaughtered twenty million combatants during that war for no military gain. War became less heroic, less personal. The winning side needed not only a sufficient number of soldiers with courage and skill but an edge in the technology of war. Again, although aircraft had been used to a limited extent in World War I, it was World War II that gave them prominence. What is happening to just war theory when both sides justify the intentional obliteration of civilian populations in massive air raids with few military consequences?

Perhaps the single most important advance in war technology was the atomic bomb—first of all the fission bombs and then within a few years the fusion bomb (the so-called "hydrogen bomb"). The debate will go on about whether Hiroshima and Nagasaki saved more lives, both Japanese and American, than they destroyed, but there is little doubt that on just war premises, taking out Hiroshima with a single bomb was no more justified than the fire-bombing of Tokyo—both of which targeted noncombatants predominantly. Whether the dropping of an atomic bomb or two on some remote area or on some more narrowly military target would have had adequate psychological impact to end the war is a question that cannot be answered; but from the perspective of just war theory, that is certainly what should have been done. To reply, "There wouldn't have been a Hiroshima if there hadn't been a Pearl Harbor," is undoubtedly true, and it is more than a little disappointing to visit the Hiroshima Memorial and see that this elementary point has been skirted. But that truth does not affect what *we* should have done *had we been committed to just war theory* and not only to crushing the enemy as quickly as possible.

The massive and indiscriminate slaughter that nuclear weapons can effect introduced new factors that made just war theory extremely difficult to apply.[42] The threat of MAD (mutual assured destruction) offered only the most fragile of securities. To look back and say rather smugly, "Well, it worked," is to forget how breathtakingly close we were to nuclear holocaust at the time of the Cuban missile crisis. But the genie cannot be put back in the bottle. Christian commitments, not to say mere sanity, demand that we try to limit such armaments, reduce their number, and try to put in place measures (such as assured verification) that will enhance mutual security. But now that more and more countries are gaining access to these weapons, the world is becoming even less secure than it was when the weapons were largely restricted to the two superpowers and their allies. It is not clear to me that just war theory ever coped with such realities. Or, more precisely, various just war modifications were proposed, but none captured wide assent.

September 11 has introduced new factors into the way we must think about war. One or two writers have drawn comparisons between the destruction of the World Trade Center and other catastrophic disasters, e.g., the sinking of the *Titanic* (April 14-15, 1912), the destruc-

---

[42]See, for example, John R. W. Stott, *Issues Facing Christians Today: A Major Appraisal of Contemporary Social and Moral Questions* (London: Marshall, Morgan and Scott, 1984), 80-108. Whether or not one agrees with all of Stott's conclusions, one must admire the commitment to think things through in an informed way out of a deep theological matrix.

tion of the *Hindenburg* (May 6, 1937), and the explosion of the shuttle orbiter *Challenger* (January 26, 1986).[43] I suppose something can be said for those comparisons, at least in terms of the shock-impact they achieved. Even then, I am a long way from being convinced that the comparisons are helpful (though my own memory reaches back only to the last of these three), because a substantial part of the shock of the World Trade Center attack was not the destruction itself or even the scope of the destruction, but that the destruction was the product of a savage attack by a means never before attempted by an enemy at that juncture still vaguely defined. None of the other three was the result of an attack; none commanded months of cleanup and body-finding by countless teams of rescue workers; none provoked a military call-up and a new kind of war; none had quite the same impact on the stock market.

But for our immediate purposes, we must identify some of the features of 9/11 that presage a new kind of war. None of these is absolutely new, but their collocation is new, and this newness demands that we think afresh about certain elements of just war theory. Four elements contribute to this newness.

First, from the side of the attack, the right term to use, I think, is genocide. Small-time guerrillas and terrorists have often targeted non-combatants. There is nothing new about that. But these men used technology—i.e., jet aircraft—to kill thousands. We cannot say that the terrorists used weapons of mass destruction; rather, they turned a modern invention into a genocidal weapon in a manner not done before. Moreover, by their private and public pronouncements, these terrorists are clearly trying to obtain or manufacture weapons of mass destruction—biological, chemical, and nuclear.

Second, and still more to the point, these terrorists represent no nation. They are a multinational group drawn from one religious/civilizational entity, Islam, attacking another.[44] One may reasonably hold certain nations responsible for aiding, abetting, and harboring them, but

---

[43]Brian Rosner, "The Twin Towers of Babel?" *The Briefing* 278 (Dec. 2001), 11-13.

[44]Here, too, a difference in cultural outlook prevails. "Throughout Islam the small group and the great faith, the tribe and the *ummah*, have been the principal foci of loyalty and commitment, and the nation-state has been less significant" (Samuel P. Huntington, *Clash*, 175).

that alone will certainly not stop them. In the past weapons of mass destruction, and therefore the possibility of genocide, were beyond the reach of small groups of determined fighters. But now, with the rise of the technology of the past one hundred years, plus the money provided by Arab oil wealth, not to mention the donations through masked "charities" from countless Muslims around the world who are joined in their antipathy toward Western culture, relatively small groups, whose organization is shadowy (should we think of them as more or less autonomous cells, or is there some sort of disciplined structure?), are openly committed to the genocide of noncombatants.[45]

Third, the technology of response has also changed the possibilities of the conflict. Electronic surveillance, cameras orbiting in space, and unmanned drones make it possible to target small groups more effectively than ever before. Despite the widely publicized instances of "smart" bombs or cruise missiles that went astray, the vast majority of Western ordnance can be delivered with remarkable precision. There has been no talk of fire-bombing Kabul the way we fire-bombed Tokyo in World War II. In some ways, therefore, the precision with which sites and groups of fighters can be targeted counteracts the fact that this enemy is not massed in tens of thousands of tanks or hundreds of thousands of foot soldiers.

Fourth, the global communications network generates what sociologists call instant reflexivity. If something happens, whether the destruction of the World Trade Center at the hand of suicide fanatics using hijacked planes or the accidental destruction of a Red Cross depot in Afghanistan, the information is widely disseminated almost instantaneously. This in turn solicits instant responses, many of them not thought through, not necessarily a reflection of well-developed policy. And these instant responses in turn call forth responses to the responses,

---

[45]Cf. Samuel P. Huntington, *Clash*, 187-8: "Terrorism historically is the weapon of the weak, that is, of those who do not possess conventional military power. Since World War II, nuclear weapons have also been the weapon by which the weak compensate for conventional inferiority. In the past, terrorists could do only limited violence, killing a few people here or destroying a facility there. Massive military forces were required to do massive violence. At some point, however, a few terrorists will be able to produce massive violence and massive destruction. Separately, terrorism and nuclear weapons are the weapons of the non-Western weak. If and when they are combined, the non-Western weak will be strong."

and so forth—instant reflexivity. The possibility of mistakes, misunderstandings, and misjudgments is correspondingly increased.

In the light of these developments, many of the tenets of just war theory are surely still applicable, but some need revisiting. With respect to the rules that govern going to war:[46] (1) The only just cause is defense against violent aggression, and the World Trade Center attack qualifies if anything does. (2) The only just peace is the restoration of justice to friend and foe alike. On the "friend" side, this conflict also qualifies; on the "foe" side, because these foes are driven by religious/civilizational ideals, I suspect that they will not easily concede that anything is "just" unless they wipe out the West's influence and gain great victories for Islam. Just war theory does not really address that sort of conflict. (3) Military force must be a last resort. One might legitimately argue that in this conflict America has been slow to resort to arms. The origins of the violence go back about a dozen years to a succession of attacks in the Middle East, Africa, and the Arabian Gulf.[47] Clinton was slow to take these things very seriously, partly because by temperament he was much more interested in domestic policy than in foreign policy and partly because his attempts to be the president who would bring peace to the Middle East blinded him to the seriousness of the attacks. Arguably, too, the two-year path toward his impeachment distracted him. His one missile attack was both silly and futile. But for better or worse, we went past the point of military restraint when we suffered genocide on 9/11. So it is hard to fault the West's response under this heading. (4) The decision must be made by the highest governmental authority. That certainly fits the American response; this is one of the things under just war theory that rules out the legitimacy of the attack.[48]

---

[46]I am now following the sequence I summarized earlier, pp. 107-08, adapted from Holmes.

[47]To mention only a few: February 1993—Sunni Muslims set off a bomb in the World Trade Center; April 1996—Egyptian Muslim militants opened up with machine gun fire and threw hand grenades at Western tourists outside a Cairo hotel; June 1996—Muslim radicals opposed to King Fahd bin al-Saud set off a truck bomb at the U.S. Air Force barracks in Dhahran; November 1997—the Gamat al-Islamiya killed fifty-eight foreign tourists and four Egyptians in Luxor, Egypt; August 1998—bombs exploded at the U.S. embassies in Tanzania and Kenya, killing a total of 263 persons and injuring thousands; October 2000—the USS *Cole* was attacked in Yemen by Islamic suicide bombers.

[48]This is one of the elements in most strands of just war theory that makes it hard to legitimate civil war (on the part of the rebels) or revolutionary war (assuming the rebellion succeeds). In theory, however, the American revolutionaries justified their actions precisely because before they officially took up arms, they constituted themselves an independent government of an independent nation that no longer recognized British rule. But these are invariably "fudges" to some degree because just war theory has not been worked out more comprehensively and then widely accepted.

As for the conduct of war: (5) War must be for limited ends only. So far, that has been the case in this instance. But if the limited ends are to "repel aggression" and to "redress its injustice," the phrasing does not fit the present pattern very well. Just war theory was framed when aggression meant sustained attack and taking over territory, and so it could be "repelled" and the related injustices "overturned." But international terrorists with a global reach do not attempt a form of aggression that can be "repelled" in that sense.

(6) The means of war must be limited by the proportionality of the offense. Granted the weight of ordnance we have already dropped on Afghanistan, those of more pacifist persuasion are already doubting that we have stayed within this boundary. But if we measure this criterion in terms of lives lost on both sides, we are certainly within the boundary. Yet the issue is more complicated. Because these terrorists are avowedly committed to using weapons of mass destruction, are we permitted to preserve proportionality not only with respect to what has been done to us so far, but also with respect to what will almost certainly be done to us if we do not prevent it? To what is the violence that must be undertaken to prevent such an attack proportional? These questions are raised not only by our technology but by the speed with which attacks can take place. By the time a weapon of mass destruction has been deployed, it cannot be "repelled," and notions of proportionality to a nuclear attack may be abhorrent when only relatively small groups of scattered terrorists are guilty. What, then, is the just force that may be used to stop the detonation of a nuclear device in New York Harbor?

(7) So far, noncombatant immunity from intentional and direct attack has been respected. In fact, it has been the advance in technology that has made the bombing in Afghanistan as restrictive and as effective as it has been. But that does not mean, nor does just war theory require, that there be no "collateral damage"—a dreadful expression, admittedly, when we are talking about human beings. War is savage; it is not pretty. More than the bad guys get hurt. But facing the alternatives squarely means that most of us will conclude that sometimes it is still the *just* thing to do, the *loving* thing to do.[49]

---

[49]It may not be entirely inappropriate to point out that "collateral damage" is a function of *many kinds* of decisions that diverse groups think are morally defensible, not just decisions about war. The Chinese

(8) Just war theory tells us that combat should not be prolonged when there is no reasonable hope of success within the limits just set out. So far, I think, the West can say it has complied with this criterion. But suppose America, with or without its allies, decides to go into, say, Yemen, Iraq, or some other place. The envisaged success is extremely hard to sort out over against the damage that will be caused. If we are virtually certain that failure to go in will bring us, say, a smallpox horror or a nuclear explosion, surely we must conclude that this criterion is being met. But such a calculation necessarily depends on our assessment of the relations between the terrorist groups and the nations in view, and on the genuine potential of these groups to achieve their stated aims. Those may be very difficult things to determine. How much does measuring up to this criterion of just war theory depend on intelligence officers?

The current war on global terrorism, as it is being pursued while I write these lines, fares pretty well by the standards of just war theory (at least, the eight points of this particular version of just war theory). But note how many of the points urgently need rethinking, probing, revising in the light of the new forms of violence. Under (2), we may be satisfied that we are engaging in a "just war," but what shall we do with the "just peace" clause when the opponents want nothing less than your destruction? If this conflict is not being fought over territory or trade or slavery or the like, but over fundamental and civilizational differences, triggered by such matters as whether or not Saudi Arabia has the right, though a Muslim state, to ask the United States to place some of her forces on her territory and whether the U.S. policy on Israel and the Palestinians meets the unbridgeable demands of both sides, precisely what would a "just peace" look like? How should this criterion

government's one-child-per-family policy, combined with the strong cultural preference for boys rather than girls and the resulting selective abortions, has resulted in a population in which there are about one hundred million more men than women in China. In particular, there are about twenty-five million more men of marriageable age than women. This in turn results in rising rates of homosexuality, prostitution, and aggression. In the name of women's rights and ostensibly to stop the barbarity and injustice of back-room abortions, *Roe v. Wade* has managed to kill upwards of twenty-eight million potential citizens—many of them in final term, by crushing their skulls—neither of which factors was clearly foreseen when the *Roe v. Wade* decision was made. That seems to be a stunning amount of collateral damage. My sole point in these observations is that questions of collateral damage apply to countless decisions requiring a moral determination. To restrict to questions of war the factoring in of collateral damage is morally myopic.

be revised? Under (4), the assumption in the past was that the attacking force would be state-sponsored, and only the highest level of another government had the right to respond. But here we are attacked by a nonstate entity. Our own response meets this criterion, but just war theorists clearly did not think about this kind of attack. Under (5) and (6), we have already noted that the present conflict demands that we expand on what it means to "repel aggression" and qualify what it means to "redress injustice"; the notion of limiting violence by proportionality needs a great deal more thought, especially where the aim is to prevent genocide by a weapon of mass destruction. Under (7), so far in this conflict the West has been pretty careful not to target noncombatants directly, but more thought must be given to this category when we evaluate whether or how to go after those who harbor and shield terrorists. Do we largely ignore such people? How much "aid" must a nation-state give to a cell of terrorists before the nation becomes morally responsible for the mass violence of the terrorists? At what point should people who are nominally noncombatants be viewed as combatants? Suppose they provide arms, moral encouragement, and money, but do not know what the targets are in advance? Suppose they do these things and congratulate the terrorists after the event? Suppose they know about the plan, applaud it, and do nothing to warn the targets? More thought is needed.

And finally, under (8), doubtless it is true that just war is not to be prolonged beyond a reasonable hope of success within these limits. But what a "reasonable" hope is in this new kind of war is a bit squishy at the moment, and "success" itself will be hard to measure—the more so if some al-Qaeda members fade back into their cultures, to reappear perhaps in some new group equally committed to acquiring weapons of mass destruction but for the moment hidden from prying eyes. Clearly "success" cannot refer to the destruction of every person who has the potential for constituting this sort of "global reach" terrorist cell; and even if it did, new generations of such persons would quickly come forward, perhaps in part elicited by the destruction of the very people whom they wish to replace. But what, then, does "success" mean? Do we simply declare "success" when we think we have the most important leaders? Or when we are not going to be able to continue without causing more resentments than we are eliminating? Or must there be an ongoing vigilance now that this kind of violence has won a certain credibility for itself? At what point does such vigilance threaten this eighth point? Does the point need revision?

I have included this discussion to show that in broad terms the war against Osama bin Laden and his buddies fits within the traditional categories of just war theory. To that extent, we manifest a deficiency of justice, and thus a want of virtue, even a want of love, if we fail to make the sacrifices necessary to win in this conflict. On the other hand, some far-sighted Christian ethicist with a firm grasp of biblical theology and solid knowledge of contemporary culture and of the realities of this new kind of war would do the Christian world a great deal of good if he or she would successfully and convincingly rework just war theory to take into account the sorts of questions I have raised.

(5) As with racism, so here: Christians need to reflect on how some of the fundamentals of the faith bear on just war. I shall not go over the same doctrinal matters again (see above, pp. 97-103). It would, however, be a good exercise for a young theologian to reflect on the same doctrinal categories—justice and forgiveness, creation and the fall, the glory of the cross, the importance of the tension between the "already" that we have received in Christ Jesus and the "not yet" that awaits the consummation, and the centrality of the church—and think through how these and other biblical and theological categories have a controlling bearing on how Christians should view September 11, mass destruction, just war, and Osama bin Laden.

I shall not take up that challenge myself. Instead, I want to offer four theological reflections that extend a little beyond such points.

First, although much has changed, little has changed. The media are constantly telling us that 9/11 has changed everything. Certainly for those who lost loved ones at the World Trade Center, at the Pentagon, or in the airplane that came down in a field in Pennsylvania, an enormous amount has changed; certainly the nation has a heightened security awareness, and in some measure our economy has been placed on a war footing. Perhaps the deepest changes are psychological: we are vulnerable, and the security we have long associated with the fortunate gift of our isolated geography has been breached by a determined handful of men willing to give their lives to kill others.

Nevertheless, though it may at first seem almost sacrilegious to say it, little has changed. One recalls the challenge faced by C. S. Lewis in the autumn of 1939. On September 1 of that year, German forces surged across the Polish border, and World War II began. In Oxford the minister of the University Church of St. Mary wondered what should be said to undergraduates for whom studying would surely seem irrelevant in the light of the impending cataclysm. He invited Lewis, then at Magdalen College and himself a wounded veteran of the trenches of World War I, to give a lecture that has since been published many times under the title "Learning in War-Time."[50]

On October 22 Lewis climbed into the high pulpit and spoke to the students. He began by subverting his theme. How can anyone study when countless thousands are dying? But surely, Lewis said, at all times and in every place Christians must ask a still more fundamental question—"how it is right, or even psychologically possible, for creatures who are every moment advancing either to heaven or to hell, to spend any fraction of the little time allowed to them in this world on such comparative trivialities as literature or art, mathematics or biology."[51] Lewis's profound point exposes the shallowness of contemporary analysis: "The war creates no absolutely new situation: it simply aggravates the permanent human situation so that we can no longer ignore it."[52]

So also with 9/11. It creates no new thing; rather, it reminds us of the brevity of life, the destructive power of evil, the fragility of any cul-

---

[50]His sermon has been reprinted many times. My copy is in the volume of collected essays: C. S. Lewis, *Fern-seed and Elephants and Other Essays on Christianity*, ed. Walter Hooper (Glasgow: Collins, 1975), 26-38.

[51]Ibid., 27.

[52]Ibid. He goes on to say: "But there is no question of death or life for any of us; only a question of this death or of that—of a machine-gun bullet now or a cancer forty years later. What does war do to death? It certainly does not make it more frequent: 100 percent of us die, and the percentage cannot be increased. It puts several deaths earlier, but I hardly suppose that that is what we fear. Certainly when the moment comes, it will make little difference how many years we have behind us. Does it increase our chances of a painful death? I doubt it. As far as I can find out, what we call natural death is usually preceded by suffering; and a battlefield is one of the very few places where one has a reasonable prospect of dying with no pain at all. Does it decrease our chances of dying at peace with God? I cannot believe it. . . . Yet war does do something to death. It forces us to remember it. The only reason why the cancer at sixty or the paralysis at seventy-five do not bother us is that we forget them. War makes death real to us, and that would have been regarded as one of its blessings by most of the great Christians of the past" (37-38).

tural artifact such as the Tower of Babel—for all our pomp and strength will someday be one with Babylon, Nineveh, and Tyre.

Second, in the light of biblical priorities, we must see in the events of September 11 a strong call to the church and then to the nation to repent. When two prominent religious figures publicly blamed homosexuals, abortionists, and feminists for this act of judgment upon us, it was not long before the public clamor drove them to apologize. But they almost got it right. The problem was that they pointed to two or three sins that they particularly disliked and which were clearly the sins of *other* people and not theirs. It was a divisive thing to do at a time that demanded national unity; worse, it was theologically inept. When Isaiah sees the exalted Lord, he begins by confessing his *own* sins within the context of the national sins (Isa. 6:5). By pointing fingers to *other* people and *their* sins, these two prominent preachers simultaneously managed to be divisive and to project an image of self-righteousness. But at least they recognized that September 11 was, among other things, an act of judgment and a call to repentance.

We must be careful how we word this. We should make clear what we are *not* saying. Certainly we are not saying that those who died on September 11 were in any sense more wicked than those who did not die. But when Jesus was confronted with a disaster in his day and was asked if the people who had recently been murdered in the temple or who had perished when a tower collapsed were somehow more wicked than others, he did not reply with either a stern "Of course!" (which at least would have explained why *they* died and not others) or with a dismissive "Of course not!" (which might have comforted those who mourned their loss but explained nothing). Rather, he says something unexpected: "But unless you repent, you too will all perish" (Luke 13:5). What that means is that *all* of us deserve to die. It is of the Lord's mercy that we are not consumed; repentance is urgent for all of us. And large numbers of deaths, even where they are brought about by evil men, remind all of us that we live and die under the curse, and we will one day give an account to God.

If judgment begins with the family of God (1 Pet. 4:17), it follows that God's people must constantly be first to repent. It does not take much understanding of today's church to recognize how little different we are from the surrounding culture—and with less excuse, for we should know better. Just as Nehemiah repented for himself and his people before the Lord appointed him to leadership (Neh. 1:5-7), so we too must repent for ourselves and our nation.

We cannot duck this responsibility on the ground that this cannot be what is going on here, since the attackers are clearly more evil than the attacked. But those who draw such an inference simply do not know their Bibles. The peculiar providence of God often uses a more wicked people to bring chastening to a less wicked people (e.g., Isa. 10:5ff.; Habakkuk).

We live in perilous times. This will not be the last terrorist attack; the efforts of a Saddam Hussein or an Osama bin Laden to obtain and deploy weapons of mass destruction are going to be with us for a long time: the scientific genie cannot be put back in the bottle. One can imagine a dozen possible frightening scenarios, conjuring up scenes of hundreds of thousands of deaths, perhaps millions of deaths. Charles Colson is right:

> Let's say, for the sake of argument, that God is using these attacks as a sign of judgment. What will save us, then, are not the marines, cruise missiles, satellites or smart bombs; the only thing that will save us is deep and genuine repentance. William Wilberforce was a Christian member of Parliament who fought to abolish slavery in the British Empire. During a crucial moment in that campaign he said that his hope for Britain depended "not so much on her navies and armies, nor on the wisdom of her rulers, as on the persuasion that she still contains many who love and obey the gospel of Christ, that their prayers may yet prevail."[53]

None of this exonerates us from the responsibility of trying to hunt down the terrorists and prevent them from pressing on with the next ghastly step of their vision. It means that only the Lord himself can enable us to prevail; it means that whether we prevail or not, we Christians have been given a somber call to repent and renew our covenantal vows. Ultimately, only the name of the Lord is our strong tower (Prov. 18:10).

Third, September 11 and the events that have followed, including

---

[53]Charles Colson, "Wake-up Call," *Christianity Today* 45/14 (12 Nov. 2001), 112.

the release of the amateur videotape that shows just how calloused and hard Osama bin Laden is, have resurrected some national discussion, still far too shallow, over the nature of evil. We have already had reason to remark that considering the evil, violence, and loss of life that characterized the twentieth century, it is more than a little shocking that we should reach the end of that century and the beginning of the next with so many of our intellectual elites assuring us that there is no such thing as objective evil: there is only evil as perceived by some interpretive community or another. But now we are talking about evil again, even on national TV. The discussion has not led to much thought about evil in God's eyes or to personal or (still less) national repentance, but at least a little space has been opened up for the category of evil.

This matter is something that Christian apologists and other thinkers should be working on. For already the spin doctors of postmodernism are assuring us that 9/11 provides no justification for the support of moral absolutes. In an "Op-ed" piece in *The New York Times*, Stanley Fish argues that we in our culture have very good reasons for preferring our own values, but we cannot fall back on "false universals" or abstract notions of justice.[54] We take our side because it is ours, and that is enough. The moral bankruptcy is staggering. He is right to demand that we try to understand the opponent's perspective. But cannot we in some measure understand a Pol Pot or a Stalin or a Hitler and yet condemn him for utterly evil actions? It has been widely reported that ABC News president, David Westin, in an address to students at Columbia University, announced that his standard of "objectivity" [*sic*!] forbade him to render a moral judgment on the propriety of flying an occupied jet into the Pentagon.[55] By contrast, Fox News at the moment seems to delight in showering opprobrium on the opposition. Serious Christian engagement must surely decry evil wherever it is found—in our own hearts, in our own culture, and among those who fly passenger jets into buildings and threaten nuclear holocaust. In short, the horrific events of September 11 are a banner to rally serious ethical discussion to address the challenges raised by postmodern epistemology.

[54]For 15 Oct. 2001; available from http://query.nytimes.com/search/abstract?res=F50617FE385B0C 768DDDA90994D9404482.
[55]That item has been widely quoted. See, for instance, *Imprimis* 30/12 (Dec. 2001), 6.

Fourth, the civilizational struggle between the world of Islam and the West turns on numerous conflicting perspectives. But one of these is (to use the Western categories) how we are to understand the relationship between church and state. In Islam, there is no debate as to whether the word of Allah takes precedence. How that word is interpreted is another matter—but it is impossible at the moment to imagine an ostensibly Muslim state long sustaining a largely secular system of civil government. Probably the most daring experiment, and the closest thing to a contradiction of this assertion, was the heritage of Mustafa Kemal Ataturk. Turkey's more recent leaders, however, have tended to adopt Muslim fundamentalist practices and enlist fundamentalist support. The jury is out on where the experiment will end up. Whatever the future of Turkey, however, it is at most the exception that proves the rule.

By contrast, most Western countries are accelerating toward increasing secularization (which does not necessarily mean that there are fewer people going to church!). In the United States, court rulings exclude Christian confessionalism from many venues (not least publicly funded schools), while in Germany the number of theological students has dropped by 85 percent in the last decade, and in France no church, including the Roman Catholic Church, offers much more than a blip on the cultural screen. In the West, so-called Christianity has largely become privatized, democratized, domesticated. The heritage that gave us the separation of church and state is being pushed to the periphery. *And it is this secularization, much more than Christianity itself, that is so loathed and feared in the world of Islam*. At the very least we should precipitate large-scale debates about whether the peculiar relationships that are developing between Christianity and civil society in various Western countries are the best that can be devised. Certainly recent judgments in the United States regarding the "wall of separation" are far removed from the assumptions of the founding fathers. One cannot help but ask whether a modern Isaiah or Paul would interpret some of our exercises in multifaith civic religion as worthy examples of nation-building or horrible examples of idolatry.[56]

---

[56]Implicit in this sentence is the fact that Christians who live in Western nations where there is a strong tradition of the distinction between Christ and Caesar must try to work out what Scripture says on these matters and not utterly give themselves over to the empiricists: *pace* Robert Wuthnow, *Christianity and Civil Society: The Contemporary Debate* (Valley Forge: Trinity Press International, 1996), 7.

We urgently need some fresh theological thinking along these lines, while acknowledging with gratitude that the roots of the separation between church and state are profoundly Christian (it was Jesus, after all, who gave us Matt. 22:21).

(6) One more theological reflection is relevant to the concerns of these lectures. Complex discussions about justice, forgiveness, enemies, and just war theory may entice us to forget that they were all precipitated by the effort to think exegetically and theologically about love. There are two more ways in which love bears on the discussion in this section.

First, I have already noted that Cicero (106-43 B.C.) developed a pagan form of just war theory before the Christian era dawned. The heart of the difference between his theory and that articulated by Augustine was this: Cicero allowed war either as an act of defense or to avenge dishonor. By contrast, Augustine restricted just war to defense alone because he understood that love does not seek vengeance.

Therefore, in the present struggle, even while we must try to prevent the terrorists from doing more violence, we must eschew a vendetta mentality. Love demands that we do not demonize Osama bin Laden. He is a human being made in the image of God. He is an evil man, and he must be stopped, but he is a man, and we should take no pleasure in destroying him. Vengeance is the Lord's alone. Do not offer the alternative, "Should we weep for Osama bin Laden or hold him to account for his genocide and prevent him from carrying out his violent intentions?" The right answer is yes.

Similarly, even if there are very good reasons for not according the status of POW to those detained at Guantanamo Bay or in Afghanistan,[57] America must not only be "clean" but be seen to be clean in its treatment of its captives, so far as food, shelter, clothing, medical

---

[57]Especially in Europe, there has been a lot of finger-pointing against the United States for allegedly breaching the standards of the Geneva Conventions for prisoners of war. I do not know how accurate those reports are; I am quite certain that brutality in the treatment of these prisoners is without excuse. But I also think that most of the media in Europe have not tried to understand why America is hesitant to assign POW status to these detainees. Under the Geneva Conventions, lawful combatants must wear a uniform or visible insignia, have a commander who is responsible for their conduct and who is part of a chain of command back to a recognized government, and conduct their operations "in accordance with the laws and customs of war." That is why, for instance, the Geneva Conventions did not forbid the execution of a spy (such were not considered lawful combatants since they were out of uniform). None of these conditions applies to al-Qaeda. Here, too, I suspect, careful rethinking and redefinition are needed as to what a combatant is under just war theory in this age of high-tech, global-reach terrorism.

help, and the like are concerned. And we who are Christians should be at the forefront of pushing for such treatment of those who are made in the image of God.

Second, while it is important for Christians to think through the issues discussed in this lecture, none of what I have said should lessen our passionate commitment to herald the good news—not least among Muslims. Both Christianity and Islam are monotheistic missionary religions. The means of expansion are often radically different, but each side is convinced that what it holds to be the truth is so important and precious that others should enjoy it, too. So while we may find it necessary to make war against some Muslims who are intent on bringing death and destruction to untold thousands, we had better not demonize *any* Muslim. It is virtually impossible to evangelize, in Christian terms, people whom we despise or hate. Here, too, Christian love must prevail. Otherwise evangelism of Muslims, already challenging and now made so much more difficult by 9/11 and its aftermath, will tragically dissolve in the acidic hates of war.

5

LOVE AND THE DENIAL
OF THE GOSPEL

A. INTRODUCTION

Western culture likes to think of itself as fundamentally tolerant. In comparison with most cultures in the history of humankind, a great deal could be said to support the view that, for all our faults, tolerance has found much more welcome here than in any other major civilization. But before we hunker down in the warm glow of self-commendation, our reverie needs to be modified by a little realism. Five things need to be said.

(1) We should be the first to admit that the West has not always been tolerant. The heritage that we now largely take for granted had to be earned, argued for, even fought for. The "Great Ejection" from key pulpits of two thousand ministers after the restoration of the monarchy was not a high point in the history of the Church of England. Most of the American colonies were not open to any and every denomination; Rhode Island was the first, founded by a Baptist who had been on the receiving end of persecution. And what shall we say of the Inquisition, of repeated manifestations of anti-Semitism, of various forms of racism? Western countries have enough sins in their heritage that their moral urgings of others should always be combined with humility, historical perspective, and vigilance.

(2) When we speak of "the West," we are including highly diverse

nations with equally diverse histories and tolerance levels. Consider the Reformation: the Germans divided over it (roughly north and south); the English formally embraced it and yet changed their tolerance levels (and the direction in which *in*tolerance was expressed) according to who was in power (contrast Oliver Cromwell and Bloody Mary); the Spanish clamped down with the Inquisition; the French, at first receptive, organized the genocide of the Huguenots. The effects of these historical realities are still with us in some fashion or another. There was overt persecution of evangelicals in Quebec a bare half-century ago (Baptist ministers alone spent a total of eight years in jail between 1950 and 1952), just as there are still outbreaks of similar persecution in parts of Latin America today. And this is merely a summary of certain kinds of *religious* intolerance.

Yet having said all this, by and large the West has forged a path toward tolerance of diversity and difference that is unparalleled in history. Part of this is the fruit of democratic institutions; part of it, in many countries, is the fruit of extraordinarily complex immigration patterns, feeding on the ideal of democracy;[1] part of it is tied to some form of separation of church and state, which itself is a fundamental Christian insight. Whatever the causes, the fact remains that every year hundreds of thousands of people try to move into Germany, France, the United Kingdom, Canada, the United States, Brazil. One cannot find hundreds of thousands of people trying to get into Saudi Arabia, the former USSR, China, and other totalitarian regimes, except on occasion as guest workers to earn some money to send home, with little thought of settling there.

(3) A case can be made that the long pursuit of tolerance has been a mixed blessing. A. J. Conyers has forcefully argued that the checkered history of the rise of tolerance has not in fact been in support of racial or religious diversity, but has ultimately served to solidify central government and a profitable capitalism.[2] The primary reason for these conclusions is that by dissolving the loyalties that once bound people to their church, to their family, and to other mediating institutions, toleration

---

[1] Diverse immigration patterns alone are insufficient, for there are many examples where immigrants have moved to totalitarian regimes without achieving similar levels of tolerance.

[2] *The Long Truce: How Toleration Made the World Safe for Power and Profit* (Dallas: Spence, 2001).

has left isolated citizens to confront the unmediated power of the state. Even if his thesis needs qualification, it is at least arguable that the price of "toleration" has been the silencing, or at least the relativizing and diminishing, of the very voices in our culture that at their best serve as a prophetic check against the raw materialism of the culture and the pretensions of an ostensibly "neutral" government. Conyers himself prefers the voice of preached humility in pre-Reformation Christianity to the indifference to religion, which (he asserts) predominates today.

(4) More serious is the change in the very meaning of tolerance that has installed itself in much of the Western world during the last couple of decades. It used to be that a tolerant person was one who insisted that those who disagreed with him had rights no less than his own to speak their own positions freely. The slogan was, "I may detest the things you are saying, but I will defend to the death your right to say them." The tolerance, in other words, was directed toward people, not their ideas. In fact, the idea implicit in this notion of tolerance is that the tolerant person *disagrees* with some idea or other: that is precisely why tolerance is needed. One does not "tolerate" someone with whom one is already in perfect agreement!

By contrast, the new tolerance is directed not to people who are permitted or even encouraged to articulate repugnant views, but to the ideas themselves: under the priorities of postmodern ideology, it is wrong to say that any worldview or set of ideas or religious opinion is wrong or untrue or evil. Ideas alien to us may be "bad" in the relative sense that our own system sees the other system as flawed. But (postmodernist tolerance urges) it is wrong to say that a contrary view is wrong, at least in any objective or absolute sense.

It is unclear to me why such a view of tolerance should be labeled "tolerance." If an idea is neither wrong nor bad, what is there to tolerate? If all ideas are equally valid or good, what is there to tolerate? Strictly speaking, postmodernism does not advocate a broader tolerance; rather, it removes the need for any tolerance. As a result, genuine tolerance withers and dies. The most compelling evidence that this is the case lies in the fact that postmodernists are notoriously *in*tolerant of those who do not share their epistemology. And this fierce intolerance is often directed against the *people* whose views are disliked, not simply against the views themselves. People with non-postmodern views are systemat-ically marginalized, ignored, dismissed, not hired, refused a voice. In short, they are not tolerated.

In today's world, more and more views are welcomed to the table, on the condition that none of them says the others are wrong or infe-rior. That is the one wrong and inferior thing to say. The forces of polit-ical correctness maintain the stance.

(5) To add to the complexity of this subject is debate over the place of traditional or confessional bodies in such a society. We might well agree that all-male clubs in which a lot of business is informally trans-acted prejudice the opportunities of the rising number of women-led businesses; we might well agree that all-white clubs in which a lot of business is informally transacted prejudice the opportunities of the ris-ing number of minority-led businesses. Pretty soon both cultural and judicial pressures squeeze such clubs to open their memberships to the wider community. But by and large we do not coerce synagogues to admit people who have no sympathy with the purpose of the synagogue; we do not demand that mosques in America admit non-Muslims; we do not force churches to admit members who disagree with stances they have adopted. That is part (but only part) of religious freedom.

In the previous lecture I briefly indicated how most Muslims view these developments: these developments are an insult to Allah, an immoral vice. But are not many confessional Christians also more than a little uneasy about the moral and religious compromises that characterize our existence? An interfaith service may unify the nation in a time of crisis, but at what cost? If the philosophical pluralists are right, there is no cost to pay: interfaith services are unmitigated triumphs. But if believers think that there are real and unbridgeable differences that separate faiths in profound ways, then the state-sponsored interfaith service is not only an implicit denial of this confessionalism (and thus a state-sponsored support of plu-ralism) but is also the illegitimate meddling by the state in matters of reli-gion. It is the elevation of the state over religion.

Nevertheless my purpose in this lecture is not to explore these issues again, this time by examining the changing face of tolerance. Rather, I now wish to focus on a further problem that is becoming acute within many churches and parachurch organizations. Christians are not

immune from societal pressures. If a local church has certain doctrinal
and moral standards for membership, and if those standards are tested
and upheld by the expulsion of members who no longer meet those standards, commentary in the broader culture is largely negative. After all,
they remind us, Jesus himself taught, "Do not judge, or you too will be
judged" (Matt. 7:1). Aren't Christians supposed to love their enemies?
So don't such expulsions prove that Christians are mean-spirited and
intolerant? The result is that many Christians become intimidated, too
frightened to do what is right. We who are Christians are also citizens,
and we necessarily pick up many of the cultural stances of the broader
citizenry. When the cultural imperatives denigrate any form of exclusion
and then forcefully exclude those who disagree with this stance, it is easy
for Christians to feel marginalized when their local churches insist on
church discipline. One of the results is that fewer and fewer churches
practice much discipline.

As we saw in previous lectures, however, the New Testament writers, even while writing the texts on love and forbearance that we are trying to understand and obey, condemn false apostles, expel the man who
is sleeping with his stepmother, declare that it would have been better
for Judas Iscariot if he had not been born, assure readers that the evil of
Alexander the metal-worker will be required of him, and solemnly warn
of eternal judgment to come. Sometimes, of course, churches with right-
wing passions use these same texts to bully their members into unflag-
ging submission to the local dictator. The threat of church discipline can
degenerate into a form of manipulation, of spiritual abuse. Where, then,
is the line to be drawn? To a postmodern relativist, any form of confessional discipline will seem to be nothing more than intolerant, manipu-
lative abuse. From a Christian perspective, what lines must be drawn
and why? How does Christian love work itself out in such cases?

In the next two sections of this lecture, I propose to examine the
famous confrontation between Paul and Peter. That will set us up for
some concluding pastoral reflections. Before proceeding, I should explain
how that apostolic interaction contributes to a book reflecting on what
it means for Christians to love in hard places. The obvious point, of
course, is that here we find an apostle rebuking an apostle: is this a man-
ifestation of love or a failure of love, or something else? As we shall see,

the scene itself must have been emotionally gut-wrenching. But although Paul writes with his customary forcefulness, he does not write with bitterness. Moreover, here and there throughout this letter, Paul writes movingly of Jesus' love (Gal. 2:20) and displays his own deep passion for the well-being of his readers (4:19-20). He encourages them to "serve one another in love," not least because the entire law "is summed up in a single command: 'Love your neighbor as yourself'" (5:13-14). After all, the fruit of the Spirit is, among other things, love (5:22). Thus unless we are prepared to charge him with international-class hypocrisy, the apostle Paul is fully persuaded that his rebuke of the apostle Peter is entirely within the constraints of Christian love. Indeed, at one level, it is motivated by Christian love. Isn't this the letter in which Paul reminds his readers that if they are called upon to confront a fellow believer who is caught in a sin, they should restore that person gently (6:1)? That, doubtless, is what Paul believes he was trying to do with Peter.

B. PORTRAIT OF AN APOSTOLIC REBUKE (GAL. 2:11-14)

[11]*When Peter came to Antioch, I opposed him to his face, because he was clearly in the wrong.* [12]*Before certain men came from James, he used to eat with the Gentiles. But when they arrived, he began to draw back and separate himself from the Gentiles because he was afraid of those who belonged to the circumcision group.* [13]*The other Jews joined him in his hypocrisy, so that by their hypocrisy even Barnabas was led astray.* [14]*When I saw that they were not acting in line with the truth of the gospel, I said to Peter in front of them all, "You are a Jew, yet you live like a Gentile and not like a Jew. How is it, then, that you force Gentiles to follow Jewish customs?"*

The exact nature of the confrontation between Peter and Paul in Antioch has long been disputed. From Paul's perspective, Peter's offense was serious: "he was clearly in the wrong," Paul writes—and the verb means more than that he was inconsistent or happened to be mistaken. It means he was frankly in the wrong before God; he was condemned by God himself.

How we understand the confrontation turns in no small measure on how we understand two expressions in verse 12, namely "certain men . . . from James" and "the circumcision group." In what is probably the most common view among contemporary Bible readers, the two expressions refer to the same people,[3] and the scene unfolds something like this: Peter arrives in Antioch where Barnabas and Paul have been ministering for some time (the former longer than the latter, Acts 11:22-26). During the first part of his visit, Peter was happy to eat with Jews and Gentiles alike, including, no doubt, the Lord's Supper. After all, by this time he had well learned the lesson that he was not to call anything impure that God had made clean (Acts 10:15, 28; 11:9; cf. Matt. 11:15). It may have been that even in Antioch there were some conservative Jews who could not bring themselves to eat with Gentile believers, while others had no objection. Whatever the breakdown, Peter initially had no scruples in this regard.

But then "certain men came from James" (2:12), and Peter began to change his practice. The text gives the impression that the change did not happen all at once. Perhaps he began to eat with the Jewish group more often. Whether this Jewish group was restricted to the "men . . . from James" or included some restrictive Jews in Antioch, we cannot say. But it was not long before Peter ate only with the Jews. And why did Peter take these steps? Paul tells us that it was because Peter "was afraid of those who belonged to the circumcision group"—which, on this reading, are the Jewish "men . . . from James." It would appear, then, that Peter was happy to adopt a non-kosher lifestyle when he was in Antioch, but he would not want word of his habits slipping back to Jerusalem where the stories could damage his reputation and authority with the more conservative wing of the Jerusalem church.

Inevitably, some of the Jews who had been well integrated into this mixed-race church drifted toward Peter and his kosher practices. Perhaps their choice was partly driven by a desire to be with their "own." But with the theological discussions of the day brewing in the background, certainly some must have asked questions such as these: "If Peter is restricting himself to kosher food, why shouldn't I? Does Peter think it is somehow more holy or more acceptable to God to adopt restrictive eating practices in line with the laws of the old covenant?

[3]Ernest de W. Burton, *A Critical and Exegetical Commentary on the Epistle to the Galatians* (Edinburgh: T & T Clark, 1921), 107.

Perhaps Paul has been a bit too liberal: wasn't Peter the great hero of the day at Pentecost? Isn't he the powerful and Spirit-anointed preacher who has proclaimed the gospel from the beginning?" Eventually "even Barnabas" (2:13) was led astray.

On this reconstruction, it does not take much imagination to grasp the growing resentments and confusion among the Gentile believers. Probably some of what they felt was painful abandonment. But at least some of them must have wondered if perhaps the Jews did have an inside track with God. Perhaps it really was important not only to trust Jesus but to preserve the kosher food laws of the old covenant Scriptures. Perhaps Gentile Christians would never be more than second-tier members of the church unless they became Jews—and what would that mean? Circumcision?

Whatever the mental processes of the Gentile believers, Paul is horrified by what is happening. His summary displays his judgment: "The other Jews joined [Peter] in his hypocrisy, so that by their hypocrisy even Barnabas was led astray" (2:13). The word rendered "hypocrisy" does not always have the moral weight of the English term; sometimes it might better be rendered "play-acting." But in any case, what is the precise nature of the "play-acting" or "hypocrisy" that Paul finds in the action of Peter and the Jewish believers he influenced? Paul explains by summarizing the initial rebuke he delivered in public: "You are a Jew, yet you live like a Gentile and not like a Jew. How is it, then, that you force Gentiles to follow Jewish customs?" (2:14). The charge is that Peter has long since learned to "live like a Gentile," that is, to live free (in this context) of kosher food laws. So how is it that by his current conduct, by the power of his own example, he now drives Gentiles toward the kosher food laws he does not himself consistently observe? Granted his common liberal practice, does not his current restrictive practice seem like play-acting?

This is probably the most common interpretation of the passage. It depends on identifying the "certain men . . . from James" with "the circumcision group." But this reading of the passage is not intrinsically strong. No doubt Peter made some spectacular blunders in his life as a disciple of Jesus Christ, but this one—that is, the blunder presupposed by this interpretation—does not sound very likely. After all, Acts 10—11 make it pretty clear that the visionary experience that prepared Peter to meet Cornelius and his household was decisive for him. More importantly, when Peter was called on the carpet by the Jerusalem church (Acts 11:3), he defended himself by relating the entire incident, recalling the words of the Lord Jesus and recounting the conversion of Cornelius (Acts 11:4-17). We are told that the church as a whole had no further objections—not, at least, at this juncture!—and praised God. With this background in mind, it is hard to believe that Peter would be intimidated by the mere presence of conservative Jews from Jerusalem who preferred to eat kosher food on their own.

In fact, there is a more believable reconstruction of what happened. But it will be easier to understand it if we first grasp two points.

(1) As the church grew and became more diverse, with more and more Gentiles being added, there arose a spectrum of opinion about how Christians should relate to the law of Moses. At the risk of providing neat cubbyholes for positions that were doubtless more complex and more fluid, we might think of the spectrum resolving into the following array of positions:

(a) Eventually some Gentile Christians thought that the law had no claim on their lives whatsoever. The Old Testament could be abandoned, and some of the New Testament as well. This extreme position, exemplified by Marcion and his followers in the second century, is not clearly attested in New Testament times. But mild forms of this stance can be spotted in the New Testament among those who advocated some kind of libertinism. Perhaps they reasoned that if they were not under the Mosaic covenant, and if the grace of Christ forgives all sin, they could be careless about sin. They were at liberty (hence "libertinism") to do anything they liked. Possibly some Gentiles in Galatians held such a view; it is certainly the sort of error presupposed in Romans 6:1, 15.

(b) Others, like Paul himself, insisted that Christians are not under the law covenant even though they are certainly not free from God's demands (see 1 Cor. 9:19-23). That leaves quite a bit of room in which to work out the nature of the connections between the Mosaic covenant and the new covenant, but for our purposes it is enough to observe that it left Paul and Christians like him free to practice circumcision and observe kosher food laws, or not, as pastoral wisdom dictated. Included in this large category were growing numbers of Gentile believers who felt under no obligation whatsoever to observe the stipulations of the old covenant, the Mosaic covenant.

(c) A little farther along the spectrum were Christian Jews who fully understood and accepted Paul's position but whose personal "comfort zones" meant that they chose, at least most of the time, to be observing Jews. They did not, however, think that their own kosher practices were necessary for either salvation or maturity, and they certainly did not insist that they be imposed on Gentile believers.

(d) Still farther along the spectrum were Jews who probably thought it was acceptable for Gentile Christians not to see themselves as being under the Mosaic covenant, but that Jewish Christians should observe the Mosaic code. One suspects that many in Jerusalem who heard Peter's defense of his visit to Cornelius (Acts 11:1-18) belonged either to this position or the previous. In other words, they were genuinely happy that Gentiles were being converted and given the gift of the Spirit, but they themselves were Jews and were either more comfortable to remain in their traditions or genuinely thought that such traditions should be maintained by Jewish believers, even if not by Gentile believers. Initially, they probably did not think through the implications of such a position for a mixed church, since they were comfortably ensconced in Jerusalem where such problems could not be central. But the challenge of the mixed church could not be ducked in a city like Antioch.

(e) Snuggled into the spectrum at about this point were Jews who fully admitted that Gentiles could be saved simply by repenting and trusting Christ, but who probably thought that the really spiritual among the Gentile Christians would want to obey the Mosaic covenant even if such obedience was not strictly necessary to their salvation. In some instances this was probably not so much a mature theological conclusion as an inherited cultural bias, but the effect was the same: Christian maturity and deep spirituality were tied to observing the Mosaic covenant rather more than they were tied to Christ. If I am not mistaken, the "false apostles" of 2 Corinthians 10—13 belonged to this camp.

(f) Farther yet along the spectrum were Jews who believed that Jesus is the Messiah and that he rose again and ascended to the right hand of the Father, but they thought that his life and death and resurrection restored God's people to faithfulness to the Mosaic covenant. Jesus was a *Jewish* Messiah, and his messianic ministry reformed and purified *Jews*. The new covenant was a renewal of the old covenant. Gentiles, of course, were welcome, but they could not truly accept Jesus as the Messiah unless they first became Jews—and that meant submitting to circumcision, observing Sabbath and kosher food laws, and so forth. At least initially, people on this part of the spectrum would have been accepted in Jewish Christian circles as Christians in good standing, since after all they did accept that Jesus was the Messiah and that he had risen from the dead and that it was vital to trust him. Almost certainly the people who sometimes trailed Paul in his ministry and tried to persuade Paul's converts to accept circumcision (and thus commitment to the entire Mosaic code) as a condition for salvation belonged to this group (see Acts 15:1). Later history has called them "Judaizers." They were progressively disenfranchised within the church, as their position was gradually recognized to be incompatible with the gospel (Acts 15:1-35; Titus 1:10), but they did a fair bit of damage before such steps were widely taken.

(g) Finally, many devout Jews remained who did not accept Jesus as the Messiah. In their view, what they thought of as the Jewish sect that followed the Nazarene were not only mistaken regarding Jesus' identity, but they were opening up the boundaries of Jewishness to Gentiles—a still more grievous offense, one that could not be left unchecked. Hence the vehemence of the opposition against Paul when he returned to Jerusalem for the last time (Acts 21:27—23:11). In this case, "the circumcision party" may simply refer to non-Christian Jews (e.g., Rom. 4:12b).

With this spectrum in mind, we must ask in a few moments where the parties of Galatians 2:12 fit along it.

(2) The second point to make is that the two expressions, "certain men . . . from James" and "the circumcision group," refer to two *different* groups of people, and these two groups find themselves at *different* places along the spectrum I have just laid out.

The expression "certain men . . . from James" probably means more than "certain men from the Jerusalem church [where James served as senior elder]." The expression most naturally reads as referring to men sent by James, perhaps carrying a message of some sort from him. What that might be we shall consider in due course. But if they are "from James" in this sense, then presumably he has confidence in them, and in general terms they share his outlook, his theological stance. According to Paul, there was no fundamental difference of opinion between himself and the genuine Jerusalem leaders (like Peter and James) as to what the gospel was about (2:1-3, 9). They even agreed to a basic division of labor—Peter to the Jews, Paul to the Gentiles (2:9). Even this was not absolute, since Peter was sent to Cornelius (a Gentile), and Paul's regular practice in any new town was to begin with the synagogue, i.e., primarily with Jews. These observations are in line with the way James handles himself at the Jerusalem Council, reported in Acts 15: He sides strongly with Paul and Barnabas against those who were trying to make circumcision necessary to salvation and clearly regards them highly as fellow servants of the gospel. This marks James out as occupying position (d) or position (c) above—and similarly, in all likelihood, these "men . . . from James" who arrived at the church in Antioch.

The expression "the circumcision group" can in the New Testament refer simply to Jewish Christians in a completely nonpartisan way, i.e., in a way that does not place them at any particular point along the spectrum I have just laid out (e.g., Acts 10:45; Col. 4:11). But to whom does the expression in Galatians 2:12 refer? Peter, we are told, takes the actions he does "because he was afraid of those who belonged to the circumcision group": This statement makes it easy to rule out certain theoretical possibilities. Peter was certainly not afraid of Jewish Christians in Antioch who doubtless belonged to positions (b) or (c), or in some cases even position (d). In the light of what had already taken place in Jerusalem over the Cornelius episode, it is hard to imagine that Paul is frightened of Christians in position (f), the so-called Judaizers. If the visitors were truly "men . . . from James," then judging by what we know of James, doubtless they sprang from positions (b) or (c) or (d). There is no evidence that makes it likely that Peter would fear people holding position (e), the view that although people are saved exclusively by Christ, somehow it is more spiritual to obey such stipulations as circumcision and kosher food laws.

The most likely identification of "the circumcision group" is that the expression in Galatians 2:12 refers to unconverted Jews. The reconstruction then falls into place. The "men . . . from James" probably brought a message from James along these lines: "Peter, you know that you and Paul and I agree on the heart of the gospel. Nevertheless, you ought to be aware that the religious and political situation in Jerusalem is becoming increasingly dangerous. Word keeps arriving in Jerusalem that you habitually enjoy table-fellowship with Gentiles. Primarily I'm worried about the rising hostility of the unconverted Jewish authorities. Persecution keeps breaking out. Almost as troubling is the fact that some of the more conservative of the Christians here in Jerusalem, egged on by the rising pressure from the Zealots, are beginning to stress the importance of the law. You may have won many of them over temporarily when you gave your magnificent address on the conversion of Cornelius and his family, but under these pressures some are wondering if you were drawing the right theological inferences. And now their fears are being inflamed by these reports from Antioch. So in addition to the pressure from the surrounding culture and the ubiquitous authorities, it is not impossible that these developments could split the church.[4] At the very least, Peter, please be careful, and understand that what you do, granted your high profile, affects a lot of your brothers and sisters in Christ here at home."

This is entirely plausible. The mid-forties of the first century saw the renewal of militancy among the Zealots and other nationalists. Some of it was directed against Christians, who as far as the Zealots were concerned were dangerous compromisers. The trouble was bad enough that about A.D. 46-48, Procurator Tiberius Julius Alexander crucified two of the nationalist leaders, Jacob and Simon, who were sons of Judas the Galilean, who a generation earlier led the revolt against a provincial census (A.D. 6). About A.D. 52 the Zealot militancy intensified. Peter's visit might have been in the late forties before the Jerusalem Council of Acts 15 (A.D. 49); alternatively, it might have been in the early fifties during one of the periods when Paul was back "home" in Antioch between mis-

---

[4]On this latter point, see Robert K. Jewett, "The Agitators and the Galatian Congregation," *NTS* 17 (1971), 198-212.

sionary journeys (e.g., Acts 18:22-23). Whatever the exact date, the known political and religious circumstances increase the initial plausibility of this reconstruction to a high degree of likelihood.[5]

If this or something like it is what is going on, then what Peter fears from "the circumcision group" is nothing as insignificant as a bit of damage to his personal reputation but two far worse things. He is afraid that reports of his conduct may result in fellow believers back in Jerusalem having to face harsh persecution, perhaps even death. And also he may be afraid that these same pressures will drive the more law-oriented believers in the Jerusalem church to precipitate a schism. Besides, as Paul himself acknowledges, there had been a rough division of labor agreed between Paul and the Jerusalem Three (2:9): Paul was primarily responsible for ministry to the Gentiles, while they were primarily responsible for ministry to the Jews. So shouldn't Peter accept some restrictions on his lifestyle in Antioch in order to preserve and further his own primary sphere of ministry, this ministry to Jews, not least the Jews in Jerusalem? Peter might even have talked himself into believing that he was taking the high road; he was being compassionate toward brothers and sisters back home and thinking strategically about what was best for the mother church. Peter being Peter, it is hard to imagine that he did not articulate his thoughts on these matters—and that may well account for the fact that he won over the Jews in Antioch and even the doughty Barnabas to his position.

But Paul does not see things this way. Doubtless he is deeply disappointed by the withdrawal of Jewish believers in Antioch from table-fellowship with their Gentile brothers and sisters; doubtless he is shattered by the decision of Barnabas. But Paul recognizes that the crisis has been precipitated by Peter's action (and probably by Peter's arguments, stemming from the report from Jerusalem). One cannot be certain, of course, but quiet discussions may have been going on for some time. But now things have gone so far that although Paul addresses Peter directly, he does so in public, "in front of them all" (2:14), since he is now facing schism in the Antioch church.

---

[5]For useful discussion, see T. W. Manson, *Studies in the Gospels and Epistles* (Manchester: Manchester University Press, 1962), 178-181; F. F. Bruce, *Commentary on Galatians*, NIGTC (Grand Rapids: Eerdmans, 1982), 129-131; Richard N. Longenecker, *Galatians*, WBC 41 (Dallas: Word, 1990), 73-75.

The charge he levels against Peter is that he is play-acting; Peter is guilty of hypocrisy. If it were merely a matter of some Christian Jews finding it difficult to enjoy table-fellowship with Gentile Christians, Paul would not have been entirely happy, and in some circumstances might have disapproved, but he would not have charged them with play-acting. In part, it was the fact that Peter normally enjoyed table-fellowship with Gentile believers and had gone on record to justify this stance theologically—before the Jerusalem church, no less—that earned the charge of play-acting, of hypocrisy. But there was more to it than that. It was not simply that Peter acted differently in different circumstances. After all, Paul himself often adopted flexible policies. He was prepared to live like a Jew to win the Jews and to live like a Gentile to win the Gentiles (1 Cor. 9:19-23): Paul certainly knew the importance of tactical flexibility in the great calling to evangelize Jews and Gentiles alike. His charge against Peter lies at a deeper level. Paul is utterly candid about his tactics. He enjoys these liberties (and he would certainly want Peter to enjoy them, too) because of his freedom in the gospel. But Peter's conduct involves play-acting, that is, pretending that he is following one course of action when in reality he is following another. That is hypocrisy, regardless of the high level of Peter's motives.

Moreover, in this instance, it is not just a question of deceit, of play-acting. Paul understands that the gospel itself is at stake. Peter may think he is acting with wisdom and compassion, but in fact he has become confused. Not only does he think that his newly adopted restrictive practices with all of their falseness are going to quell the problems back home, but the moral influence of his example is precipitating a crisis in Antioch.

The crisis is double-edged. On the one hand, the church in Antioch is dividing into two parts, a Jewish Christian church and a Gentile Christian church, and the moral influence of Peter's conduct is causing it. And on the other hand, from the perspective of Gentile believers who are observing the conduct of Peter and Barnabas and the other Jewish believers in the congregation and who may not fully grasp all the political realities in Jerusalem, becoming observant Jews is now the high road. Whether these Gentile believers were wondering if they needed to be circumcised and adopt kosher practices in order to be just like Peter and Barnabas, or whether some of them were tempted to think that they might go along with these practices in order to help fellow believers in Jerusalem is, for Paul, irrelevant, since the result would be the same: Christians would be giving in under the pressure of Judaizers and of non-Christian Jews (groups [f] and [g] above). In the long term, that would force Christianity to become a subset of Judaism; it would abolish all claims to the exclusive *sufficiency* of Jesus and his death on behalf of sinners. Gentiles would be driven to become Jews.[6] Peter's tactics might be finely motivated, but the gospel itself was being jeopardized.

Paul had thought long and hard about these things. He was, as I have said, a remarkably flexible man himself. Thus, he could happily circumcise Timothy so that this young man could have as ready access to synagogues as the apostle himself (Acts 16:3). By contrast, Paul refused absolutely to allow Titus to be circumcised (Gal. 2:1-5), precisely because the demand for his circumcision was being made in a context that jeopardized the gospel. In other words, if someone argues that a Gentile must be circumcised in order to be a true Christian, Paul forbids it absolutely, because that would annihilate the exclusive sufficiency of Christ; if no one is making that sort of demand, Paul is happy to circumcise a believer if it will advance the interests of the gospel. In all of this, Paul is quite open. But Peter's conduct, Paul argues, not only involves play-acting but openly succumbs to the demands of Judaizers and unconverted observant Jews.

Perhaps I should say in passing that Paul does not tell us what the outcome of this public rebuke was. Many have suggested that his silence means that at least initially he lost the debate, since (it is argued) if he had clearly won, news of that outcome would surely have increased the strength of his argument with the Galatians to whom he was writing.[7] That is a strong argument, and it may be right. But four additional things need to be said.

First, on the assumption that he won this debate, Paul's reticence to speak of his own victory may have been motivated by a certain pastoral

---

[6]There is good reason to think that the Greek at the end of 2:14 should not be rendered "to follow Jewish customs" but "to become Jews." In other words, the danger was not only external conformity to certain practices, but it was also the idea that for Gentiles to become full members of the Christian church it was necessary to convert to Judaism.

[7]See the references and discussion in Longenecker, *Galatians*, 79-80.

reserve that does not want to appear to score points. This is not as far-fetched as it might initially seem. After all, elsewhere in this letter Paul writes, "Brothers, if someone is caught in a sin, you who are spiritual should restore him gently. But watch yourself, or you also may be tempted" (6:1).

Second, and more plausibly, one need not think of an instantaneous "winning" or "losing." The rebuke probably sparked tense, complex discussions. The fact that both Acts and the later letters of Ignatius hold Paul in very high regard, along with Peter, strongly suggest that this was not a prolonged dispute and that Paul's position won out. Otherwise it would have been difficult for the Antioch church to send him out on further missions or for Paul to have been so warmly received by the genuine believers in Jerusalem when he went there toward the end of his life in the fateful visit that would finally send him on to Caesarea and Rome as a prisoner (Acts 21:17—28:31). Perhaps, then, Paul's reticence does not mean that he lost, but that the subsequent debates were sustained, complicated, and painful. Even if he finally won, the precise course of these protracted debates added nothing to the fundamental theological position he sets out in this letter to the Galatians. So he finds it simpler to omit them.

Third, it is important that toward the end of his life, Peter has left evidence of what he thought of Paul at that time: "Bear in mind," Peter writes, "that our Lord's patience means salvation, just as *our dear brother Paul* also wrote you with the wisdom that God gave him. He writes the same way *in all his letters*, speaking in them of these matters. His letters contain some things that are hard to understand, which ignorant and unstable people distort, as they do the other Scriptures, to their own destruction" (2 Pet. 3:15, emphasis added).[8] On the face of it, these comments suggest that at this juncture Peter thinks very highly of Paul, regards at least some of his writings as Scripture, certainly thinks he is telling the truth, but recognizes that some people, whether out of malice or ignorance, sometimes twist what Paul says. There may even be a gently ironic admission that out of ignorance he, Peter, has managed to get things wrong in the past himself. Peter's witness is all the more

---

[8]Of course, those who think that 2 Peter is pseudepigraphical will not be impressed with this observation.

impressive when we recall that on any responsible dating of both Galatians and 2 Peter, the former had been circulating for some time before the latter was written—which may well mean that 2 Peter approves the account given in Galatians 2:11-14.

Fourth, and most importantly, the precise nature of the outcome, immediate or protracted, is not what binds us as Christians, but what the canonical books actually say. The outcome of Paul's public rebuke of Peter is interesting and has its own historical importance, but for our purposes we need to attend the argument of Galatians itself.[9]

C. RATIONALE OF AN APOSTOLIC REBUKE (GAL. 2:15-21)

It is not entirely clear whether we are to take 2:15-21 as part of the rebuke delivered on the occasion, and thus a continuation of verse 14, or as Paul's later theological reflection on the incident. There were no quotation marks in the ancient text. Transparently, the New International Version opts for the former. It does not really matter. Undoubtedly the historical occasion of the rebuke found Paul saying more than the few lines of verse 14, and verses 15-21 may be a summary of what he said. On the other hand, undoubtedly Paul had time and reason to reflect on the crisis in Antioch again and again, and verses 15-21 may represent a summary of his mature reflections. Either way, for Paul it is the theological argument that is important, not the venue when it was first delivered.

The first part of the argument is clear, but the going is soon tight enough that it is a bit hard to understand. "We [Christians] who are Jews by birth," Paul begins, "and not 'Gentile sinners' [using one of the slighting terms by which many Jews referred to Gentiles] know that a man is not justified by observing the law, but by faith in Jesus Christ" (2:15-16).[10] In other words, that is the crucial step that any Jew has taken to become a Christian; Paul and Peter stand on common ground at this

---

[9] I should perhaps add that the rhetorical function of this section is in line with the sustained argument of all of Galatians 1—2, viz. the establishment of the apostle Paul's relative independence from Jerusalem and its apostles. But that point, though it is immensely important in the letter, is less important for our purposes.

[10] Despite the work of Richard B. Hays (*The Faith of Jesus Christ*, 2nd ed. [Grand Rapids: Eerdmans, 2002]), the objective genitive is the more convincing reading. In any case, for my argument it matters little, since the undisputed verbal form "put our faith in Christ Jesus" is also found in this verse.

point, and Peter has publicly defended the same truth (Acts 11). Christian Jews have fully appreciated that their justification, their status before God, is grounded not in observing the law, "because by observing the law no one will be justified" (2:16): they have put their faith in Christ. So now if while we Christian Jews hold to justification by faith in Christ and not by observing the law, it becomes evident that we are as much sinners as the "Gentile sinners" we previously loved to condemn, doesn't that mean that Christ himself must be promoting sin? After all, on these assumptions, this "law-free" gospel actually increases the total number of admitted sinners. Doesn't this mean that Christ becomes, literally, a "minister of sin," a promoter of sin?

"Absolutely not!" Paul fumes—one of his favorite expressions and frequently found in contexts where opponents suggest that his understanding of the gospel promotes sin (e.g., Rom. 6:1-2, 15). After all, the gospel does not increase the number of sinners or increase the amount of sin. Indeed, Paul will shortly argue that it was the law that did that (3:19). Therefore, there is no sense at all in which Christ can be legitimately seen as an agent of sin.

In the original language, Galatians 2:18 begins with a "For. . . ." In other words, verse 18 offers an explanation as to why the charge that Paul's gospel makes Christ a minister of sin is so ridiculous. The logic runs something like this: If I as a traditional, law-abiding Jew take the position that I am in fact a sinner and turn to Christ for justification, that does not mean that Christ himself is promoting sin (v. 17), *for* consider this: If someone who receives justification through Christ then decides to reinstate the law in Christ's place, that person simply becomes a sinner all over again (v. 19)—and surely Christ can't be blamed for that.

In other words, if the law-covenant is still in force (as the Galatians are being urged to think), then those who abandoned it to turn to Christ became transgressors, and if they now try to rebuild it, they are merely saying in effect that when they became Christians they became transgressors. If the law-covenant is *not* still in force because it has been replaced in the stream of redemptive history by the new covenant inaugurated by Christ, then to adhere to the law-covenant means one is not justified. That is why Paul will later warn the Galatians, "Mark my

words! I, Paul, tell you that if you let yourselves be circumcised, Christ
will be of no value to you at all" (5:2).

Verses 19-21 are among the best known of all that Paul wrote. They
have provided endless comfort and encouragement to countless generations of Christians. But that does not mean they are readily understood.
Verse 19 is difficult, and verse 20, I think, has sometimes been interpreted out of its context.

Begin with verse 19: "For through the law I died to the law so that
I might live for God." We recall that elsewhere Paul speaks of dying to
sin (Rom. 6:2, 11), i.e., dying in relation to sin. In one sense, that death
to sin is true of all Christians. If we are dead to sin, sin can make no
demands of us. But Paul's point here is that not only have Christians died
in relation to sin but in relation to the law-covenant—that is, they find
that because they are not under the law-covenant, the law-covenant's
demands on them are not in any sense directly binding, for Christians
are under a new covenant. In short, they are dead in relation to the law-
covenant. This is particularly true of Jewish believers. Paul makes the
point in the first person: he no longer lives under the power of the law.
For him, death to sin and death to law (Rom. 6:2; 7:4-6) are bound
together, precisely because "the power of sin is the law" (1 Cor. 15:56).
If you are under the power of the law-covenant, you are necessarily
exposed to all of its commands and prohibitions, and the temptations
to break at least some of them are so strong that you can be said to be
exposed to the power of sin. Those who have entered into new life in
Christ Jesus and have had their sins forgiven stand in a new relation to
both sin and law: "For *sin* shall not be your master, because you are not
under *law*, but under grace" (Rom. 6:14, emphasis added).

Two more details must be observed. *First*, what is the force of the
initial "For"? What is the logical connection between Galatians 2:19
and what precedes? The flow, I think, is something like this: "Do not
think that the Christian position means that Christ promotes sin or that
Christians have become lawbreakers (vv. 17-18). *For* the truth of the
matter is this: Far from becoming a lawbreaker, I died to the law. I died
in relation to law." Paul did this so that he might "live for God," literally "live to God." But *second*, in what sense did Paul do this "through
the law"? What does that phrase mean? It may simply mean that the law

showed him his moral bankruptcy and therefore directed him toward faith in Christ. But there may be something more. Paul will shortly argue that "Christ redeemed us from the curse of the law by becoming a curse for us" (3:13). Thus there is a sense in which Christ himself died "through the law": by taking on himself the law's penalties and by bearing its curse, Christ died through the law. And the believer then died on account of Christ's death, for, as Paul is about to say, we have been crucified with Christ (2:20). "The law has no further claim on him who in death satisfied its last demand, and the believer who has 'died with Christ' is similarly 'discharged from the law' (Rom. 7:6)."[11]

That brings us to verse 20. Probably the most common understanding of this verse is that, on the one hand, believers have died to the law because they have been crucified with Christ, and now Christ lives in them (by his Spirit?) in much the sense that Jesus announces in John's Gospel that he will come and take up residence in his followers by the Holy Spirit (John 14:16-17, 23). That is an important theme in Scripture. But I am not persuaded that it is the theme with which Paul is working in this passage.

"I have been crucified with Christ," Paul writes, "and I no longer live." If we have rightly followed the flow of the apostle's argument so far, this is reasonably clear: Since Christ died on my behalf, bearing my penalty, then because of Christ's death I am clear of that penalty imposed by the law. I am dead in relation to law because of Christ's death; I am crucified with Christ. In that sense, I no longer live. (Paul is certainly not saying that there is *no* sense in which he lives since after all Paul is writing these lines!) "I no longer live," Paul writes, "but Christ lives *in me.*"

What is the meaning of this prepositional phrase? If we take it as referring to location, even in some sort of metaphorical sense, then we return to the interpretation that makes this passage sound a bit like John 14. But the phrase in Greek, ἐν ἐμοί (or for that matter, ἐν + dative of any personal pronoun), is frequently not locative, i.e., it does not refer to location. Consider, for example, the last line of Galatians 1. Paul there tells his readers that when the churches in Judea heard of his conversion, they rejoiced that the man who once persecuted them was now preach-

---

[11]F. F. Bruce, *Commentary on Galatians*, 143.

ing the faith he once tried to destroy. "And," Paul adds, "they praised God ἐν ἐμοί"—lit., "in me," which in English makes no sense at all. They were not "in Paul" praising God; nor were they praising the God who was "in Paul." No, as the New International Version rightly para-phrases, "they praised God *because of me.*" The Greek phrase often means something like "with respect to me" or "in relation to me." "They praised God *in relation to me* or *with respect to me.*" In the con-text of 1:24, that is best rendered in English "because of me." Similarly in Galatians 2:20: "I no longer live, but Christ lives *in relation to me* or *with respect to me* or *in my case.*" In the context, the point is not that Christ by his Spirit takes up residence in Paul (even though that is a bib-lical truth taught elsewhere), but that just as Christ's death is Paul's death, so Christ's life is Paul's life. In both cases the idea is forensic, sub-stitutionary, judicial.

None of this means that there is no sense in which Paul continues to live. In fact, the apostle goes on to speak of his own life: "The life I live in the body, I live by faith in the Son of God." In other words, as far as the penalty of sin and the demands of the law-covenant are con-cerned, Paul is dead, because Christ died in his place; as far as living "to God" is concerned (v. 19), Christ's life is counted as Paul's, and Christ lives ἐν ἐμοί, "in my case." But the life Paul is actually living in his body—questions of Christ's forensic substitution aside—he lives by faith in the Son of God: Jesus Christ the Son of God is the object of his faith, and that is enough. His confidence is in him, not in the law-covenant. In fact, this is so unimaginably glorious that Paul bursts out in spontaneous acclaim. It is as if he cannot mention the Son of God without adding, "who loved me and gave himself for me." For Paul understands well that his forgiveness, his right standing before God, his freedom from the curse of sin and the penalties of the law, all turn with-out exception on the love of Christ—love that brought him to an odi-ous cross where the just died for the unjust to bring us to God.

The argument is tight. But the punch line, which shows that Paul has not lost his way but is still providing the theological rationale for his public rebuke of Peter, is reserved for the last verse of the chapter: "I do not set aside the grace of God, for if righteousness could be gained through the law, Christ died for nothing" (2:21). Paul is certainly not saying that Peter wants to draw that conclusion. Rather, he is saying that Peter's actions in this context will have the long-term effect of driving people to that conclusion. If Christianity becomes one of the sects of Judaism, if it is necessary to become a committed follower of the law-covenant in order to become a Christian, if one is somehow more acceptable to God by submitting to circumcision and eating only kosher food, then Christ's death must be ineffective. That is the only possible explanation: Christ died in vain. And neither Peter nor Paul nor any other genuine Christian will ever be comfortable with that conclusion.

Implicitly, of course, Paul is willing to face the consequences. If the preservation of the gospel means that some Christians in Jerusalem or elsewhere will have to suffer under the brutal hand of persecution, so be it. If it means that the church in Jerusalem divides over the very meaning of the gospel, so be it. Paul will not draw back from the glory of Jesus' death on our behalf; he will not jeopardize the exclusive sufficiency of the cross-work of Christ.

D. Some Pastoral Reflections

Certain things follow from this rebuke of Peter by Paul and the theological rationale that Paul provides.

(1) Where the gospel is at stake, *nothing* is more important—not even apostolic unity. Paul says as much in the first chapter of his letter to the Galatians: "But even if we or an angel from heaven should preach a gospel other than the one we preached to you, let him be eternally condemned! As we have already said, so now I say again: If anybody is preaching to you a gospel other than what you accepted, let him be eternally condemned!" (1:8-9). This is far removed from the stance that says, "Whatever I say is the truth. I am an apostle, and so my opinions must go unquestioned." Rather, Paul is saying that the gospel itself is so absolute that should he himself change his message, his readers should stick with the gospel and not with Paul. If Paul can relativize himself with respect to the gospel, small wonder that he can also relativize Peter.

Four reflections will clarify this first observation.

First, Paul is not saying that Peter is damned, eternally condemned. Between this passage and the record of the rebuke, Paul points out that he and the Jerusalem Three, including Peter, essentially saw eye to eye on the gospel (2:1-10). So in his rebuke of Peter, Paul does not charge him with heresy; rather, he charges him with play-acting, with hypocrisy. Peter was "not acting in line with the truth of the gospel" (2:14). Nevertheless, Paul is making the case so strongly that he is saying in effect that this inconsistent, play-acting behavior actually supports anti-gospel stances that both Peter and Paul reject.

Second, the reason why Paul can put the matter so sharply is because of the gravity of the issue. It is a *gospel* issue—the gospel that alone frees a person from sin and all its consequences. Without the gospel, there is only eternal condemnation; that is precisely the reason why Paul can say that if anyone preaches any other gospel, "let him be eternally condemned" (1:8).

Third, this gospel has been brought about by the love of Christ (2:20); it is this gospel that produces the fruit of the Spirit, which includes love (5:22); it is the freedom of the gospel that produces transformed behavior, characterized by the love that sums up the law (5:13-14). Passionate love for the Galatians forces Paul to take such pains to guard the gospel (4:17-20). Not for an instant does Paul think he is pitting the gospel's truth against love. To recognize the peerless worth of the gospel is to make one eager to preserve it, zealous to see it undiluted, and lovingly committed to making it known.

And *fourth*, as an aside, Paul's insistence on this point—that where the gospel is at stake, *nothing* is more important, not even apostolic unity—discounts the view that the locus of the church is determined by the succession of bishops that descend from the apostles. Apostles *as such* cannot determine what the church is or who is in it. *It is the gospel itself* that calls the church into being, and one of the essential marks of the church is that it faithfully proclaims that same gospel.

(2) Implicitly, this example reminds us that biblical truth is hierarchialized. To put it bluntly, not every dispute over doctrine or practice warrants rebuking an apostle—or anyone else, for that matter.

Any complex system results in the need to hierarchialize the components. Jesus himself points out that under the Mosaic code the Sabbath ordinance forbids work on the seventh day while the law demands that a male child be circumcised on the eighth day. So when the eighth day falls on the Sabbath, should the priest perform the work of circumcision? In fact, he did so (John 7:22-23)—which means that obedience to the circumcision law takes a certain precedence.

In some extremely authoritarian Christian traditions, super-pastors become mini-popes. Their decrees on a very wide range of topics, from doctrine to morals to customs and mores, hold absolute sway for the people of that church. To dissent is to invite excommunication. By contrast, the same Paul who openly rebukes Peter can be very relaxed about some matters. For example, after explaining certain points to the Philippians, he goes on to say, "All of us who are mature should take such a view of things. And if on some point you think differently, that too God will make clear to you. Only let us live up to what we have already attained" (Phil. 3:15-16). To the Romans, Paul says, "One man considers one day more sacred than another; another man considers every day alike. Each one should be fully convinced in his own mind. He who regards one day as special, does so to the Lord. He who eats meat, eats to the Lord, for he gives thanks to God; and he who abstains, does so to the Lord and gives thanks to God" (Rom. 14:5-6). Part of the bearing and forbearing theme that we explored in the second lecture clearly applies to differences of opinion on many doctrinal matters.

Such considerations force us to ponder in what cases a Paul would think himself justified in rebuking a Peter. To put it differently, even after we have agreed that the components of any complex system must be hierarchialized, we must then decide, at least in general terms, which belong toward the top and which toward the bottom of the hierarchy.

Numerous approaches to resolving this challenge are possible. But for our purposes, it is worth reminding ourselves that in the New Testament only three classes of offense warrant excommunication, which is the ultimate disciplinary action within the church. The first is gross doctrinal error that jeopardizes the gospel itself (e.g., Gal. 1:8-9); the second is gross moral lapse (e.g., 1 Cor. 5); and the third is persistent, loveless divisiveness (e.g., Titus 3:10). Remarkably, these three areas align with the three positive tests of 1 John: a truth test (in that case, bound up with certain Christological confessions), an obedience test, and a love test. And John makes it plain that it is not "best two out of three." Where there is flagrant disavowal of the truths essential to the gospel, where there is persistent and high-handed disobedience to the commands of Jesus, or where there is chronic, selfish lovelessness, there, John insists, we find no authentic Christianity.

So it will not do in such cases to appeal to Christian "love" and Christian "forgiveness" and say the breaches do not matter. Doubtless some forms of Christian love will still be displayed, and rightly so, to those who fall into such stances. But the love we show such persons will not be the love of Christian for Christian. And precisely because we love men and women in these positions, we will want to be faithful to the gospel that alone can save them.

In one sense, of course, I have ducked the hardest questions by not specifying which truths are so bound up with the gospel that they cannot be denied without disowning the gospel itself. That brings us to the next observation.

(3) The most dangerous errors in any generation are those that many Christian leaders do not see. That is surely one of the lessons to be gleaned from Paul's rebuke of Peter. At least initially, and perhaps for some time, Peter simply did not see the danger. If an apostle could be snookered, we had better admit that the potential for being undiscerning is dangerously high. And part of the gift of discernment lies not only in perceiving the theological ramifications of a particular stance, but its long-term implications. If some position or other, superficially useful or good on the short haul, is allowed to flourish unchecked for fifty years, what will be the result? On the matters discussed in this chapter, Paul understood where Peter's action would inevitably lead; Peter himself did not.

It is easy to spot yesterday's dangers. Not many evangelicals are going to be deceived today by classic liberalism. Today's dangers are the things that fewer people perceive to be dangers: several new forms of traditionalism that jeopardize the Bible's exclusive authority; appeals to postmodern spirituality on the one hand or to modernist approaches to truth on the other, which jeopardize a mature and genuinely Christian epistemology, and ultimately the uniqueness of Christ; and much more.

In North America several books have recently appeared chronicling the decline of Christian commitment in numerous universities and colleges that began as Christian foundations.[12] The patterns are complex. Commonly, for instance, there is a drift to a social-science approach to religion, instead of a biblical and theological approach. As institutions become larger and more successful, the dreams and visions of the initial founder, usually a pastor-scholar, give way to the pressing need for administrators. These may be good and loyal people, but their focus of interest and their tolerance levels, not to mention the degree of their theological acumen, cannot handle the pressure that comes from new stances that invariably parade themselves as being on the cutting edge. Similar developments, of course, have also taken place in student movements, mission agencies, and entire denominations, until the controlling consensus is a long way removed from the gospel-driven vintage of the founders. The most dangerous errors in any generation are those that many Christian leaders do not see.

(4) In the New Testament, church discipline does not offer us the reductionistic antithesis, excommunication or nothing. There are many passages that mandate mutual admonition, mutual instruction, warning, encouragement, even rebuke (e.g., Rom. 15:14; Gal. 6:1-2; 2 Thess. 3:15). These sorts of things are also part of church discipline. Plainly, the Pastoral Epistles stipulate that the primary responsibility for such mediating "discipline" falls upon the shoulders of the elders.

Such encouragement is not to be confused with what often passes for encouragement today. Under the influence of postmodern distortions of "tolerance," many today think that encouragement means one must never disagree with a brother or sister in Christ: that would be discouraging. I know more than one senior pastor mightily endowed with the gift of "encouragement," who never offers constructive criticism of his assistants and associates. They learn from his even temperament and gracious spirit, but they are slow to correct their mistakes precisely because no one with the advantage of learning and experience is telling them how to improve. In one or two cases, the associate is falling into significant theological errors, but the senior pastor, committed as he is to "encouragement," is not demanding more exegetical rigor, wider

---

[12]Among the best of these is James Tunstead Burtchaell, *The Dying of the Light: The Disengagement of Colleges and Universities from Their Christian Churches* (Grand Rapids: Eerdmans, 1998). See also George M. Marsden and Bradley J. Longfield, ed., *The Secularization of the Academy* (New York: Oxford University Press, 1992).

reading, engagement with the error—for any of those steps would be "discouraging." Psychological pleasure with oneself is thus elevated above more substantive "encouragement."

But I would go further and say that such senior pastors are lacking in love. They are confusing niceness and psychological encouragement for the real thing—the tough love that will in a spirit of meekness rebuke and correct, encourage in the ways of truth and righteousness, warn, and even on occasion rebuke a brother or sister who needs it.

And this, too, Paul understood. His rebuke of Peter was not only for the gospel's sake, not only for the sake of Gentile believers who were receiving mixed signals, and not only for the sake of Jewish believers who might be tempted to elevate the law-covenant above Christ—*but for Peter's sake.* Peter was in error, and on a serious matter, *regardless of how good his own motives were.* "Brothers, if someone is caught in a sin, you who are spiritual should restore him gently. But watch yourself, or you also may be tempted. Carry each other's burdens, and in this way you will fulfill the law of Christ" (Gal. 6:1-2)—which is of course the law of love. We must learn to speak the truth in love (Eph. 4:15).

Suppose, then, we think that someone more senior than we—our pastor perhaps—has made a mistake of some kind. What then? Let us be frank. Some people are always going to criticize pastors or other leaders. Some just love to hear themselves speaking; they always know better than everyone else, especially those in authority. I am not speaking of them. But if you are the sort of genuine Christian who prays for your pastor that he will be "a good minister of Christ Jesus" (1 Tim. 4:6) and seeks to respect and honor him in his work and calling, and then, sadly, you find yourself in disagreement with him, what next?

If the disagreement is over trivial things—length of the meetings? temperament? style?—then quite frankly there are things you should simply put up with. Bear and forbear; love and overlook. If you are gentle, and your pastor is not easily intimidated, you may be able to discuss these things and improve them; if not, remember: "Love is patient, love is kind. It does not envy, it does not boast, it is not proud. It is not rude, it is not self-seeking, it is not easily angered, it keeps no record of wrongs" (1 Cor. 13:4-5).

If the disagreement has arisen because the pastor has sinned against you in some way, Matthew 18:15-19 tells you what to do. But if the disagreement has arisen because the minister is unethical or is not preaching the gospel faithfully, then you will have a choice to make. You may try to convince him of a better path, as Paul tried to convince Peter (though of course, that was apostle to apostle, and not the sort of circumstance we are thinking about now). If you cannot convince him, you may feel it best to leave; or in rare instances, you may think it best to bring others into the discussion; in some cases, where there are few choices, you may think it best to stay and put up with things as they are for the good of other ministries and people in the church. All of these possibilities, however, must be motivated by love and by a transparent loyalty to the gospel and its fruit.

My chief point in all this, however, is that in the New Testament, discipline does not mean excommunication or nothing.

(5) Finally, just as love for fellow believers, even for Christian leaders, does not mean they are above gentle but firm rebuke, so love and forgiveness for *fallen* Christian leaders does not necessarily mean restoration to office. It depends on the circumstances. In Galatians 2, Paul does not think that Peter is acting in a perverse way but in an inconsistent way. Although the evidence is not overwhelming, there is good reason, as we have seen, to think that on the long haul Peter saw his way more clearly. At any rate, this is a very different case from that found in 2 Corinthians 10—13. There the egregious preaching of the "false apostles, deceitful workmen, masquerading as apostles of Christ" (2 Cor. 11:13) had resulted in a picture of Jesus so different from the real one that Paul dismissed the message as "a different gospel" (11:4). He clearly hoped the church would take disciplinary action before he arrived, when he would feel constrained to use his apostolic authority in harsh ways (13:10).

The more difficult cases arise when a leader has been unambiguously sinful in one of the three great areas that demand firm church discipline, and then he repents. Let us suppose that, so far as responsible Christians can see, the repentance is genuine. May such a leader be "restored"? After all, is not the Christian gospel rich in forgiveness? Is not forgiveness in such a case an extension of Christian love?

Everything depends on what is meant by "restored." Restored to what? There is always room in the fellowship of believers for repentant

Christians. Christians, after all, make up a congregation of sinners—sinners called by grace, repentant and restored.

But restoration to leadership is a slightly different matter, for the conditions for Christian leadership depend in no small measure on the consistency of conduct that breeds credibility both with insiders and with outsiders (e.g., 1 Tim. 3:2a, 7). If a pastor has been caught in fornication, and if the matter has come to light, and the pastor has (so far as anyone can see) genuinely repented, the demands of love nevertheless remain complex. Those who make decisions about that pastor's future must love, among others, the spouse and the children and the congregation who were betrayed. They must love the Savior himself and ask what course will maintain his glory; they must love the congregation and ask whether there will be a cynical snicker when the pastor speaks anytime soon on any subject related to sex, temptation, or even sin more broadly and the forgiveness the gospel offers. And they will have to love the fallen pastor, whose good in biblical terms may well be tied up with discipline, with facing consequences—and even with being kept away from circumstances where the temptation is likely to recur, since not a few pastors who have been dismissed for fornication and then restored to office fall again in the same way. Recidivism is painfully high. And love for God demands that we try with every part of our being to follow the stipulations and examples of his Word as we work through these matters. To appeal instead to some ill-defined and sentimental notion of love as the ground for contravening Scripture may be a lot of things, but it is not Christian love.

———

I have tried in this lecture to think through some of the relationships between Christian love and matters of church discipline, especially those that bear on the denial of the gospel. Here is another of the "hard places" where current notions of "love" prove thin and disquieting and where Christian teachings on love are invariably more complex and more robust.

But love, not least Christian love, can be strangled and stultified by many things. I shall reflect on a few of those things in the last lecture.

6

LOVE AND THE INTOXICATION OF
THE DILIGENT ROUTINE

For all of their complexities, the challenges inherent in loving enemies and in loving those whom we must discipline because they are denying the gospel are in some ways less subtle than those bound up almost exclusively with our own weaknesses. How easily does the intensity and purity of our love—for God and for others—shrivel and shrink. At a certain level, we may handle the external pressures with a fair degree of responsibility and maturity, partly because the problems are "out there," outside of us, and therefore more easily analyzable and more readily confronted than when the desiccation of our love cannot so easily be blamed on others. Like a married couple who feel helpless while their marriage grows cold and distant from want of attention, even while it retains its formal boundaries and predictable duties, so Christians may feel helpless while the hot flame of their Christian love dies down to an ash-coated ember. All the while they deny no cardinal truth nor even relinquish their ongoing Christian responsibilities. But inside they are dying; they know it, and they feel they cannot escape.

Perhaps the place to begin to think about this sort of degeneration is with one of the best examples of it in the New Testament. The church in Ephesus faced exactly this problem toward the end of the first century.

Probably the gospel first took root there almost half a century earlier, under the witness of Priscilla and Aquila in A.D. 51 or 52 and under the impact of the preaching of Apollos (Acts 18:18-22). Paul made Ephesus the center of his very fruitful ministry, a ministry that reached out and touched all of "Asia"—that is, all of the Roman province of Asia, the western third of modern Turkey—during a two-and-a-half-year period (A.D. 52-55; Acts 19:1-10). Eventually he was followed by Timothy (1 Tim. 1:3). From this one church, effective witness sprang up in Laodicea, Colosse, Hierapolis, and other centers. Paul himself foresaw that there would be problems for these churches. It is not surprising, therefore, to hear him warning the Ephesian elders of impending dangers (Acts 20:17-35) or writing a letter to the Colossians to help them overcome what was later called "the Colossian heresy." Shortly before he died, Paul knew that there had been a substantial turn against him in the province of Asia (2 Tim. 1:15).

Nevertheless, that was not the end of the story. When Jerusalem was attacked and destroyed by the Romans (A.D. 66-70), Christians fled the city and scattered to various corners of the Empire. There is very good reason to think that the apostle John settled in Ephesus, which he made the center of his own ministry for the next quarter of a century. His choice was not surprising. With a population of about one-third of a million people, Ephesus was the capital of the Roman province of Asia. The city straddled three major trade routes—toward the Euphrates by way of Colosse, toward Galatia by way of Sardis, and south and east through the Meander Valley.

Despite the fruitfulness of gospel ministry in that city, it had never been an easy place. Port cities are often tough towns. Already it was a center for the imperial cult: it included a temple built in honor of the dead Emperor Claudius. (Later on it would erect two more, one in honor of Hadrian and the other in honor of Severus.) More importantly, it was the primary center for the worship of Artemis (or Diana). The temple dedicated to Artemis was one of the seven wonders of the ancient world. It was about four times larger than the Parthenon in Athens and was spectacularly adorned by the work of great artists. It stood 425 feet long and 220 feet wide. Ephesus also included a huge stadium cut into the western slopes of Mount Pion, large enough to seat about 25,000 people.

Despite its wealth and prestige in Paul's day and in John's day, however, Ephesus was headed for long-term decline. Silt from the Cayster River was clogging up the harbor, and the dredges of the day were not adequate to compete with the river. Today the ruins of ancient Ephesus lie about half a dozen miles from the coast. The sludge won.

This is more than a bit of esoteric archaeological information. All seven of the churches addressed in the famous "letters" of Revelation 2 and 3 took on something of their surrounding culture or reacted against something in the culture.[1] In that light, the letter to the Ephesian church (Rev. 2:1-7) implicitly warned the believers. Just as those with eyes to see could discern that the city, though prosperous and powerful, could not go on in its present fashion but would decline and wither, so those with eyes to see would discern that the church, though currently strong and influential, could not go on in its present fashion, but would decline and wither.

The text deserves careful reading:

> [1]*To the angel of the church in Ephesus write:*
> *These are the words of him who holds the seven stars in his right hand and walks among the seven golden lampstands:* [2]*I know your deeds, your hard work and your perseverance. I know that you cannot tolerate wicked men, that you have tested those who claim to be apostles but are not, and have found them false.* [3]*You have persevered and have endured hardships for my name, and have not grown weary.*
>
> [4]*Yet I hold this against you: You have forsaken your first love.* [5]*Remember the height from which you have fallen! Repent and do the things you did at first. If you do not repent, I will come to you and remove your lampstand from its place.* [6]*But you have this in your favor: You hate the practices of the Nicolaitans, which I also hate.*
>
> [7]*He who has an ear, let him hear what the Spirit says to the churches. To him who overcomes, I will give the right to eat from the tree of life, which is in the paradise of God.*

Who the "angel" is that is being addressed is not certain. The two most likely views are: (a) the "angel" is simply God's "messenger" (the Greek word ἄγγελος sometimes refers to a non-angelic messenger) to

---

[1]See especially the important book by Colin J. Hemer, *The Letters to the Seven Churches of Asia in Their Local Settings*, JSNTSS 11 (Sheffield: JSOT Press, 1986).

the church, perhaps a senior elder; or (b) the "angel" is a true angel, perhaps the angelic counterpart to the church, pictured as receiving the message from the exalted Christ on the church's behalf. In some ways, it makes little difference, for the message is in any case to the church, the local church in Ephesus.

Far more important is the one who is speaking and how he is described. In each of the seven letters of Revelation 2—3, he is described in terms of one or more of the components of the inaugural vision of Revelation 1: this is the risen and exalted Jesus (see especially 1:12-16), addressing the churches of Asia Minor. Here he is described as the one "who holds the seven stars in his right hand and walks among the seven golden lampstands" (2:1). The language is drawn from 1:12-13 and is carefully explained to the reader in 1:20: the seven lampstands are the seven churches of this Roman province of Asia, and the seven stars are the seven "angels" (the messengers to those churches, whether "angelic" or not). The idea is that in the case of these churches, Christ is holding his messengers in his right hand, the hand of his power, and he is on an inspection tour of the seven churches themselves. He is evaluating them, telling them their strengths and their weaknesses. In two cases, he finds only strengths and faithfulness (even though those two churches are small); in the other five cases, he finds something to criticize—and the exalted Savior carefully warns of the consequences that will follow if those sins and weaknesses are not dealt with.

I shall begin with the strengths of this church and then turn to its cardinal weakness before reflecting on the bearing of this passage for the obligations of Christians to nurture their love today.

A. PORTRAIT OF A WONDERFUL CHURCH

Jesus commends this church in Ephesus primarily for three virtues:

(1) Jesus commends these Christians for their disciplined and persevering labor. "I know your deeds," Jesus says, "your hard work and your perseverance" (2:2a); and again, "You have persevered and have endured hardships for my name, and have not grown weary" (2:3). These were not fickle or apathetic people. Still less did they belong to the "flash and fizzle" crew—short-termers with large promise and only

the briefest performance. Thoroughly unlike the seed that falls on "rocky places" (Mark 4:5, 16-17), where initially there is so much promise of life and quick growth, but where life cannot be sustained, and there is never any long-term fruit, these Christians pressed on and on and on. They had no history of merely "going to church" or "coming to sit." They had persevered in evangelism and church planting (as the existence of several churches in this province attested), enduring "hardships," and doing so, Jesus says, "for my name." There was a sense of deep religious and personal loyalty among them, not mere traditionalism.

(2) Jesus commends these Christians for their abhorrence of evil, their scrupulous discernment. "I know that you cannot tolerate wicked men, that you have tested those who claim to be apostles but are not, and have found them false" (2:2b). Precisely who these "wicked men" were whom the believers in Ephesus could not tolerate is not specified. Were they some amalgam of Diana worshipers and greedy materialists, like Demetrius (Acts 19:23-41)? Were they involved in the Emperor cult? Or were they nothing more than fine representatives of graft in the city? We do not know. The point to observe, however, is that Jesus commends these Christians for their intolerance: "You cannot tolerate wicked men," he says. Doubtless this does not mean that they were rude or dismissive toward them. It means, rather, that wickedness was to be opposed, and these Ephesian Christians opposed it. There is a form of "tolerance" that is highly commendable and even self-sacrificial; there is another form of "tolerance" that is merely an excuse for moral apathy or even gross wickedness—and in such cases it is no virtue.

If the "wicked men" to whom the text refers are the same as those who are mentioned in the rest of the sentence, then perhaps they were not so much wicked because of their participation in the evils of the city, but because of their machinations, false claims, and spurious teachings in the church. Whether the exalted Jesus has two groups in mind here—the "wicked men" of the surrounding culture and the false apostles within the believing community—or just one, certainly the latter are roundly condemned while the church is praised for its careful discernment: "You have tested those who claim to be apostles but are not, and have found them false." This church has been neither dismissive nor gullible. It has not instantly rejected every teacher who came along; nor has it accepted everyone at face value. Rather, it has "tested" people and built up an enviable reputation for exposing those whose authority and teaching have been spurious.

This discernment was especially important during the first century or two of the church's life. There were no universities as we know them, but a large number of traveling lecturers or preachers. The best of these were very good, and they often set up small "schools" to which well-to-do people sent their sons. Many others earned their money with speeches, some extempore and some well-rehearsed, in the market-places. Inevitably, the system was so fluid that not a few charlatans with a gift of the gab and precious little substance could also earn a fine living this way. With the church multiplying quickly and with far too few excellent Bible teachers to meet the need, pretty soon thirst for biblical teaching called into existence Christian itinerant preachers, who would have been perceived in the broader culture as more or less the Christian equivalent of the traveling speakers with whom everyone was familiar. And once again, there were fine Christian teachers involved in this crucial ministry, and there were charlatans who were in it for the adventure, the prestige, and the money, and who could do a lot of damage by disseminating at best a superficial knowledge of the gospel and at worst a blatantly false understanding of it.

Young, small churches with few experienced Christian leaders were inevitably the most likely to be snookered by a warm personality and smooth talk. If such churches were located anywhere near a major church—one with many more years of Christian experience and with many more teachers with a record of faithfulness—they could ask that major church to check out itinerant preachers who came their way. In this fashion, some churches eventually began to preside over the affairs of other churches. At a functional level, this was not entirely bad, for it added to the doctrinal and moral security of churches still ill equipped to sift the good from the bad in the world of traveling preachers.[2] Whether the church in Ephesus gained a reputation for discernment only

---

[2]Although this is not the place to explore the phenomenon, it is easy to imagine that in some instances the larger church, which could also have been the "mother" church (i.e., the one that had planted the surrounding smaller churches), did not so much foster discernment in the "daughter" church as simply tell it what to do. Here, almost certainly, is one of the factors that went into the rise of monarchical bishops (a function they did not have in New Testament times).

in the case of its own needs to assess traveling preachers or also with respect to the needs of churches in the surrounding area, Jesus commends them.

That is an important point. The church is responsible to evaluate the teachers and preachers they appoint. Many churches discharge this responsibility abysmally. Some are narrow, controlling, merely traditionalist; more commonly today (at least in the West), in the name of tolerance and love churches appoint teachers and preachers with subtly shifting values and beliefs that are leading people away from the gospel. And sometimes those with moral and doctrinal discernment are sidelined by well-intentioned but immature appeals for "love," "openness," and "forgiveness." But the Ephesian church made none of these mistakes: "You have tested those who claim to be apostles but are not, and have found them false" (2:2).

(3) More broadly, Jesus commends these Christians for their disciplined doctrine and conduct in the face of notoriously subversive opposition. "But you have this in your favor: You hate the practices of the Nicolaitans, which I also hate" (2:6).

We know almost nothing about the Nicolaitans. We must infer that our ignorance in this case does not matter, for the point of this passage is not to denounce a particular error but to commend the church in Ephesus for the moral repugnance it displayed when confronted with the error. In this respect, it followed Jesus himself. Jesus hates; in this passage he hates the practices of the Nicolaitans. Not only does he expect his followers to join him in his hate, but by commending the Ephesians so warmly on this point, he clearly implies that failure to follow his example and hate the practices of the Nicolaitans would be a serious lapse and a cause for rebuke.

Like many passages of Scripture, it is possible to rip this one out of its context and deploy it to authorize poisonous, self-righteous, hypocritical hatred. It does not help the cause of the gospel to have fundamentalist preachers hoisting placards at the funeral of a slain homosexual, announcing that "God hates fags." In a profound sense, of course, it is true—just as God also hates liars, proud people, self-righteous religious hypocrites, thieves, those who cheat on their income tax, those who abuse their spouses, idolaters, and many more. It is also true that he loves them. As we saw in the first lecture, the Bible can depict God as loving the just and the unjust equivalently, sending his sun and his rain to nourish them; he loves sinners everywhere and pleads with them to turn to his Son; he loves his elect—and they certainly include in their number stellar representatives of every group of sinners on the face of the earth.

But not all of this can be said on every occasion. One passage talks of God's love in one way; another passage talks of God's love in another way. But there is more. The Bible talks of God's wrath. If the Bible talked only about the love of God, carefully delineating different ways of speaking of that love, but never spoke of God's hatred or his wrath, we would be dealing with a quite different God.[3] Just as we are called to imitate God's love in various ways, so are we called to imitate God's wrath and hatred in various ways. And in this passage, the Ephesians are commended for hating the practices of the Nicolaitans, which the exalted Jesus also hates. If contemporary Christians ask themselves how much of their love reflects the love of God in its various dimensions, they should also ask themselves how much of their hatred reflects the hatred of God. Just as we can prostitute love, so we can prostitute hatred.

Suppose, for example, that someone in the church turns out to be a pedophile who has sodomized half a dozen boys in the congregation. Or suppose the treasurer has walked off with large sums of money that were being accumulated for a substantial mission project among the hungry of war-torn Ethiopia and Eritrea. Or suppose some influential leaders, masking their intentions in the pious jargon of familiar clichés, manage to smuggle in false teaching that is dividing families and obscuring the gospel. Is there *no* sense in which wrath and hatred are called for? That is not *all* that is called for, but it is surely *one* of the things called for. A parent whose kids have been the victims of a pedophile had better have more than wrath in his or her heart, or the damage done by the perversion will be multiplied several times over by the nurtured bitterness and obsessive-compulsive rage. But is there not *some* place for outrage, for wrath, and, in the best sense, for hate—

---

[3] I tried to work out some of the relations between the love of God and the wrath of God and even the Bible's references to the hatred of God in the fourth chapter of *The Difficult Doctrine of the Love of God* (Wheaton, Ill.: Crossway, 2000).

along with courage, understanding, forgiveness, not to mention wisdom and resolve to prevent it from happening again, plus candor, hope, tears, and love?

All of these reflections take on a certain intensity when we turn to this church's failing, which I'll take up in a moment: it has lost its first love. Despite that failing, Jesus does not say, "Your problem is that you have got the balance wrong between love and hate. You have become far too condescending and critical. Lighten up a little; become a little more positive, a little less negative." Not a bit of it: Jesus commends this church for its hatred of the practices of the Nicolaitans, for in this respect they were closely following him.

On so many fronts, then, this was a good church: doctrinally sound, discerning, hard-working, disciplined, persevering. And that makes its central failing the more wrenching.

B. PORTRAIT OF A DOOMED CHURCH

"Yet I hold this against you: You have forsaken your first love" (Rev. 2:4). The charge is sad and troubling beyond words.

The words "first love" do not refer to the *person* who is loved "first," in the way in which a man who has lost his wife and then married another might speak of his first wife as his "first love." In this context, such a usage would imply that the Ephesian church has turned away from loving God or from loving Jesus to loving some other. In biblical terms, that would be the rawest idolatry; it would be a breach of the first commandment. There is no way that Jesus would then be commending the church for its fidelity and perseverance on so many fronts. The church would simply be apostate.

The words "first love," then, must refer, not to the person first loved, but to the character of that love as it was first expressed. Something burned low or perhaps was extinguished. And it is not easy to see exactly what it was.

It is more than a question of mere intensity. For when the intensity of love for God wanes, customarily one finds a rise in apathy, a slackness in industry. But this church is commended for its faithfulness, industry, perseverance, and even discernment. Nor is this failure of love merely at the hidden level of emotion and thought, since Jesus tells the believers to repent and "do the things you did at first" (2:5). Despite the highly commended hard work and perseverance, this church is no longer *doing* something that it once did, and Jesus is displeased.

Perhaps the best guess is that these Christians have succumbed to numbing, resolute faithfulness. When they were first converted, their love for God and their love for each other lay at the heart of all their service, and this love transformed work into pleasure and faithfulness into covenantal joy. Now they maintain the work and the faithfulness and the discernment, but they are no longer driven by transparent and effusive love for God and love for one another as brothers and sisters in Christ. Their Christianity is a bit like a marriage in which all the formal pieces are still in place: the couple work hard at their relationship, remain faithful, honestly commit themselves to meeting the other's needs, budget time together, sleep together, pray together, work out a common front in rearing their children and managing household finances. Yet somehow the spark has gone. Each hides this fact from the other; no casual observer would spot the problem. But the magic has evaporated.

I am not suggesting for a moment that mature love must retain all the marks of the exuberant immaturity that characterizes young passion: in the best marriages, the love grows deeper—and deep waters run still. Similarly, I am not suggesting for a moment that mature Christian love for God and for other believers must retain all the marks of the zestful enthusiasm of the fresh convert: in the best examples of Christian maturity, the love grows deeper—and deep waters run still. But these believers in Ephesus have lost their first love. No longer intoxicated with God's love, no longer returning that love to him as they had at first, now they are content with the more mundane delights of diligent routine.

Why is the exalted Jesus so hard on them? After all, they could be a lot worse. The answer surely lies in Jesus' own teaching, teaching on which we have already reflected. The first and most important commandment is to love God with heart and soul and mind and strength; the second is to love your neighbor as yourself (Mark 12:28-34). We have already seen that failure to follow this pair of commands is implicated in every other sin we commit; worse, failure to obey the first commandment is nothing less than idolatry. God is de-godded. The forms and disciplined zeal may remain, but this church in Ephesus is in the throes of overturning the sheer centrality of God. Deep down, Christians in this lamentable condition, if they will be honest with themselves, will be aware of how much has changed. That is why Jesus says, "Remember the height from which you have fallen!" (2:5).

There is only one way back: "Repent and do the things you did at first" (2:5). In the light of the commendations Jesus has given this church for all its faithful and persevering activity, returning to the things they did at first cannot possibly refer simply to *more* things. The idea is not that the church's problems will get sorted out if only the Christians add one more duty or a few more duties to the plethora of their other Christian activities—things that perhaps had been neglected. Rather, when Jesus tells these believers to repent "and do the things you did at first," he is surely referring to the *quality* of the things they did at first. All of their Christian service and work, discernment, and discipline were then motivated by profound and transparent love for God and for one another. They had better return to that place, or judgment awaits.

That judgment is spelled out in the last sentence of verse 5: "If you do not repent, I will come to you and remove your lampstand from its place." Recalling that the lampstand is the local church itself (1:20), this can only mean that the Lord of the church, Christ Jesus himself, will take away this church. The church will cease to exist. This will be an act of judgment by the exalted Christ himself, the decision he takes in the wake of his inspection tour of these churches in Asia Minor. Of course, individual Christians nevertheless still have the responsibility to be "overcomers," and they will be fully rewarded (v. 7). But the church will be destroyed.

If this church does not repent, it is doomed. The destruction might take two or three generations; it might take longer. But sooner or later the candlestick is removed; sooner or later the church that no longer finds obedience to the first and second greatest commandments a delight is sinking into the mire of idolatry and self-love—regardless of how orthodox, active, and zealous it is. Here is our first duty, our fundamental privilege, our basic worship: to love God with heart and soul and mind and strength, and our neighbor as ourselves. In the midst of suffering, persecution, disability, disappointment, infirmity, tiredness, duty, discipline, work, witness, discernment—in short, in the midst of everything—that love remains our first duty, our fundamental privilege, our basic worship still. When we grow old and calamitously weak, we must love God still; when we look after the chronically ill and think that our horizons are shriveling up, we must love God still; when we are bereaved, we must love God still; when we study and work and build and witness, we must love God still; when we exercise theological discernment, we must love God still. And still, too, must we love our neighbors as ourselves.

So we have returned to love in hard places, the first of the hard places—the hard places of our own hearts, our own souls.

C. REFLECTIONS ON AN OVERCOMING CHURCH

Suppose, then, that not only a few individuals in the church in Ephesus learn to "overcome" (2:7) their loss of first love, but the whole church in Ephesus "overcomes." Suppose the church as a whole follows the counsel of the risen Lord to remember the height from which it has fallen, repents, and does the things they did at first. What will that church look like? More broadly, what will be characteristic of any church that learns to "overcome" in this domain?[4]

The following list of five suggestions merely pulls together some of the strands of these lectures and draws in preliminary thoughts on a selection of related passages and themes.

(1) An overcoming church will try to obey the first two commandments—that is, the double-love command. The substance of the double-love command I laid out in the first lecture. From Revelation 2:1-7 we observed that, regardless of the other virtues that a church may possess, if it loses the passionate desire to conform to God's Word in this respect, it is doomed. We may add three further comments.

---

[4]It is important to remember that although the theme of "overcoming" is maintained throughout these seven letters, the precise shading of what it means for each church to "overcome" is constrained by the themes of the individual letters. What victory and overcoming look like depends in no small measure on what the particular dangers are, on what kind of defeat is most imminent. My focus at the moment is exclusively on overcoming the loss of first love for God and for others.

First, especially in our culture where sentimental or romantic notions of love have sometimes masked the richness of the biblical treatments of the subject, we must constantly remind ourselves that the double-love command is deeply constrained by the double object. So far as the greatest command is concerned, we are not simply to love, to love in the abstract, but to love *God*. Nor does this mean that we are to love any god or the god of our choosing, but the God and Father of our Lord Jesus Christ. To love this God means, among many other things, that we will be hungry to get to know him better; conversely, in learning his words and ways, his attributes and his glory, what he loves and what he hates, we will find that our understanding of what it means to love God, what it means to love enemies, what it means to love brothers and sisters in Christ, will all be progressively modified and enriched. Precisely because, as created, dependent, and redeemed creatures, we are called to love our Creator, our Sovereign, our Redeemer with heart and soul and strength and mind, we will be firmly led to think robustly about what *he* is like, how *he* views evil, what rights and responsibilities *he* gives to the state in a fallen world, *his* role both in making peace and in judgment, and, above all, his commitment to his own glory as God. That is what forces us to avoid mere sentimentality. The fact that we are called to love *this* God and not, say, Allah, Shiva, or Marxism constrains the way we think about everything, including love.

Second, we dare not forget that although in his teaching the two love commands hang together, the Lord Jesus himself makes a distinction between the first and the second commandment. The first is to love God with heart and soul and mind and strength; the second is to love our neighbor as ourselves. The latter is neither the equivalent of the first nor a replacement for the first; nor should it be confused with the first. This is not a matter of mere counting, of mere prioritization. It is a matter of the structure of reality. God alone is God; God alone is our Maker and Redeemer; to God alone we acknowledge our absolute dependence. And then this God insists that we must love other creatures who have been made in his image as we love ourselves.[5] To reverse or confuse the

---

[5]Cf. 1 John 4:20-21: "If anyone says, 'I love God,' yet hates his brother, he is a liar. For anyone who does not love his brother, whom he has seen, cannot love God, whom he has not seen. And he has given us this command: Whoever loves God must also love his brother."

first and second commandments is to return to idolatry by another route: it is to love the created order more than the Creator himself, who is blessed forever.

Third, the second of the two greatest commands has sometimes been weakened or trivialized by a discussion controlled by the current psychological agenda. Discussion of this command must be controlled by the biblical categories themselves. We are to love our neighbors as ourselves—and that standard of comparison, *as ourselves*, is often taken as an implicit command to love ourselves. On this view, the wording not only permits self-love but commands it; it not only sanctions self-esteem but reinforces its importance. On the face of it, however, self-love in Mark 12 is merely presupposed, not advocated. To read much of the contemporary literature, evangelical and otherwise, on self-esteem is to inhabit a domain a long way removed from the second great commandment.

There is of course a place for thinking through matters of self-esteem from a theological point of view. Interestingly enough, passages that speak most powerfully about human worth are not found in contexts commanding us to love others. There is a strong implicit emphasis on human significance in the creation narratives: only human beings are made in the image of God. The same emphasis on the sanctity of an individual human life leads to the sanction of capital punishment: human life is so valuable that when it is violently taken, the murderer must die as a way of pointing out how awful the crime is (Gen. 9:6).[6] The Master's insistence that his disciples not worry about the necessities of life, such as food and drink and clothing, brings up the relative importance of human life in yet another context: God looks after the birds and feeds them; he clothes the fields with wild lilies. If God does all that, should we not expect him to look after his own people, who are so "much more valuable" than birds and lilies (Matt. 6:25-34)?

But there is no passage that commands us to love ourselves. True, we Christians are to remember that our body is the temple of the Holy Spirit and act accordingly (1 Cor. 6:19-20). But this theme does not emphasize the intrinsic importance of human existence so much as the holiness of

---

[6]The reasoning, of course, is far removed from that commonly deployed today: because human life is so valuable, we must abolish capital punishment. Whatever the value of other arguments against capital punishment, that particular argument, it seems to me, turns biblical logic on its head.

the Holy Spirit, who is offended when we sin, and the fact that we do not belong to ourselves anyway, since we have been bought with an unimaginably great price, obliging us to honor God with our bodies.

Where the abysmal pressures of contemporary life have contributed to a truly bankrupt level of self-esteem—as in cases of child abuse and early sexual molestation, for instance—there are huge healing resources in the gospel itself. When men and women, regardless of background, come to grasp something of God's love for them in Christ Jesus, this is transforming knowledge (about which I'll say more in a moment). When men and women recognize their creaturely status, not only does it smash their idolatries (they are dependent creatures, not autonomous gods), but it assigns them enormous significance in the universe, for they alone of all the creatures have been made in God's image. And when men and women come to Christ in the context of a strong and loving church, the amount of healing and restoration that takes place in such a body is past finding out. They may have come from an abusive family, but now they enter a family much larger and more caring than they could have dreamed.

I suspect that one reason why the Bible does not foster self-love and self-esteem in the fashion of several strands of popular psychology is because God, unlike popular psychologists, is infinitely aware of the danger of fueling idolatry. The first temptation was the temptation to de-god God and turn self into god. Appeals to self-love and self-esteem, even at their best and even when well-intentioned, can never be far from that danger. Far better to seek the powerful remedies of the gospel.

Moreover, the first principle of Christian discipleship is self-denial: "If anyone would come after me," Jesus insists, "he must deny himself and take up his cross and follow me. For whoever wants to save his life will lose it, but whoever loses his life for me and for the gospel will save it" (Mark 8:34-35). Of course, self-denial is not the same as the kind of self-loathing that results from abuse. But when such self-loathing is treated by fostering self-love (at least, self-love of the most popularly encouraged varieties), then self-denial becomes an alien notion. Yet the irony lies in the paradox: Christians discover, in line with Jesus' teaching, that losing yourself for Christ means you find yourself; self-denial results in life and vitality and in the growing graces connected with

Christian maturity. Self-focus and self-love may produce a superficial and transient high, but they result in death.

These elementary Christian perspectives prepare us for meditative reading of the love chapter, 1 Corinthians 13. Love is more than self-sacrifice and altruism: all the self-sacrifice and altruism and religious power and mountain-moving faith in the world is barren without love (13:1-3). But on the other hand, genuine Christian love issues in astonishingly countercultural behavior: "Love is patient, love is kind. It does not envy, it does not boast, it is not proud. It is not rude, *it is not self-seeking*, it is not easily angered, it keeps no record of wrongs. Love does not delight in evil but rejoices with the truth. It always protects, always trusts, always hopes, always perseveres" (13:4-7, emphasis added). In 1 Corinthians 12—14, Paul insists that the diversity of gifts that God showers on the church is distributed to Christians variously. But all Christians without exception are to follow the "way" of love (14:1).

(2) An overcoming church will manifest such love in the sub-ecclesiastical unit of the family.

So far I have said almost nothing about the expression of Christian love in the home. Yet the New Testament itself can draw various analogies between the family and the church (e.g., 1 Tim. 3:5). To attempt even a superficial treatment of Christian love in the home, in conjunction with related themes of husband/wife, parent/child relationships, would have added another chapter, a long one. Here I shall say only two things.

First, the Christian church has often so emphasized the purpose of sex as procreation that not infrequently it has overlooked the Bible's happy emphasis on sex within marriage as something far richer and more wonderful. This is not to deny the importance of procreation; it is to say that in its concern for spirituality and sometimes for asceticism, the church has sometimes treated erotic love with a reserve not found in Scripture.[7] When God created Eve for Adam, it was not initially so that they could make babies together, but because "for Adam no suitable helper was found," and because, God insisted, "It is not good for the

---

[7] The book to read, though sometimes it goes over the top, is Jack Dominian, *Let's Make Love: The Meaning of Sexual Intercourse* (London: Darton, Longman & Todd, 2001).

man to be alone" (Gen. 2:20, 18). The Song of Songs celebrates erotic love in a marvelously rich and evocative way.

Most surprising perhaps for those who are inclined to think that sexual intercourse is intrinsically soiled or at best morally inferior, the Bible chooses marriage as a "type" of the relationship between Yahweh and Israel (think especially of the prophecy of Hosea!) and of the relationship between Christ and the church. The final consummation can be thought of as the marriage supper of the Lamb. It is as if the only pleasure and intimacy in this life that comes close to anticipating the pleasure and intimacy of the church and her Lord being perfectly united on the last day is the sexual union of a good marriage. And, conversely, that invests each marriage with a kind of typological value that should make thoughtful Christians all the more eager for the Lord's return, for the coming of the Bridegroom, for the consummation. Hence the spectacular intertwining of the pairs husband/wife and Christ/church in Ephesians 5:25-33.

Second, although Scripture sometimes says that wives should love their husbands (e.g., Tit. 2:4), more characteristically Scripture tells husbands to love their wives and in one remarkable passage adds a compelling qualifier: "Husbands, love your wives, just as Christ loved the church and gave himself up for her" (Eph. 5:25). The double pairing of husband/wife, Christ/church is not some nice bit of abstract theology without ethical entailments. If the love of Christ for the church is the standard of the husband's love for his wife, the least that this standard means is that the love must be self-sacrificial and for her good, for that is the way Christ loved the church. Always, therefore, the Christian husband must be thinking of expressing his love for his wife not only in terms of the characteristics found in 1 Corinthians 13, but with these two immensely practical tests: In what ways am I diligently seeking her good? And how is this pursuit of her good costing me something, prompting me to sacrifice something, as an expression of my love for her—in exactly the same way that the Savior sought the church's good at the cost of his life?

(3) An overcoming church will seek to nurture the kind of love and therefore unity that will make that church a reflection, even if only a pale reflection, of the unity of love in the Triune God. For did not the Lord

Jesus pray to that end? "I have given them the glory that you gave me, that they may be one as we are one: I in them and you in me. May they be brought to complete unity to let the world know that you sent me and have loved them even as you have loved me. . . . I have made you known to them, and will continue to make you known in order that the love you have for me may be in them and that I myself may be in them" (John 17:22-23, 26).

(4) An overcoming church will recognize that both the demonstration of Christian love within the body and the demonstration of Christian love for those who are on the outside combine to drive us toward evangelism. The prayer of Jesus, we have just seen, is not only for loving unity among believers, a loving unity that reflects the loving unity of the Godhead, but at least one of the purposes of such love is, Jesus says, "to let the world know that you sent me and have loved them even as you have loved me." Paul insists that it is Christ's love that compels the ambassadors of the new covenant to exercise their ministry of reconciliation, imploring men and women on Christ's behalf, "Be reconciled to God" (2 Cor. 5:14, 20). Christ's love for us reminds us that we did not deserve this wonderful salvation. So in a sense we are debtors to all so that they may hear, too. Because we have been the objects of Christ's seeking and redeeming love, so we become the mediators of that love to others.

(5) Finally, the overcoming church recognizes that the love it offers up to God and to others is always by way of response.

One of the dangers of these lectures, where most of the focus has been on the different ways the Bible has of talking about the love Christians should display, is that this focus will eclipse the more important reality, the reality of God's love. "We love," John writes, "because he first loved us" (1 John 4:19). Love is so much inherent in God's nature that love is a necessary mark of every person who is born of God: "Dear friends, let us love one another, for love comes from God. Everyone who loves has been born of God and knows God. Whoever does not love does not know God, because God is love (4:7-8). In fact, the most spectacular way in which God has shown his love is in the giving of his Son. In the most profound sense, then, we join the apostle in saying, "This is how God showed his love among us: he sent his one and only Son into the world that we might live through him" (4:9). All the initiative is his; if we display Christian love, it is in response to his redemptive love. "This is love: not that we loved God, but that he loved us and sent his Son as an atoning sacrifice for our sins" (4:10). And here it is again, the move from God's love to our love: "Dear friends, since God so loved us, we also ought to love one another" (4:11).

All of this suggests that Christians cannot begin to approach maturity in love unless they approach maturity in grasping something of the dimensions of God's love—which is exactly why Paul prays for the Ephesians as he does: "And I pray that you, being rooted and established in love, may have power, together with all the saints, to grasp how wide and long and high and deep is the love of Christ, and to know this love that surpasses knowledge—that you may be filled to the measure of all the fullness of God" (Eph. 3:17b-19). We love in response to God's love (Col. 3:12-15; 1 Pet. 1:8), and our love is nothing less than the fruit of the Spirit (Gal. 5:22).

Thus we have gradually worked our way into the position where we begin to perceive some remarkable parallels. On the one hand, the Bible speaks of God's love in different ways; on the other, it speaks of the love of Christians in different ways. In neither case does this mean that there are different "loves" that are turned off and on for the occasion. Rather, the perfection of God's love, in perfect harmony with all of God's other perfections, is inevitably displayed in different ways in the varied relationships he maintains. Similarly, mature Christian love should be nurtured as a reflection of the very being of God, in harmony with those other divine perfections we must emulate (e.g., "Be holy because I am holy," Lev. 11:44, 45; 19:2; 1 Pet. 1:16)—and this love will be displayed in different ways in the varied relationships we maintain.

The parallels will never be exact, for a very good reason: there are differences whenever one puts God and his image-bearers into the same sentence. Sometimes one is driven toward analogical language; sometimes the difference between the Creator God and his created, rebellious image-bearers necessarily means that our love cannot reciprocate his exactly nor emulate it entirely. His love for us is the love of Creator for creature; ours is the love of creature for the Creator. In some instances, the descriptions of his love for us are clearly redemptive, the love of a holy but a redeeming God for sinners; our love for him is never redemptive, but the response of hearts grateful for being loved. Our love is properly centered on him, with heart and soul and strength and mind, because he alone is God. When his love is fastened on us, it is most certainly not because we are God, but because he is God—that kind of God.

Despite the differences, however, the parallels are striking. God's intra-Trinitarian love is to be mirrored in the peculiar love that binds Christian to Christian. Moreover, the love of the Father for the Son is the standard by which he loves the world and the fundamental motive behind the Father's commitment that all should honor the Son even as they honor the Father, while the Son's love for the Father issues in perfect obedience to him, even to death on the cross. Thus God's intra-Trinitarian love spills out into redemption. God's even-handed, non-distinguishing, providential love for the world tells us something of the way we should love our enemies, for God sends his sun and rain upon the just and the unjust. God's yearning love to see men and women saved is repeated in us: the God who loved the world now commands us to preach the gospel to every creature, driven by the same love to implore a dying world, "Be reconciled to God." God's sovereign love for the elect is reflected not only in Christian love within the community of faith, but also in Christian marriages: as Christ loved the church and gave himself for her, so the Christian husband is to love his wife and give himself for her—and that, too, is a restrictive and selective love, even as it is sacrificial and seeks the other's good. Moreover, God's love for his people never allows them to forget that when he set his love on them, they were enemies (e.g., Rom. 5:8-11), for we are all by nature "objects of wrath" (Eph. 2:3). And if in some contexts God's love is made conditional on obedience, in some contexts ours is too: as we rear our children, exercise discipline in the church, deal with evil in a fallen and broken world. Indeed, just as the Bible's diverse ways of talking about God's love cannot responsibly be deployed to eradicate other things of which the Bible speaks—God's wrath, his judgment, his jealousy, his perfect holiness, his justice—so the Bible's diverse ways of talking about the Christian's love cannot responsibly be deployed to eradicate or domesticate the fullness and complexity of what the Bible says about our dealings with sin, injustice, war, brokenness, and judgment in this life and in the life to come.

In this world, despite all the pleasure and healing it brings, Christian love will always be a matter of loving in hard places. But none of it is as hard as what God himself did: "God demonstrates his own love for us in this: While we were still sinners, Christ died for us. . . . For if, when we were God's enemies, we were reconciled to him through the death of his Son, how much more, having been reconciled, shall we be saved through his life!" (Rom. 5:8, 10). One day the hard places will be gone. But the love will remain, unalloyed, immensely rich, reflecting in small but glorious ways the immeasurable love we have received.

General Index

INDEX OF NAMES

Scripture Index